THE Child WITNESS

THE Child WITNESS

LEGAL ISSUES AND DILEMMAS

NANCY WALKER PERRY
LAWRENCE S. WRIGHTSMAN

SAGE PUBLICATIONS
The International Professional Publishers
Newbury Park   London   New Delhi

For information address:

SAGE Publications, Inc.
2455 Teller Road
Newbury Park, California 91320

SAGE Publications Ltd.
6 Bonhill Street
London EC2A 4PU
United Kingdom

SAGE Publications India Pvt. Ltd.
M-32 Market
Greater Kailash I
New Delhi 110 048 India

Printed in the United States of America

Library of Congress Cataloging-in-Publication Data

Perry, Nancy W.
  The child witness: legal issues and dilemmas / Nancy Walker
Perry, Lawrence S. Wrightsman.
      p.   cm.
  Includes bibliographical references and indexes.
  ISBN 0-8039-3771-7. — ISBN 0-8039-3772-5 (pbk.)
  1. Children as witnesses—United States. I. Wrightsman, Lawrence
S. II. Title.
K9672.P465 1991
347.73′66′083—dc20
[347.30766083]   91-331
                                                                    CIP

FIRST PRINTING, 1991

Sage Production Editor: Michelle R. Starika

Contents

Preface   vii

Acknowledgments   ix

1. Children as Witnesses in Court: Issues and Dilemmas   1

    Introduction

    Four Basic Issues and Dilemmas   10

    Goals and Coverage of This Book   21

2. In the Eye of the Beholder: Reactions to Children as Legal Witnesses   23

    Reactions to Children as Legal Witnesses   24

    Legal Views of Child Competence   37

    Summary   52

3. The Developing Child: A Psycholegal Perspective   55

    Physical and Mental Development   58

    Emotional and Social Development   80

    Special Considerations   85

    Summary   93

4. Children in Court: Issues of Comprehension, Memory, and Communication   97

    Children's Understanding of Legal Personnel and Proceedings   99

    Memory   106

    Language and Communication   124

    Summary   129

5. With Liberty and Justice for All: Protecting the Rights of Child Witnesses, Defendants, and the Public   131

    Protecting Children From Traumatization   135

    Protecting Defendants From False Charges   139

    Protecting Defendants' Constitutional Rights   140

    Examination of Children as Witnesses in Court   145

	Procedures Designed to Reduce Traumatization of Child Witnesses	155
	Summary	172
6.	Resolving the Dilemmas: The Marriage of Social Science and the Law	175
	Differing Roles in the Justice System	178
	The Issues Revisited	181
	Summary	219
7.	In the Aftermath of *McMartin*: Society's Rights to Accurate Testimony	223
	The Issue of Accuracy Revisited: Whose Responsibility Is It?	224
	What Psychologists, Psychiatrists, and Social Workers Need To Do	228
	What Interviewers Need To Do	236
	What Officers of the Court Need To Do	248
	Policy Recommendations	255
	Conclusions	257
	Summary	258
	References	261
	Legal Cases Cited	277
	Name Index	279
	Subject Index	285
	About the Authors	289

Preface

Twenty years ago the issue of child sexual abuse was seldom discussed in the United States. Now reports of such abuses have become commonplace, and the arrests and trials of alleged abusers have become a staple of the evening television news reports.

The onslaught of disclosures about children who report being sexually abused creates a dilemma for all of us, but especially for those who, as social scientists or service-delivery professionals, must make policy-oriented decisions about children. Furthermore, children who report being victims or witnesses to other crimes, as well as sexual abuse, are increasingly being called upon to testify in court. What rights do they have, if any, to special treatment? Are they competent to testify? How does the court balance their needs with the right of a defendant to a fair trial?

The purpose of this book is to provide a professional audience an integrated, up-to-date review of social science research, legislation, and recent court decisions that relate to children as witnesses in court.

The book is organized around four issues: children's competence as witnesses, their credibility, the rights of children, and the rights of the accused. Child and adolescent development is reviewed from a psycholegal perspective. Recent research on issues of comprehension, memory, and the communication skills of children is evaluated within a context of the requirements of courtroom testimony. Reactions of various audience—attorneys, judges, jurors—to the credibility of children are described. Procedures designed to reduce the traumatization of children who testify in court are described and evaluated, including their relevance to recent Supreme Court decisions that have responded to alternative ways of testifying by sexually abused children.

This book concludes with recommendations for judges, attorneys, and service-delivery professionals who work with children who might be called on to testify. These guidelines are based on a consideration of both the case law and the social science data that were presented in preceding chapters. Facts and details from actual cases are used to supplement the findings; more than 350 references to psychological research studies and cases are cited.

Nancy Walker Perry
Lawrence S. Wrightsman

Acknowledgments

This book is one of a series of scholarly books that apply social science findings to the criminal justice system. Others published previously in the series include *The Psychology of Evidence and Trial Procedure, In the Jury Box,* and *On the Witness Stand.* We want to thank Charles T. Hendrix of Sage Publications for his encouragement of the development of this series and his suggestions for new topics.

It has been a pleasure to prepare this book. Completion of the task was facilitated by the research assistance of Jeff Kearney, Rebecca Kellen, Linda Monroe, and Barb Whitehill, and by the typing and computer assistance of Karen Wright. Elizabeth Dahl, Chairperson of the Department of Psychology, Creighton University, and Edwin Martin, Chair of the Department of Psychology, University of Kansas, were responsive to our urgent requests as we completed the manuscript.

We want to thank Robert Belli of the Creighton University Department of Psychology and Lucy McGough of the Louisiana State University School of Law for their useful comments on chapter drafts.

We offer this book to our loved ones—Douglas J. Perry, Kristen and Laura Perry, and Bernadine Gray—as a tangible show of appreciation for the emotional support and encouragement they gave us during its preparation.

N.W.P.
L.S.W.

1

Children as Witnesses in Court: Issues and Dilemmas

Introduction

Four Basic Issues and Dilemmas

Competence
Issue #1 • Dilemma #1

Credibility
Issue #2 • Dilemma #2

Children's Rights
Issue #3 • Dilemma #3

Defendants' Rights
Issue #4 • Dilemma #4

Goals and Coverage of This Book

The courtroom is filled with an electrifying intensity. Spectators whisper among themselves as the prosecution's star witness approaches the stand. All eyes are riveted on the diminutive figure of a child who has come to offer testimony about her sexual assault.

How will the judge and jury react to this small visitor? Will she be viewed as a capable historian, one who has accurately perceived and remembered a traumatic event? Will she be able to communicate a chronology of the alleged abuses accurately and persuasively? What weight will the jurors give to her testimony? Will this courtroom experience, intended to generate justice, actually reactivate all the traumatic reactions she experienced before?

At the defense table sits the man accused of committing a sexual assault on this child. His name has appeared on the front page of the local newspaper, as well as on all the evening news programs. In the eyes of the public, he may already be judged guilty, and his professional reputation has been tarnished at least or perhaps even destroyed. Where he will reside for the next several years—at home or in prison—depends in large part on the reactions to the testimony about to be provided by his small accuser.

Will the defendant receive due process of law in this matter? Will his constitutional rights be protected? Or will the testimony of the child so impress the jurors that they will vote for conviction even if the defendant is in fact innocent?

What is at issue in this example? On the one hand, people need to feel secure and safe, to believe that lawbreakers will be prosecuted and punished for the crimes they have committed and that society at large will be protected from further harm. Packer (1964) refers to this set of values as the *crime-control* model of criminal justice. On the other hand, our society is founded on the premise that individuals possess certain inalienable rights and that one function of the legal system is to ensure that these rights are protected for each and every citizen. Our system of law rests on the assumption that each person accused of a crime is innocent until proven guilty and that equal protection under the law will be afforded to all citizens. These views reflect the second model of criminal justice, the *due-process* model, as described by Packer. Thus, the due-process model places primary value on the protection of innocent citizens from the possible abuses of police, prosecutors, and the law-enforcement system generally, whereas the crime-control model seeks the punishment of lawbreakers.

Looking at these two models psychologically, we may describe the tension between them as the psychological dilemma of "the rights of individuals versus the common good" (Wrightsman, 1991). Decisions reached by the United States Supreme Court over the last 30 years have reflected this tension, especially those decisions concerned with the rights of suspects and defendants versus the rights of victims of crimes. Under Chief Justice Earl Warren, the Supreme Court of the 1960s established or extended a number of principles that provided explicit rights for those suspected of breaking the law. In other words, the Warren Court focused on the due-process rights of the defendant. The Supreme Court under Chief Justices Warren Burger and William Rehnquist, on the other hand, has shifted emphasis toward the crime-control model. Specifically, the court has increased the surveillance opportunities of the police, diminished the opportunity for some suspects to escape prosecution, and emphasized the rights of crime victims.

Each time a child is called to the stand to testify, these conflicting values in society must be confronted. In a given case, such as the scenario sketched above, the court must decide whether its procedures will favor the due-process or the crime-control model of criminal justice.

Unfortunately, in the United States such cases are not rare; indeed, cases involving children as witnesses are appearing on court dockets with increasing frequency (Leippe, Brigham, Cousins, & Romanczyk, 1989). Claims of sexual abuse are not the only type; pre-teenage children may be asked to testify for a variety of reasons. They may be witnesses to accidents (see, for example, *Rueger v. Hawks,* 1949), crimes (see *Wheeler v. United States,* 1895, as an example), or other events of legal significance (as in *Birmingham Ry., Light & Power v. Wise,* 1906). Likewise, they may be injured parties (see, e.g., *Harrold v. Schluep,* 1972) or victims of alleged wrongdoing (as in *State v. Fairbanks,* 1946), including abuse. Their opinions may be relevant to legal decisions, such as the awarding or changing of temporary or permanent custody (*Callicott v. Callicott,* 1963; *Bole v. Bole,* 1946). Finally, they themselves may be perpetrators of crimes (see, for example, *State in re S.H.,* 1972). Although children may testify in court for a multitude of reasons, they are most likely to testify as witnesses at trials dealing with the crimes of sexual or physical abuse (Whitcomb, Shapiro, & Stellwagen, 1985) because, in such cases, children typically serve not only as the victims but also as the only eye-witnesses to the crimes committed.

Although there is no universally accepted definition of the sexual abuse of children (Brant & Tisza, 1977; Kelly, 1984), pedophilic acts generally are condemned throughout the modern world (Doek, 1981). Sexual abuse of children is illegal in all 50 states (Fraser, 1981), and all have laws that make it mandatory for professional persons (physicians and social workers, for example) who become aware of the abuse of a child to report it (Meriwether, 1986). In spite of the statutory requirements, child sexual abuse is rarely reported in relation to the frequency with which it occurs (Duggan, Aubrey, Doherty, Isquith, Levine, & Scheiner, 1989); still, it is the fastest growing form of reported child abuse in America (Mac-Farlane & Bulkley, 1982). A special report by the National Center on Child Abuse and Neglect (1981) estimated that the incidence of child sexual abuse in the United States is in excess of 100,000 cases each year, while non-sexual physical abuse of children is estimated to occur at the staggering rate of nearly two million cases annually (Gelles & Cornell, 1985; Straus, Gelles, & Steinmetz, 1980).

For a number of reasons, only a small proportion of even the reported cases actually comes to trial (Whitcomb, Shapiro, & Stellwagen, 1985). Still, they represent a significant subset of court cases, and when such cases come to trial, they may receive national attention in the media.

The difficulties and dilemmas inherent in prosecuting alleged cases of child sexual assault were given national attention in the late 1980s and early 1990s by the highly publicized McMartin Preschool trial (*People v. Buckey,* 1990). (A chronology of events in this case may be found in Box 1.1.) The preschool, founded by Virginia McMartin, had enjoyed an impeccable reputation for more than 25 years. Then, in the spring of 1984, an emotionally troubled mother lodged a complaint of molestation against Raymond Buckey, grandson of the school's founder. In the ensuing months, a furor developed with dozens of molestation charges being filed against Buckey, his mother Peggy McMartin Buckey, and five other teachers at the school. Molestation was alleged to have taken place not only at the school but at a number of public locations as well—a market, a car wash, a church. More than 350 children were alleged to have been molested, taken on plane rides, and forced to drink blood and to watch animals mutilated. Yet not one of the children ever said a word to any parent, friend, classmate, doctor, or neighbor. Prosecutors said that the children had been told by Buckey that their parents would be killed if they divulged the secrets—certainly ample justification for keeping silent. After a preliminary hearing and other pretrial activities that stretched over three years, charges against five teachers were dropped. But Raymond Buckey and Virginia McMartin Buckey went to trial in April 1987. The defense argued that it was preposterous that several hundred preschoolers could keep quiet about the alleged atrocities. Moreover, the defense claimed that the interviewing and videotaping procedures used by social workers at Children's Institute International to question 400 children were inept at best and, at worst, illegal. When the trial ended in January 1990, several jurors reported that they believed some of the children had in fact been molested but that the state had failed to prove the identity of the perpetrator(s). Buckey and McMartin hence were found not guilty on 52 of the charges. The district attorney of Los Angeles County then decided to retry Buckey on 8 of the 13 remaining charges, those for which the initial jury could not agree on a verdict. For those remaining charges, the defendant again was found not guilty.

What were the financial, social, and emotional costs of this trial? This case, the longest running criminal trial in the history of the United States, cost the taxpayers between $13 million and $15 million. Trial jurors devoted nearly three years of their lives to the case before finding the defendants not guilty on most of the counts. As one news account noted, "The childhoods of alleged victims were put on hold in the expectation that the case would be speedily resolved. Some of those childhoods came to an end while the case dragged on" (*Omaha World Herald,* Jan. 21, 1990). One 10-year-old boy, for example, spent 16 days on the witness stand during a preliminary hearing. The boy's ordeal, especially under cross-examination, led parents of most of the 41 other alleged victim-witnesses to remove their children from the case.

The prime suspect, Raymond Buckey, served five years in jail before the jury even began to deliberate his guilt. His mother, Peggy McMartin Buckey, spent two years in jail. The other five teachers suffered ostracism and loss of jobs. One of them, a woman 64 years of age and who had never even had a traffic ticket, was kept in jail without bail until her attorney won an appeal (Hechler, 1988). All but one of the McMartin Preschool teachers had to sell their homes to pay their legal expenses.

Box 1.1

A Chronology of Events in the McMartin Preschool Case—
People v. Buckey, 1990

August 12, 1983   The mother of a 2½-year-old boy at the McMartin Preschool in Manhattan Beach, California, calls the local police to tell them she believes her child has been molested by a teacher at the school, Raymond Buckey. The mother says her child saw the head of a live baby chopped off, was forced to drink blood, and saw Raymond Buckey fly. Mr. Buckey is arrested but then released on the same day because of a lack of evidence. The 2-1/2-year-old boy cannot identify "Mr. Ray" from a school photo.

September, 1983   The Manhattan Beach police send a letter to 200 parents, asking if their children have reported any incidents of molestation at the school. The letter says: "Our investigation indicates that possible criminal acts include oral sex, fondling of genitals, and sodomy." Mr. Buckey is named in the letter as a prime suspect. Many parents send their children to Children's Institute International (CII) for diagnosis and therapy.

September 1983 to March, 1984   Approximately 400 children are interviewed by CII staff; they conclude that at least 350 have been abused. The state files a complaint, indicating that 41 of these children were victims of molestation.

February 2, 1984   KABC-TV in Los Angeles reports that more than 60 McMartin children have been abused.

March 22, 1984   After hearing reports from 18 children, a Los Angeles County grand jury indicts Raymond Buckey, Peggy McMartin Buckey, and five other teachers on charges of abusing children. Among the accused is the school's 82-year-old founder, Virginia McMartin.

March 24, 1984	Raymond Buckey and Peggy McMartin Buckey are denied bail.
April 20, 1984	The defendants plead not guilty.
June 6, 1984	A preliminary hearing begins—and lasts 17 months.
January 22, 1985	Children begin testifying at the preliminary hearing. One 10-year-old boy is on the stand for 16 days, 15½ of which are spent in cross-examination.
January 10, 1986	The judge orders a trial for the seven teachers accused of molesting children.
January 17, 1986	The state drops the charges against five of the teachers, citing insufficient evidence; the district attorney, Ira Reiner, describes the evidence against them as "incredibly weak." Raymond Buckey and his mother, Peggy McMartin Buckey, are bound over for trial.
January 23, 1986	Peggy McMartin Buckey is released on $295,000 bail after having been held in jail for 22 months. One of the attorneys mortgages his house to contribute to the payment of the bail bond.
December 19, 1986	Judy Johnson, the mother whose complaint initiated the inquiry, is found dead in her home at the age of 44, of a liver disease associated with alcoholism. It is learned that in 1985 she had been diagnosed as having paranoid schizophrenia.
April 20, 1987	Jury selection for the trial begins. It lasts three months.
July, 1987	The trial begins.
February 15, 1989	After spending nearly five years in jail, Raymond Buckey is released on $3 million bail raised by 20 people who put up property.
May 16, 1989	Peggy McMartin Buckey takes the stand and denies that she sexually assaulted her students.
July 26, 1989	Raymond Buckey also takes the stand and denies that he ever molested children.

November 2, 1989	After presentation of 124 witnesses (including 9 of the allegedly molested children) and 917 exhibits, presentation of the evidence concludes, and the jury begins its deliberations.
December 15, 1989	The jury takes a two-week holiday break.
January 18, 1990	Verdicts are announced: acquittal on 52 of the counts. The jury reports deadlock on 13 other charges against Raymond Buckey, so Judge William R. Pounders declares a mistrial on these. One of the jurors says, "We didn't find out so much what the child knew as what the interviewer wanted to know." Other jurors report feeling that some of the children had been molested but that the prosecution had not proved beyond a reasonable doubt that the defendants were the abusers.
January 19, 1990	One day after the announcement of the verdicts, Peggy McMartin Buckey and Virginia McMartin announce that they are filing a multimillion-dollar lawsuit against the Manhattan Beach police, Los Angeles County, Kee MacFarlane of CII, and others for malicious prosecution, defamation, and violation of their civil rights.
March 6, 1990	The prosecution decides to retry Raymond Buckey on 8 of the remaining 13 charges. These counts involve three girls (ages 11 to 13 in 1990) who assert that Mr. Buckey molested them while they were students at the McMartin Preschool.
March 26, 1990	The U. S. Supreme Court lets stand a lower court ruling throwing out the civil suit filed by Peggy McMartin Buckey and Virginia McMartin.
April 9, 1990	Jury selection begins for the second trial.
May 7, 1990	Opening statements in the second trial are presented.

June 3, 1990	Ted Gunderson, a retired FBI agent, reports that a team of archaeologists have uncovered evidence that two tunnels and a secret room once existed beneath the McMartin Preschool, potentially substantiating claims made by students that they had been molested in an underground room. Gunderson says his team of experts has found (a) evidence of the remains of a trapdoor leading to an elaborate tunnel system, (b) dirt foreign to the dig site, (c) two tunnels, (d) a nine-foot wide room, and (e) a total of 2,000 artifacts—many dating from times after the preschool was built, and some commonly used in Satanic rituals.
July, 1990	Verdicts in the retrial of Raymond Buckey are announced: Not guilty on all counts.

Three people associated with the case died under mysterious circumstances. The young mother whose allegations started the case apparently drank herself to an early death. (She had alleged that her two-and-one-half-year-old son had been molested not only by Buckey but also by three witches, by a member of the Los Angeles Board of Education, and by an AWOL Marine. She also claimed that McMartin teachers had put staples into her son's ears, nipples, and tongue, and had stuck scissors in his eyes; she also alleged that he had had encounters with a lion and an elephant and that he had been involved in a ritual in which a human was sacrificed.) A second death occurred when one suspect, who never was formally indicted, apparently took an overdose of pills after several children implicated him. A defense investigator killed himself the night before he was to testify. Los Angeles Superior Court Judge William R. Pounders, who presided at the trial, aptly noted that the case had "poisoned" the lives of everyone it touched.

Given these circumstances, was it worth it to prosecute the McMartin case? Opinion is sharply divided on this point. Stanley Goldman, a professor at Loyola Law School in Los Angeles, queried, "How could you say it was worth it the way it was handled? Society has no business spending that amount on one proceeding like this" (*Omaha World Herald*, Jan. 21, 1990). Phillip E. Johnson,

Professor of Law at the University of California, Berkeley, disagreed: "You've got these accusations that people in charge of small children committed these horrible acts . . . and you're going to say that it costs too much to look into it?" (*Omaha World Herald,* Jan. 21, 1990).

These comments capture well society's dilemma in legal cases involving children as key witnesses. How can we protect the rights of individuals in society and simultaneously serve the common good?

FOUR BASIC ISSUES AND DILEMMAS

Whenever we attempt to resolve this dilemma, four basic issues must be addressed. First, we must consider the competence of children as witnesses. Are children accurate recorders and reporters of events that have transpired? Second, we need to assess the credibility of children and their testimony that forms a part of the evidence. When should the court believe the evidence provided by children who have been judged competent to give testimony? What rules should govern the ways in which testimony is obtained from children? Third, we must protect the rights of children as citizens. Does the experience of testifying in court serve the best interests of the particular child, or does it further traumatize someone already victimized? Finally, we need to protect the constitutional rights of the accused. If a child takes the witness stand, will her or his testimony be given undue weight? Or conversely, if the child does not provide testimony, is the defendant denied his or her Sixth Amendment right to confront an accuser?

An actual case illustrates these issues. In describing it we have drawn extensively from the report by Jones and Krugman (1986); the case also is described by Goodman (1984a). (The name of the child has been changed.)

In the summer of 1983, three-year-old Susie was abducted from the street outside her home by a man driving an orange car. Her four-year-old brother witnessed the act and ran inside the house to inform his father. He reported that the man had said, "Take off your pants and get in the car," and that Susie had complied. Seventy hours later Susie was found in the cesspit of a mountain outhouse by two birdwatchers. She had been dropped through the toilet ring and into the fluid material six feet below. Because the cesspit was slightly leaking and only contained one foot of sewage, and because she had gathered sticks that were down the pit and made them into a platform to escape some of the fluid, she survived. When her rescuers asked her what she was doing inside the pit, she replied, "I live here," and then cried for her mother.

Susie was flown by helicopter to a nearby hospital where she was medically evaluated. Her physical examination generated the following observations: (a) marked dehydration; (b) bilateral "immersion foot"; (c) multiple scratches on the legs and back; (d) some bruises around the buttocks and near the anus; (e) a "normal" genital exam result. Within one-half hour of her arrival, the press reported that the physicians said she had not been sexually abused and that laboratory studies, including gonorrhea cultures, were negative. She was rehydrated intravenously and her immersion foot resolved. The nurses noted that her sleep pattern was a restless one, and it was reported that she occasionally cried out unintelligibly. On the sixth hospital day she was discharged and taken home.

Susie was interviewed by police five days after the abduction. She described her ordeal, including the kidnapping and outhouse, and, from a group of six photographs, identified a police suspect as the "bad man."

Five days later (10 days after the abduction) she viewed a videotaped lineup of the suspect and four other men, each of whom was instructed to come forward and say, "Get into the car." Susie sat on her mother's lap and watched the lineup on a television monitor while her response was videotaped. When the police's suspect appeared, she began to rub her eyes, seemed distressed, and declared, "That's him, that's the bad man who put me in the hole."

Four days later (14 days after her abduction) Susie was re-interviewed to assess the reliability of her account and of her identification and to determine how suggestible she was. The interview was conducted by Susie's psychiatrist while her pediatrician videotaped the session. During this interview she said, "a bad man put me down the hole." She was shown the original photo lineup, but with the police's prime suspect removed, and it was suggested that the set of 11 photographs contained the "bad man." She studied the photos intently, and then firmly stated that he was not among the photographs. After a snack, she was shown the same series of photos but with the suspect's photo included in the display.

This time, when she viewed the series and saw the suspect's photo, she pulled backward and gasped, saying, "He want to put me in the hole . . . he got a car." She appeared shocked and frightened. The interviewer suggested that he did not look like a bad man, whereupon she emphatically stated, "He's a *mean* man." Finally, with the 12 photos spread on the table, the interviewer pretended to have lost the photo of the bad man. With an expression of exasperation, Susie picked it out and held it up.

Three days later (17 days after the abduction), a fourth interview was held, this time to evaluate Susie's treatment needs. This session also was videotaped. Toys and materials were provided that allowed her to re-create the abduction if she wished; these included a doll's house, a car, three-inch doll-people figures, a barn (similar to an outhouse), and anatomically-correct dolls. During this session she provided more detail about the abduction, including the fact that her abductor had fondled her and had forced her to fondle his genitals while they drove the 30 minutes to the mountain park. She reported that while in the outhouse toilet he made her sit on his lap while he sat on the seat and fondled her further. She said, "He tried to go poop," and made her do the same. Then he pushed her through the toilet ring, dropping her into the fluid below; he then left and never returned.

On the basis of the information obtained in this interview, as well as his prior history of sexual offenses, the suspect was arrested and charged with attempted murder, kidnapping, and sexual assault of a child. Meanwhile, Susie received individual psychotherapy and her family attended counseling sessions. The suspect maintained his innocence as the case filtered through the courts.

At the preliminary hearing held five weeks after the kidnapping, the judge ruled that the evidence was sufficient to hold a trial. Four and one-half months later a hearing was held at which a central issue was whether Susie could testify. The judge heard testimony that she had been experiencing the following symptoms: frequent night terrors in which she would scream, "Get me out, get me out"; anxieties related to the place from which she was abducted; a relative lack of interest in those everyday activities that previously had delighted her, such as family trips or outings; posttraumatic play in which the game "kidnap" was played many times each day with a monotonous regularity; and weight loss of about four pounds. On the basis of this testimony, the judge decided she was "unavailable" for testimony in court. The psychiatrist suggested to the judge, however, that her testimony could be obtained under controlled conditions that protected her emotional well-being. Because attorneys for the two sides agreed to these conditions, six and one-half months after the abduction Susie was interviewed for a fifth time.

This interview also was videotaped, although the camera, attorneys, and judge's representative were obscured by a one-way glass. The psychiatrist conducted the interview with a microreceiver in one ear so that the attorneys could relay questions through him to the child. He had the Court's authority to veto questions if they seemed inappropriate for her age or potentially harmful to the child.

Susie reiterated her account of the abduction, sexual abuse, and attempted murder. Although she incorrectly identified the color of the suspect's car as "black," this perception was accurate from her perspective because the interior of his car—the part she saw most often—was black. The issue of whether the suspect had a female accomplice remained uncertain through all the interviews. Although Susie was not as spontaneous or detailed as she had been in the earlier interviews, which were closer in time to the trauma, Jones and Krugman (1986) suggest that Susie was not disturbed by the procedure. It should be noted, however, that it took two sessions to reestablish a therapeutic relationship between Susie and her psychiatrist.

Fifteen months after the abduction, the suspect made a full and detailed confession, admitting that he had sexually abused Susie in the exact manner the child had described. Under a plea bargain arrangement, he received a sentence of ten years imprisonment for sexual assault and attempted murder.

Four identifiable and separate psycholegal issues are raised by Susie's case and others like it.

Issue #1: Competence. How should the courts and society view the capabilities of children as witnesses?

Dilemma #1: To provide the means necessary to allow children to communicate what they know but also to protect defendants' rights.

This issue is complex and must be attacked from several angles: (a) What are the capabilities of children with respect to attending to, perceiving, encoding, storing, and retrieving memories? (b) What are the receptive and expressive communication skills of children? (c) How do children's perceptions of what is expected of them by parents, peers, and authority figures affect what they remember and report? (d) How do children perceive the procedures and players in the legal system, and how do these perceptions influence their ability to recall and to report important information? (e) What strategies maximize the accuracy of children's reports of events? (f) Conversely, how suggestible are children? (g) How do children's capabilities fare when they are compared with those of adults? (h) Regardless of the capabilities of children in general, what are the specific abilities of a particular child in a certain set of circumstances associated with a given legal case?

As these questions suggest, assessing the competence of the child as a legal witness is a complex task. All of the factors noted above must be considered when assessing the competence of a child as a potential legal witness. It is incumbent upon the court to provide the means necessary to allow children to communicate valuable evidence about a given legal case. The dilemma the court faces in this regard, however, is to provide those means while simultaneously protecting the constitutional rights of the defendant.

In Susie's case a number of sound, innovative procedures were used to help the child communicate her account of the events she had experienced. Some of her interviews were videotaped, as were her reactions to the videotaped lineup of suspects. She was provided photo arrays of suspects that did or did not include a picture of the accused. She was allowed to use toys and materials that provided her with an opportunity to play through the abduction, thereby adding detail that is difficult to obtain from a young child using verbal means alone. In short, Susie was able to communicate her competence because the court allowed the use of controlled procedures appropriate for working with a small child. The defendant's rights were protected by having his attorney present during the psychiatrist's questioning of Susie. He had ample opportunity to object to questions posed by the psychiatrist and to offer his own questions for the child to answer. Thus, although the defendant was not allowed to confront his accuser directly in court, he was allowed to confront the victim indirectly through his attorney.

Issue #2: Credibility. When should the courts and society believe the testimony of children who have been judged competent to give evidence?

Dilemma #2: To apprehend and convict criminals but also to detect false accusations.

At age three, Susie was able to remember and communicate the details of her victimization in a heinous crime, details that later were confirmed by the perpetrator. Clearly, had the case gone to trial, she *should* have been believed by the triers of fact. But, as with the issue of competence, the issue of credibility of child witnesses raises some intricate questions: (a) What factors influence a child's credibility in the eyes of the judge and jury? (b) Are the influential factors substantive (e.g., memory abilities of children in general, the suggestibility of children during cross-examination, or the capabilities of the particular child who takes the stand) or are they tangential (e.g., the physical appearance of the child or the facility with which she expresses herself)? (c) How do triers of fact judge the credibility of children versus that of adults as eyewitnesses? (d) Do jurors' pretrial assumptions or biases about children's abilities affect the perceived credibility of a particular child witness? (e) Is the child as witness more credible under some circumstances than others? All of these questions must be considered when assessing the credibility of a given child witness.

In the example provided by Jones and Krugman (1986), how would Susie have fared on the issue of credibility? Because Susie never testified in the courtroom, we have no way of knowing how she might have been perceived by jurors. All we know is that because of the posttraumatic symptoms she was displaying, the judge ruled that she was "unavailable for testimony in court" (p. 255). We know from the corroborating statement by the perpetrator that Susie *should* have been believed, but research evidence and anecdotal reports from other legal cases suggest that Susie's testimony might not have been given much weight. Ross, Miller, and Moran (1987), for instance, found that children's testimony tends not to be weighed heavily in making the final decision about guilt or innocence. Rather, jurors seem to rely on other available evidence, for example, the testimony of an eyewitness who is an adult. But, as we noted earlier, in sexual abuse cases the child usually is the *only* eyewitness. Even so, jurors seem reluctant to place much weight on the child's testimony. For example, immediately after acquitting the defendant in a case of sexual abuse of a child in Maryland, one member of the jury said, "It's very difficult to put someone in prison for something so serious, *based on a child's story*" (Beach, 1983, p. 58). Similar comments were made by jurors in the McMartin Preschool case. In other words, even when a child is judged competent to give testimony and the child's account of events is accurate, she or he may not be perceived as credible by those who will decide the verdict.

Moreover, not all children are as competent as Susie in providing legal evidence. (Indeed, many adults would pale by comparison! [See, for example, Loftus, 1979, or Loftus & Davies, 1984]) And, even if their memories are accurate, their ability to communicate clearly may be hampered either intentionally or unwillingly by the interviewer's questions. Consider this example provided by Berliner and Barbieri (1984):

[A] 5-year-old child, on direct examination, told the jury about her father putting his penis in her mouth. On cross-examination by the father's defense attorney, the following exchange took place:

Defense Attorney:	And then you said you put your mouth on his penis?
Child:	No.
Defense Attorney:	You didn't say that?
Child:	No.
Defense Attorney:	Did you ever put your mouth on his penis?
Child:	No.
Defense Attorney:	Well, why did you tell your mother that your dad put his penis in your mouth?
Child:	My brother told me to.

At this point, it looked as if the child had completely recanted her earlier testimony about the sexual abuse and had only fabricated the story because her brother told her to. However, the experienced prosecuting attorney recognized the problem and clarified the situation:

Prosecuting Attorney:	Jennie, you said that you didn't put your mouth on daddy's penis. Is that right?
Child:	Yes.
Prosecuting Attorney:	Did daddy put his penis in your mouth?
Child:	Yes.

Prosecuting Attorney:	Did you tell your mom?
Child:	Yes.
Prosecuting Attorney:	What made you decide to tell?
Child:	My brother and I talked about it, and he said I better tell or dad would just keep doing it. (p.132)

Thus, the credibility of the child as a witness hinges not only upon the accuracy of the account given, but also upon such other factors as whether the child is able to understand the questions posed, how literally the child interprets the questions asked, and how confidently the answers are given.

Issue #3: Children's Rights: What rights should child witnesses have to protection from harm?

Dilemma #3: To protect all children from further injury but also to protect specific children from further harm.

One means of seeing that "justice is done" is assuring that the guilty do not go free, but rather that they are punished for their transgressions against society. Our culture seems to have especially strong feelings in this regard when the victim is a child. But what happens when the critical testimony must be provided by a child who will suffer great emotional harm by testifying in court and reliving the nightmare in the presence of the defendant? Where is the "justice" in a system that requires that a child sacrifice her mental health in order that the guilty be convicted?

Melton (1984c) describes the potential traumatization of the child witness as follows:

The victim often must describe, and in a sense relive, the traumatic event repeatedly, and defense counsel may suggest that the victim stimulated or participated in the offense. . . . This emotional fallout of the legal process may be heightened by the requirement of testimony in open court; the victim may feel on display as he or she is forced to recall painful memories, defend against suggestions of having stimulated the offense, and confront the defendant. This feeling of public humiliation may be exacerbated by the presence of the press in the courtroom and the specter of future publicity. (p. 109)

We cannot know for certain whether Susie might have reacted similarly to the experience of testifying in the actual trial. We do know, however, that when presented with photos of the suspect, she appeared to be shocked and frightened and reported that he was a "*mean* man." We also know about the previously described emotional and physical reactions she had; according to her psychiatrist, Susie was a seriously traumatized child. Based upon this evidence, the judge ruled that Susie was "unavailable" for testifying at a preliminary hearing.

However, Susie's psychiatrist also suggested to the court that the child's testimony might be obtained under controlled conditions designed to protect her emotional well-being. In other words, the experience of giving testimony itself was not at issue, but rather the specific conditions under which the testimony was to be given. In Susie's case, with the consent of the prosecutor and defendant's counsel, the judge agreed to bend the rules. In this way, Susie was allowed to testify in a setting that was designed to minimize her re-traumatization. Of course, not all courts will agree to use such innovative procedures (see *Coy v. Iowa,* 1988).

Especially in legal systems in which the child is required to give testimony in the standard manner, the issue of retraumatization must be considered carefully. Berliner and Barbieri (1984) identify several concerns that should be addressed: (a) Will the child's testimony substantially increase the chance of conviction without doing serious harm to the child? (b) What is the child's own history? Does he or she have a history of trouble or adjustment problems that might be used to discredit the child's testimony, a process that may overwhelm the child? (c) Is the child likely to freeze or become very upset on the witness stand? (d) On the other hand, might the experience of testifying in court serve a therapeutic purpose, especially if the defendant is convicted? Berliner and Barbieri summarize the issue as follows:

> [T]he experience of testifying in court can have a therapeutic effect for the child victim. The child can learn that social institutions take children seriously. Some children report feeling empowered by their participation in the process. Some have complained, when the offender pled guilty, that they did not have an opportunity to be heard in court.
>
> Still, an acquittal can have a devastating effect on the child victim/witness. It is very difficult to explain to children that telling the truth does not always result in an outcome they consider just. (p. 135)

After studying children who had witnessed homicides, Pynoos and Eth (1984) came to a similar conclusion. They note, "[W]ith appropriate psychological consultation and intervention the child can be helped to cope with the trauma and subsequent judicial demands. In fact, satisfaction of both needs—that of the child and of the judicial system—are often found to be interdependent" (p. 88).

The task for practitioners in the field, therefore, is to determine what is "appropriate psychological consultation and intervention" for the child, in other words, intervention that promotes psychological healing in the child without subverting judicial due process.

Issue #4: Defendants' Rights. What rights should defendants have in cases involving child witnesses?

Dilemma #4: To apprehend and convict criminals but also to protect defendants' constitutional rights.

Two issues are at stake when we attempt to balance the interests of the child and the rights of the defendant. While it is morally admirable to protect children from harm, we must remember that our system of justice is founded on protection of the constitutional rights afforded to each and every citizen. Defendants must be presumed innocent until proven guilty. Moreover, the Sixth Amendment of the U. S. Constitution gives defendants the right to a public trial in which they may confront their accusers. When special procedures are invoked to reduce the potential traumatization of child witnesses——for example, use of videotaped testimony from the child, provision of a screen to shield the child from the defendant at court, or permission for the child to give testimony in the seclusion of the judge's chambers—the defendant's constitutional rights may be abrogated (Melton, 1984c). Melton (1984c) notes that in our legal system "the privacy interests of the child victim are likely to carry less weight in a balancing test than the rights of the defendant, which are constitutionally protected and therefore fundamental" (p. 111).

An ironic twist is that the defendant's constitutional rights may be breached whether the child takes the stand or not. If the child testifies and the court allows the use of special procedures (such as those noted above), it may be argued that the defendant is denied the right to a public, face-to-face confrontation with the accuser. If, on the other hand, the child is not allowed to testify, the defendant is *de facto* denied the right to confrontation. Thus, the court is faced with a unique and troublesome constitutional dilemma in cases involving children as sole eyewitness/victims.

Any case involving children as witnesses in court must come to terms with the four basic factors outlined above: (a) competence of the child to give testimony, (b) credibility of the child witness, (c) the rights of the child, and (d) the rights of the defendant. Unfortunately, making decisions regarding these issues is no easy task. Their resolution involves consideration of four broader psycholegal dilemmas (Wrightsman, 1991).

First, as noted above, child witness cases pit the constitutionally guaranteed rights of individuals against maintenance of the common good. In each case, the court must decide how to balance these conflicting values.

The second psycholegal dilemma involves the question of what should be the underlying principle in response to those who violate the law. Should defendants be treated with equality in all situations or with discretion depending upon the specific circumstances? Similarly, should adults and children be treated the same in the eyes of the court? Fundamental to our legal system is the assumption that everyone is equal before the law. Does this mean, then, that every witness, regardless of age or mental capacity, should be treated in exactly the same manner in court and at sentencing? Or should aggravating and mitigating circumstances be considered in each case? Are there relevant scientific data that speak to this issue in cases involving children as witnesses in court?

The third dilemma in our system of justice involves the clash between conflict resolution and discovery of the truth. Is it sufficient to resolve a conflict before trial in order to avoid putting the child through a possibly traumatizing event? Often, cases are plea-bargained to an admission of guilt without giving victims the opportunity to testify at trial. On the other hand, is justice better served by requiring that the child testify, even at the expense of doing psychological harm, if the truth of the matter can be ascertained?

Finally, what should be the source of decisions in cases involving children as legal witnesses? Both attorneys and social scientists may have the best interests of the child at heart; however, they also may see the same events through differing perspectives.

For example, when establishing new legal rulings, members of the judiciary are guided by case law, the rulings handed down in previous individual cases. Social scientists, on the other hand, rely on empirical evidence (for example, data from research studies) in making decisions. The methods of law and social science also differ. Law functions by the case method, with each case being viewed as an entity in its own right. In contrast, social scientists collect information via experiments, observations, and surveys, seeking to extract common factors in human behavior. Consistent relationships among variables, rather than one incident or case, are the focus of attention in the empirical approach of social science. Therefore, at times, rulings from case law and scientific evidence are at loggerheads with one another.

GOALS AND COVERAGE
OF THIS BOOK

This book seeks a reconciliation of the marriage between psychology and the law in cases involving children as witnesses in court. This chapter has raised the basic issues that must be considered in such cases.

Chapter 2 reports on research regarding the perceived credibility of children as witnesses in court. It reviews the scientific literature concerning the reactions of society in general, and more specifically of attorneys, jurors, and judges.

Chapter 3 provides a review of child and adolescent development from a psycholegal perspective. It outlines the development of the brain, perception, attention, cognition, psychosocial needs, and morality. It also addresses issues associated with working with exceptional children.

Chapter 4 raises issues of comprehension, memory, and communication relevant to children testifying in court. It provides an overview of children's understanding of legal settings and proceedings. It also discusses several memory issues relevant to children: models of memory, types of remembering, deficiencies in remembering, suggestibility, the impact of stress on children's memory, and strategies for maximizing children's memory.

Chapter 5 reviews the changing conceptions of children as witnesses in court from a historical perspective. It discusses the common-law tradition and rationale, recent trends in child witnessing, and current statutes and court decisions. Chapter 5 also covers the direct and cross-examination of children as witnesses in court, as well as special procedures that may be used when children testify.

Chapter 6 provides a social science assessment of the court's decisions regarding children as witnesses. It re-examines the basic issues raised in this chapter in light of recent empirical evidence and case law precedent.

Chapter 7 provides recommendations for procedures to be used with children who will testify in court. These guidelines are based upon a consideration of the generally accepted findings from both case law and the social sciences presented in preceding chapters.

2

In the Eye of the Beholder: Reactions to Children as Legal Witnesses

Reactions to Children as Legal Witnesses

Reactions of the public

Investigators' reactions
Police officers • *Therapists*

Attorneys' reactions

Jurors' reactions

Judges' reactions

Legal Views of Child Competence

Ancient and common-law traditions

Recent trends and statutes in the United States
States presuming incapacity below a specified age
States requiring an understanding of the oath
States following the Federal Rules of Evidence
States providing that all children are competent in sex offense cases

The competency examination

Summary

A witness wholly without capacity is difficult to imagine.
(Advisory Committee Note on Rule 601,
Federal Rules of Evidence)

What does the legal profession and the community at large have to say about the credibility of children as witnesses? When a child enters the courtroom for the purpose of providing evidence, what stereotypes and preconceived notions about children as witnesses influence the opinions of the important adults in the courtroom— attorneys, judge, and jurors? These are critical questions, for no matter how capable a young witness is, if he or she is not deemed credible by the triers of fact, the testimony given is considered worthless.

REACTIONS TO CHILDREN AS LEGAL WITNESSES

Many people—professionals and lay persons alike—believe that children are a curious mix: innocent and truthful on the one hand, yet also manipulable and devious (Goodman, 1984b). This view is not of recent origin. In 1911 psychologist J. Varendonck exhorted, "[W]hen are we going to give up, in all civilized nations, listening to children in courts of law?" (quoted in Goodman, 1984b, p. 9).

Reactions of the Public

Surveys of the public conducted by social scientists suggest that adults generally hold dim views of the capabilities of child witnesses (Leippe & Romanczyk, 1987; Ross, Dunning, Toglia, & Ceci, 1989; Yarmey & Jones, 1983). In two studies conducted by Leippe and Romanzcyk (1987), for example, young witnesses were rated as less credible than were adult eyewitnesses. This effect was especially pronounced if the witnesses demonstrated inconsistency in their testimony.

Similarly, Ross et al. (1989) found that adults believe that child witnesses are less likely to be accurate and more likely to be open to suggestion than are witnesses of adult age. Respondents in the Ross et al. study also reported that they would give less weight to testimony offered by a child than to that offered by an adult. In fact, adults in this study indicated that children do not become competent to testify until 16.1 years of age—well beyond the age children are deemed competent by statute!

In contrast, Wells, Turtle, and Luus (1989) found that although a negative stereotype of the young eyewitness probably exists, this stereotype likely is mitigated when triers of fact observe actual testimony delivered by young eyewitnesses. They note:

> The idea that a significant gap could exist between people's abstract view of the credibility of child eyewitnesses and how they judge the credibility of actual, concrete cases of child testimony should not be particularly surprising; after all, probably no one in our study or in previous studies had ever actually observed children give eyewitness testimony. (p. 33)

Indeed, Leippe, Brigham, Cousins, & Romanczyk (1989) note that very little scientific evidence is available concerning the perception and treatment of child witnesses by important actors in the criminal justice system. Surely, this is a serious omission in our understanding.

Investigators' Reactions

Any of several individuals may be the first to hear a child's eyewitness report or allegations of assault—family member, neighbor, teacher, social worker, psychologist, physician, or police officer. Typically, if the filing of criminal charges is considered, several players in the legal system will examine critically the veracity of the child's statements—the police, attorneys for the prosecution and defense, and perhaps a therapist. If these individuals are unconvinced by the child's statements and demeanor, the case is unlikely to go to court. On the other hand, if the child is viewed as credible, charges may be filed and a trial date set. It is, therefore, essential to know how the "first-line" investigators perceive children as legal witnesses.

Police Officers. Dent (1982) suggests that "some police officers at all levels simply view young children as 'innocents' who have no cause to lie and will, therefore, give accurate evidence" (p. 280). She provides no empirical evidence to support this claim, however, and additional studies in this area are lacking.

Therapists. A 1983 survey by Yarmey and Jones found that psycholegal professionals familiar with child development are particularly likely to be skeptical about children's testimonial abilities. In fact, 91 percent of the psycholegal researchers surveyed viewed children as unreliable witnesses who were both vulnerable to manipulation by the questioner and unable to answer accurately the questions posed to them. Only 69 percent of the laypersons surveyed held these beliefs.

However, more recent evidence suggests that Yarmey and Jones's (1983) conclusions are misleading. Therapists in particular are likely to believe the accounts of sexual abuse provided by young children (see generally MacFarlane). Anecdotal examples in this regard abound. Consider, for example, one social worker's comments:

> We know that children do not make up stories asserting they have been sexually molested. It is not in their interests to do so. Young children do not have the sexual knowledge necessary to fabricate an allegation. Clinicians and researchers in the field of sexual abuse are in agreement that false allegations by children are extremely rare. (Faller, 1984, p. 475)

Similarly, two researchers assert that "it has become common practice for interviewers to assume that the allegations are true" (Raskin & Yuille, 1989, p. 186; see also Young, 1986).

Attorneys' Reactions

Little empirical research has been conducted concerning attorneys' attitudes toward children as legal witnesses. We will discuss two recent studies that begin to shed light on this topic. Keep in mind, however, that both of these studies used limited samples taken only from the state of Florida, so generalization of their results may not be appropriate.

Brigham and Wolfskeil (1983) surveyed 166 defense attorneys, 69 prosecuting attorneys, and 186 police officers in the state of Florida concerning various aspects of eyewitness evidence, including testimony given by children. The authors comment, "[T]he most striking characteristic of the results was the marked differences in the responses of defense and prosecuting attorneys" (p. 103).

Brigham and Wolfskeil (1983) found that more than 90 percent of the prosecutors they surveyed believed that eyewitnesses correctly identify perpetrators. Moreover, prosecutors generally believed that eyewitness evidence was given the right amount of emphasis in court. They also strongly opposed the use of expert testimony by psychologists concerning eyewitness reliability. Finally, prosecutors were likely to believe in a positive relationship between eyewitness accuracy and the confidence with which testimony is delivered.

Not surprisingly, defense attorneys held opposing views. They estimated that only 50 to 75 percent of the eyewitness identifications they had observed were accurate and felt that jurors and judges placed too much emphasis on eyewitness evidence. As a result, defense attorneys were very receptive to the inclusion of courtroom expert testimony that questioned eyewitness reliability.

In reviewing Brigham and Wolfskeil's work, Leippe et al. (1989) note:

> [T]he bimodal pattern of the responses may reflect disagreement among attorneys and judges about children's testimony. A casual analysis of quotes by attorneys in media coverage of child sexual abuse cases suggests the same bimodal distribution of attitudes, with some attorneys viewing children as accurate witnesses and others viewing them as highly suggestible and therefore inaccurate. These discrepant beliefs usually fall along partisan prosecution/defense lines in a manner similar to that found by Brigham and Wolfskeil. (p. 105)

Leippe et al. (1989) also conducted a survey of public defenders and prosecutors. The researchers asked respondents to estimate the percentage of disputed eyewitness identifications for three age groups: (a) adults, (b) children 10 to 17 years, and (c) children nine or younger. Their results indicated both areas of agreement and specific areas of bipolarization between prosecutors and defenders.

Both groups expected younger witnesses to perform more poorly than their adult counterparts: to recall fewer details of the witnessed event, to be less likely to identify the assailant, to be more suggestible to the influence of authority figures, and to include more inconsistencies in their eyewitness accounts. Across age groups, however, prosecutors assigned a significantly higher mean accuracy estimate (83 percent) than did defenders (58 percent). On average, prosecutors gave the same high estimates of accuracy (83 to 84 percent) for adults, older children, *and* younger children, whereas defense attorneys perceived a definite age-accuracy relationship, with accuracy increasing from 46 to 67 percent with age. Interestingly, a significant number of prosecutors expected greater sincerity from a child (versus an adult) communicating an eyewitness account to police, lawyers, or juries.

Defenders did not hold the same view. In fact, a significantly greater proportion of defense attorneys than prosecutors perceived child witnesses as less able to recall important information, less able to identify the assailant from a lineup, more suggestible, and more prone to inconsistency in their eyewitness accounts. Moreoever, 25 percent of the defenders (versus only 2 percent of the prosecutors) estimated that children knowingly give false testimony on a frequent basis. Leippe et al. (1989) comment, "[T]his underscores saliently the distrust of young children among defense attorneys that was evident throughout this survey" (p. 113).

It is interesting to note, however, that although defense attorneys themselves are highly skeptical of children's testimony, "many public defenders perceive jurors as decidedly *un*skeptical about child witnesses" (Leippe et al., 1989, p. 115). Indeed, almost all of the defenders surveyed indicated that they commonly use a set of strategies designed to convince jurors of the unreliability of children's testimony. First, they highlight the youth of an eyewitness in opening arguments. Next, they point out weaknesses of the child's testimony—inconsistencies, memory lapses, and apparent compliance—during the trial. During cross-examination they also try to use to their advantage the child's vulnerabilities. Finally, during closing arguments they underscore again the reasons to distrust children's testimony. With regard to these techniques, Leippe et al. comment:

Our attorneys' candid admissions of commonly manipulating jurors' impressions of children on the witness stand are relevant to growing concerns that adversarial methods like rigorous cross-examinations may be ill-suited to truth gathering in the case of young child witnesses. (p. 127)

The prosecutors surveyed reported significantly less use of these strategies when they were confronted with child witnesses presented by defense counsel. Neither group of attorneys used two "academic" approaches: (a) calling expert witnesses (such as psychologists) to testify about children's memory abilities, and (b) citing relevant psycholegal research. In this regard, Leippe and colleagues point out that "[u]ndoubtedly, many attorneys are simply unaware of psycholegal research on child witnesses" (p. 121). Yet, in at least three states—Arizona, California, and Washington—failure to admit psychological expert testimony concerning eyewitness identification led to reversal of conviction on appeal (*State v. Chapple*, 1983; *State v. Moon*, 1986; *People v. McDonald*, 1984).

Prosecutors and defenders disagree on more than their perceptions of children as witnesses. They also have distinctly different ideas about the acceptability of alternative methods for obtaining testimony from children. As Table 2.1 indicates, prosecutors are much more likely than defenders to favor innovative methods for obtaining evidence from children.

Indeed, the only alternative method that even a small majority of defense attorneys accepted was testimony aided by anatomical dolls and other props.

Although few empirical studies have been conducted assessing attorneys' views of children as witnesses, those that do exist suggest that lawyers' perceptions are colored to a significant degree by their training and by the type of legal practice they maintain (prosecution or defense). Contrary to the commonly held view, neither group is particularly reluctant to bring to trial cases relying on a young child witness, although both groups recognize that there are special problems associated with such cases.

Jurors' Reactions

If a child is deemed credible by preliminary investigators and by at least one attorney, the case may be tried in court and the child may be asked to take the stand. At that point, the outcome of the case depends in part upon how each witness is perceived by the triers of fact—the citizens who comprise the jury. In a case involv-

Table 2.1
Frequency and acceptability of alternative ways of obtaining and
presenting the testimony of children who are witnesses or victims in
alleged crimes of sexual abuse.

Method	Attorneys' combined mean estimate of how frequently (% of the time) this method is currently used	Percentage (%) of attorneys responding that "In principle, this method is *somewhat acceptable* or *completely acceptable* to me"*	
		Defense attorneys	Prosecuting attorneys
Hearsay evidence of medical doctor	53	19	93
Testimony with aid of anatomically correct dolls and other props	48	51	98
Hearsay evidence of parents	46	7	86
Hearsay evidence of psychologist	38	16	84
Hearsay evidence of teacher	27	10	81
Hearsay evidence of other children	22	5	71
Videotaped testimony	18	13	77
Written testimony of child's account	3	1	31

NOTE: The percentage of prosecutors exceeded the percentage of defense attorneys for all eight methods at $p<.001$, according to chi-square tests.
SOURCE: From "The opinions and practices of criminal attorneys regarding child eyewitnesses: A study" by M. R. Leippe, J. C. Brigham, C. Cousins, and A. Romanczyk, in *Perspectives on children's testimony* (pp. 110-130) by S. J. Ceci, D. F. Ross, and M. P. Toglia (Eds.), 1989, New York: Springer Verlag. Reprinted by permission.

ing a child witness, the performance of the child at trial may well
be a critical factor. Therefore, it is important to know how jurors
perceive children as legal witnesses.

There is little empirical evidence assessing actual jurors' views
of child witnesses; however, anecdotal reports are not uncommon

in the press. For example, one juror in a Maryland child sexual abuse case commented, "It's very difficult to put someone in prison for something so serious, based on a child's story" (Beach, 1983, p. 58). Similarly, jurors in the celebrated McMartin Preschool trial, described in chapter 1, acquitted the defendants on 52 counts, although several members of the jury panel interviewed by the press indicated they believed that the children had in fact been molested. Jury foreman Luis Chang commented:

> What it all comes down to was the lack of a smoking gun. We felt there was evidence of molestation in some cases, but that by and large we really don't know if the children's remarks were true or if they were being led by adults. There's some truth in there somewhere, but we couldn't find it (*People Weekly*, 1990).

Although research involving actual jurors in child witness cases is not available, a number of jury simulation studies have been conducted. Generally, these studies suggest that child witnesses are deemed less credible than adult witnesses. In a series of studies, Goodman and colleagues (Goodman, Golding, & Haith, 1984; Goodman, Golding, Helgeson, Haith, & Michelli, 1987; Goodman & Michelli, 1981) found that mock jurors rated six-year-olds as less credible witnesses than young adults. The finding was robust:

> Regardless of whether the testimony was presented in written form or on videotape, whether the subjects were undergraduate students or adults from the Denver community, or whether the trial concerned vehicular homicide or murder, mock jurors rated the six-year-olds as less credible witnesses than the thirty-year-olds. (Goodman, Bottoms, Herscovici, & Shaver, 1989, p. 2)

Goodman et al. (1987) call this effect the "importance displacement hypothesis," suggesting that jurors give more weight to the testimony of other witnesses when the key witness is a child and not an adult.

Although it has been widely assumed that jurors tend not to believe child witnesses (Yarmey & Jones, 1983), recent evidence suggests that this assumption is too simplistic (Nigro, Buckley, Hill, & Nelson, 1989). While adults have a tendency to doubt the credibility of children's testimony in general, those doubts may be either confirmed or refuted when a particular child takes the stand

and a particular set of citizens is seated as a jury. Impressions of a particular witness are influenced by several factors, including the amount of incriminating evidence against the defendant and such witness characteristics as honesty, trustworthiness, consistency, certainty, confidence, and objectivity (Goodman et al., 1984).

Leippe and Romanczyk (1987), for example, report that mock jurors' assessments of bystander credibility are modified by the amount of incriminating evidence against the defendant. In their study, when the incriminating evidence was weak or moderate, age differences were not found to affect verdicts, but when the incriminating evidence was strong, the age of the eyewitness mattered. Under the strong evidence condition, the adults' testimony resulted in 100 percent of the jurors rating the defendant as guilty, while the six- and ten-year-olds' statements resulted in only 58 percent of the jurors rating the defendant as guilty.

In a second study (Leippe & Romanczyk, 1987), the researchers found that consistency of the witness's account also interacted with age. Testimonial consistency did not significantly affect the credibility of either the ten-year-old or the adult witness; indeed, "only the six-year-old paid a price for inconsistency" (Nigro et al., 1989, p. 62).

Likewise, Nigro et al. (1989) found that both powerfulness of the witness's speech style and witness age affect jurors' ratings of witness credibility. In their study, child witnesses who used a powerful speech style were rated as the most credible witnesses, even more believable than were adults who used powerful speech styles. Moreover, there were significant positive correlations between eyewitness credibility and defendant guilt in every condition. In fact, jurors did not seem to rely on corroborating evidence when the child testified using a powerful speech style. But corroborating evidence was not sought for the adult witness regardless of speech style, a finding that underscores the generally greater credibility afforded adults as compared with children.

Several researchers have offered hypotheses that attempt to make sense of the complex interactions between witness age and other characteristics that influence the perceived credibility of the witness.

Ross et al. (1989) suggest a "stereotypes" hypothesis to explain these findings. They argue that "[p]eople expect the child witness to be hesitant, vague, easily distracted, or quite eager to please the attorney questioning him or her" (p. 40). Moreover, they contend:

[t]o the extent that the behavior of the child witness conforms to these expectations, or is ambiguous enough to be interpreted as conforming to them, jurors will naturally discount the veracity of the child's testimony. (pp. 40-41)

Conversely, to the extent that the child's behavior on the witness stand violates jurors' expectations, the child is likely to be viewed as extremely credible. Ross et al. note:

Consider a child who testifies forcefully and in very precise detail. Such a child would be truly impressive, and perhaps even more credible than an adult counterpart exhibiting the same behavior. (p. 41)

This hypothesis may explain why, for example, mock jurors find a child's powerful speech style to be particularly convincing.

Goodman et al. (1989) offer other explanations. They suggest that jurors hold at least two kinds of theories that influence their perceptions of children's credibility as witnesses:

One theory is that children are generally as honest as adults, if not more honest—a theory that might predispose jurors to believe child witnesses. The second theory is that young children's cognitive abilities are less developed than those of adults, which might be expected to lead jurors to question children's testimony under many conditions. . . . Whether a child's credibility is weakened or strengthened by jurors' adherence to the second theory depends on how jurors' views of children interact with the details of a particular case. (p. 1)

In other words, the nature of the particular case may affect which characteristic—honesty or cognitive ability—is more important in assessing a specific child's credibility. When accuracy of memory is considered critical, as in a case that hinges upon eyewitness identification, a young child's lack of cognitive sophistication may reduce his or her credibility in the eyes of the jury. In cases in which honesty is deemed more important, however, as in a sexual assault case involving a younger child and a perpetrator known to the child, the child's lack of cognitive abilities actually may enhance credibility. In the latter case, jurors would not expect the child to have mature knowledge of sexual acts and behavior. Indeed, jurors well may suspect that the young child who testifies confidently about such matters has been coached.

Ross et al. (1989) draw several conclusions concerning how age stereotypes influence jurors' perceptions of child witnesses:

> First, the testimony of a child will be evaluated more positively than the testimony of an adult under two conditions: (1) when the child's testimony violates, in a positive manner, the juror's expectation about children's eyewitness abilities or (2) when witness credibility depends more on honesty than cognitive ability. Second, the testimony of a child will be viewed more negatively than the testimony of an adult when neither of these conditions are present, and when (1) the child acts like a typical youngster or (2) credibility rests mainly on the ability to remember events (p. 42).

Even when child witnesses are viewed positively, however, it is unclear whether their testimony is weighed heavily in making the final decision of guilt or innocence of the defendant. Goodman et al. (1987) found that mock jurors' judgments of the defendant's degree of guilt did not differ reliably as a function of the age of the eyewitness. Similarly, Ross et al. (1987) found that when a child testifies, jurors seem to rely on other available evidence, for example the testimony of an adult eyewitness, when reaching a verdict—a finding that supports Goodman's importance displacement hypothesis.

But Ross et al. (1989) found no support for Goodman's hypothesis. In their study, whether the key witness was a child, young adult, or senior citizen, mock jurors gave roughly equal weight to the testimony of other witnesses.

Duggan et al. (1989), however, did find an effect of age, although it was not in the predicted direction. In a simulated sexual abuse trial, Duggan et al. found that it was not the very youngest child who was considered to be the least credible witness, but rather the teenager. Still, they conclude:

> We can say that a jury is very unlikely to convict without some corroboration, especially if the victim is an adolescent or very young, although that judgment has to be tempered by the limitations of the simulation method. (pp. 91-92)

While children's testimony may not affect the verdict, it may change jurors' attitudes toward child witnesses (Goodman et al., 1987). A case in point is the McMartin Preschool trial described in chapter 1. As noted earlier, the co-defendants in the McMartin case were acquitted on 52 counts of child abuse, yet posttrial interviews of jurors indicated that the majority believed that the child witnesses had in fact been molested.

A similar result was obtained in a mock jury experiment conducted by Perry, Docherty, and Kralik (1988). These researchers assessed jurors' attitudes toward children as witnesses at three points in the trial procedure: (a) before the jurors heard testimony, (b) after they heard testimony but before deliberations began, and (c) after a verdict had been reached. Perry et al. found that the specific child's testimony had little impact on individual attitudes toward child witnesses before the jury deliberated. However, attitudes toward child witnesses in general changed as a result of deliberation. Specifically, when jurors heard a confident child witness, their attitudes toward children as witnesses became more positive following group discussion. Conversely, when jurors were exposed to a nonconfident child witness, their attitudes toward child witnesses in general became more negative following the deliberative process. In sum, although witness confidence did not affect the jurors' decisions regarding guilt of the defendant, it did affect attitudes toward children as witnesses.

What can we reasonably conclude from all of these studies of mock jurors' perceptions of children as witnesses? Dunning (1989) provides this tongue-in-cheek analysis:

> A lawyer assigned to a case involving a child witness calls the researcher to have lunch to discuss the issue. At lunch, the lawyer asks the psychologist a question of straightforward interest: "Would jurors believe a child as much as an adult?" The social scientist, armed with the rich array of data presented here and elsewhere, would be forced to answer clearly and concisely with the following: "Well, you see, it all depends. Sometimes jurors disbelieve the child. Sometimes they believe the testimony of a child more than an adult offering comparable testimony. And there is a third possibility—sometimes they believe each equally." It is easy to imagine the lawyer, on hearing this "it all depends" conclusion, rolling his or her eyes to the high heavens and wishing that social scientists would just once provide a clear and usable bottom line. (pp. 233-234)

But Dunning is correct; jurors' perceptions of child witnesses *do* vary depending upon the circumstances. On the one hand, they appear to be impressed by the honesty of children, especially of young children, and so are likely to find a particular child credible if it is assumed that he or she is too naive to employ ulterior motives. On the other hand, if the credibility of the child witness depends more on his or her ability to remember, jurors are not likely to perceive the child as believable. The stereotype of children as poor rememberers can be dispelled to some extent if the child's behaviors violate jurors' expectations—that is, if the child appears confident, alert, articulate, and not confused.

Judges' Reactions

We are not aware of any empirical studies of judges' reactions to children as legal witnesses. Goodman et al. (1989) report that the view that older children could be reliable witnesses appeared in the legal literature as early as 1910 when a German judge by the name of Gross stated that a " ' healthy half grown boy' is the best possible witness for simple events" (p. 4, as cited by Whipple, 1912). Some thirty years later, esteemed legal scholar Wigmore stated the case more eloquently:

> A rational view of the peculiarities of child nature, and of the daily course of justice in our courts, must lead to the conclusion that the effort to measure *a priori* the degree of trustworthiness in children's statements, and to distinguish the point at which they cease to be totally incredible and acquire some degree of credibility, is futile and unprofitable. . . . Recognizing on the one hand the childish disposition to weave romances and to treat imagination for verity and on the other the rooted ingenuousness of children and their tendency to speak straightforwardly what is in their minds, it must be concluded that the sensible way is to put the child upon the stand and let the story come out for what it may be worth. (Wigmore, 1940, § 509)

Historically, these are minority views among the judiciary. For the majority of legal history, child witnesses have been viewed with suspicion by the judiciary. Recent decisions, however, suggest that this view is changing. Children are appearing as witnesses in increasing numbers of legal cases, and the courts are becoming increasingly amenable to the use of alternative methods for allowing children to testify (Bulkley, 1989). For example, in 1990 the U.S. Supreme Court ruled in *Maryland v. Craig* (1990) that, upon determining that a child's courtroom testimony will result in the child suffering serious emotional distress, it is permissible to introduce into evidence the child's videotaped testimony obtained by one-way closed circuit television.

Liberalizing the standards for admitting child testimony into evidence, however, may have little effect on how individual trial judges view child witnesses. Like the public's and jurors' views of children as witnesses, the judiciary's view traditionally has been skeptical. Moreover, judges' views of the credibility of child witnesses have been inextricably linked to their definitions of witness competence. It is important, therefore, to understand the roots of the concept of legal competence to testify. This understanding helps explain why the judiciary has reacted to the testimony of child witnesses as it has.

LEGAL VIEWS OF CHILD COMPETENCE

In order to be allowed to testify, the courts insist that any potential witness must possess certain characteristics. These include the capacity to observe, sufficient intelligence and adequate memory to store information, the ability to communicate, an awareness of the difference between truth and falsehood, and an appreciation of the obligation to speak truthfully (*American Jurisprudence,* 1960). Historically, children were deemed deficient in these abilities and automatically were excluded from giving testimony at trial. However, recent legal decisions show that the courts now favor the view that a child of any age who possesses the requisite characteristics may testify (Myers, 1987). Indeed, child sexual abuse victims, regardless of how young they are, are deemed competent by statute in many states (Landwirth, 1987).

Ancient and Common-Law Traditions

For the majority of legal history, children were deemed incompetent to give testimony in court.[1] Early canon law prohibited individuals from testifying if they had not yet reached the age of puberty (Collins & Bond, 1953). For example, according to *The Jewish Encyclopedia* (1916), early Jewish tradition held that "[t]he witness must be a man, not a woman . . . of full age, that is, more than thirteen years old" (p. 277). Some cultures even excluded testimony of an adult who retrospectively reported events witnessed during childhood. In one case a judge of the ancient Sanhedrin attempted to testify concerning an execution by means of burning that he had witnessed as a child. He said, "I was a child and was being carried on my father's shoulders and I saw it [the execution by burning]." His judicial colleagues replied, "You were then a child, and the evidence of a child is inadmissible" (*Talmud*, 7:2, cited in Myers, 1987).

Throughout most of the middle ages, children younger than age 14 were excluded from giving testimony at trial (Ceci, Toglia, & Ross, 1987a). Eventually, as the English common law developed, the age limit for competency was reduced to seven years of age. Children younger than seven were believed to lack both the capacity to commit a crime and to take the oath required before offering testimony (Wigmore, 1935/1976). Children of seven or more years, however, were allowed to testify if it could be demonstrated that they understood the nature of an oath, even if they could not define the concept. Goodman (1984b, p. 12) cites this interesting seventeenth-century example (*Rex v. Braddon and Speke,* 1684):

Judge: What age are you of?
Witness: I am 13, my lord.
Attorney: Do you know what an oath is?
Witness: No.
Judge: Suppose you should tell a lie, do you know who is the father of lies?
Witness: The devil.
Judge: And if you should tell a lie, do you know what would become of you?
Witness: Yes.
Judge: What if you should swear to a lie? If you should call God to witness to a lie, what would become of you then?
Witness: I should go to hell-fire. (p. 1127)

The boy was permitted to testify on the grounds that he understood the nature of the oath.

In the American colonies, too, the English common law tradition of excluding the testimony of young children prevailed. This rule was suspended in the late 1600s, however, in a series of strange events that culminated in the Salem Witch Trials of 1692 (Ceci, Toglia, & Ross, 1987b).

During the summer and fall of that year, approximately 20 residents of Salem, Massachusetts, were accused, tried, convicted, and executed for the crime of being wizards and witches. The historical record shows that at least 100 individuals in the area surrounding Salem also were accused of witchcraft, with most accusations being leveled by children. In Salem, the so-called "circle girls"—Ann Putnam, Elizabeth Hubbard, Mary Walcott, and Mary Warren—provided the key testimony in 19 of the 20 trials that led to conviction and execution. These four girls provided "evidence" purporting to show that they had been physically afflicted by the defendants' alleged practices. At trial, for example, they went into apoplectic fits and vomited bent nails and pins that were alleged to have been placed in them by witchcraft. By the early 1700s several of the child-accusers had recanted their testimony and begged forgiveness from the surviving family of the executed defendants. The 1706 confession of the most notorious of the child-accusers, Ann Putnam, to the pastor of the Village Church is particularly poignant:

> I desire to be humbled before God for that sad and humbling providence that befell my father's family in the year 1692: that I, then being in my childhood, should by such a providence of God, be made an instrument for the accusing of several persons of a grievous crime, whereby their lives were taken away from them, whom now I have just grounds and good reason to believe they were innocent persons; and that it was a great delusion of Satan that deceived me in that sad time, whereby I justly fear that I have been instrumental, with others, though ignorantly and unwitting, to bring upon myself and this land the guilt of innocent blood . . . . I desire to lie in the dust, and to be humbled for it, in that I was the cause, with others, of so sad a calamity to them and their families. . . . (from the Witchcraft Papers, State House, Boston, cited in Ceci, Toglia, & Ross, 1987b)

For 200 years after the Salem Witch Trials, the courts noted the excesses of the Salem "circle girls," suggesting that this example provided grounds for not allowing the uncorroborated testimony of children at trial (Ceci, Toglia, & Ross, 1987b). Indeed, only recently has the uncorroborated testimony of youths been admissible at trial.

In 1779 a panel of 12 common-law judges in the United States determined that "there is no precise or fixed rule as to the time within which infants are excluded from giving evidence"; however, they noted that "the court must pose questions to determine if the child understands the 'danger and impiety of falsehood' " (*Rex v. Braiser* [1779], cited in Goodman, 1984b, p. 12).

This ruling paved the way for an important shift. Instead of relying primarily on a determination of the competence (or incompetence) of the child witness, the courts began to place more emphasis on the role of the trier of fact in assessing the credibility of the witness. The judge or jury was given more latitude in assessing the child witness's capacity and intelligence, his or her understanding of the difference between truth and falsehood, and his or her *comprehension* of the obligation to speak the truth. This trend was highlighted in *Wheeler v. United States* (1895), a case in which a five-year-old-boy testified as a witness to his father's murder. The defendant was found guilty and sentenced to be hanged. He then appealed to a higher court, claiming that the child should not have been permitted to take the stand. The appeals court rejected the defendant's claim and held:

> The boy was not by reason of his youth, as a matter of law, absolutely disqualified as a witness . . . . While no one would think of calling as a witness an infant only two or three years of age, there is no precise age which determines the question of competency. This depends upon the capacity and intelligence of the child, his appreciation of the difference between truth and falsehood, as well as of his duty to tell the former. The decision of this question rests primarily with the trial judge, who sees the proposed witness, notices his manner, his apparent possession or lack of intelligence, and may resort to any examination which will tend to disclose his capacity and intelligence, as well as his understanding of the obligation of an oath. . . . (pp. 524-525)

Under this ruling, young children still were presumed to be incompetent to testify in most states; however, a party could challenge the presumed incompetence of a given child. Thus, the burden of proof rested on the party wishing to call the child to the stand to testify.

Twenty-three years later, the Supreme Court changed the presumption to one of competence, rather than incompetence, in its *Rosen v. United States* (1918) opinion:

> the truth is more likely to be arrived at by hearing the testimony of all persons of competent understanding who may seem to have knowledge of the facts involved in a case, leaving the credit and weight of such testimony to be determined by the jury or by the court, rather than by rejecting witnesses as incompetent. (cited in Myers, 1987 p. 471)

Under this ruling, the focus changed from competence to credibility of the witness; in other words, there was a shift from the judge's responsibility to rule on competence to the jury's responsibility to decide on credibility (Haugaard, 1988). The competence of any witness still could be challenged, of course, but the burden of proof shifted from the attorney wishing to call the child to the stand to the opposing party (usually defense counsel).

Recent Trends and Statutes in the United States

As time passes, children of increasingly tender years are being allowed to testify at trial. Today, in contrast to the wording in the *Wheeler* decision above, even "an infant only two or three years of age" may be called to the stand. And yet, calling such a young witness to the stand remains a rare occurrence, even though recent legal guidelines do allow for this provision.

Case law and statutory requirements concerning the competence of child witnesses are found in each of the 50 states. Of course, variations occur from one jurisdiction to the next, but generally it is possible to group states into four categories: (a) states presuming incapacity below a specified age, (b) states requiring an understanding of the oath, (c) states following the Federal Rules of Evidence, and (d) states providing that all children are competent in sex offense cases (Myers, 1987). These groupings are not mutually exclusive, however. Some states have enacted statutes from more than one category, e.g., one presuming incompetence below a specified age *except* in sex offense cases. For this reason, in a given case it is important to check the relevant state's statutes in each of these areas.

States Presuming Incapacity Below a Specified Age

Some states hold that children below a certain age (usually 10, 12, or 14) are presumptively incompetent unless the trial judge determines via questioning that they possess the capacity to testify. Such states are tied historically to the common law rule which held that children below certain ages were incapable of understanding the nature of an oath and thus were incompetent. Consider, for example, the Idaho statute, which reads in part, "The following persons cannot be witnesses: . . . . Children under ten (10) years of age, who appear incapable of receiving just impressions of the facts respecting which they are examined, or of relating them truly" (Idaho Code § 9-202 [Supp. 1986]).

In point of fact, it may be a more accurate description of the applicable rule in these states to say that for children below the

designated age there is no presumption either way regarding
competence (Myers, 1987). Indeed, the Maine Supreme Judicial
Court so held in *State v. Pomerleau* (Me. 1976). And, in reality, the
great majority of children over the age of five are judged competent
after appropriate questioning by the court (Myers, 1987). Still, a
pretrial ruling of testimonial competence can be overturned at
trial, as the New York case, *People v. Murphy* (N.Y.Supp. 1988),
demonstrated. The case involved a defendant charged with two
counts of forcible sodomy in the first degree, three counts of forcible
sexual abuse in the first degree, one count of sexual abuse in the
first degree, and endangering the welfare of a child. Prior to jury
selection, the court held a preliminary examination, as required by
New York state law, to determine the nine-year-old alleged victim's
testimonial capacity. The judge wrote:

> At that proceeding he was so unresponsive to my questions that I
> found him incapable of providing sworn testimony. Candidly
> acknowledging the weakness of the corroborating evidence, after the
> luncheon recess the trial assistant requested a second opportunity
> for the boy to demonstrate his capacity to take and understand the
> nature of an oath. At this second interview the child was more
> responsive and articulated in a persuasive manner his understand-
> ing and recognition of the importance of testifying truthfully. . . . On
> the basis of the boy's answers, behavior and demeanor on this second
> occasion, I ruled that he was able to understand the nature of an oath
> and qualified him as a sworn witness.

> Unfortunately, in the context of the trial, this assessment turned out
> to be wrong. It became increasingly clear during [the boy's] testimony
> not only that the boy did not understand the importance of telling the
> truth but that at times he became so unnerved by the questioning
> that he did not even know what the truth was. This was particularly
> apparent during cross-examination. His manner and answers indi-
> cated that his sole interest was to end the ordeal of testifying and
> that he was answering questions without regard to the content of
> what he was saying. (p. 907)

In this case the New York Supreme Court (Kings County) ruled as
follows:

> There is no reported case of a trial court reassessing its CPL 60.20
> [New York statute] determination of a witness's testimonial capacity
> as a result of that witness's testimony at trial. As a rule, the deter-

mination of that capacity made prior to the trial is not altered by events at the trial. However, as this case demonstrates, the more informal, comfortable atmosphere in which the exploration of a child's testimonial competence is conducted *can* result in a misevaluation of the child's capacity. Under these circumstances the trial court has an obligation to alter its determination. To hold otherwise would require that court to adhere mechanically to a ruling made in the exercise of its discretion which it knows to be erroneous. (p. 908)

Similarly, the state of Washington ruled that while it may be preferable to conduct competency hearings prior to commencement of trial, there is no prohibition against conducting such a hearing after the trial has commenced (*State v. Clark,* Wash. App. 1988).

Thus, while most children over the age of five are judged competent to testify, such a ruling is not irrevocable. At any point during the proceedings, the competence of the child witness may be called into question.

States Requiring an Understanding of the Oath

Several states employ the oath as a means to ensure the witness's understanding of the obligation to testify truthfully. The purpose of the testimonial oath is two-fold: "to alert the witness to the moral duty to testify truthfully and to deter false testimony by establishing a legal basis for perjury prosecution" (*People v. Parks,* 1976, p. 366).

Use of the oath requirement harks back to the common-law practice of barring from the stand individuals who either did not understand the religious implications of an oath or would not or could not take an oath (Myers, 1987). Today, the oath continues to play a role in legal proceedings, although the states now allow witnesses to substitute a secular affirmation for a religious oath (see Cleary, 1984). For example, Rule 603 of the Federal Rules of Evidence states, "[b]efore testifying, every witness shall be required to declare that he will testify truthfully, by oath or affirmation administered in a form calculated to awaken his conscience and impress his mind with his duty to do so." The Georgia statute is representative, stating in part, "children who do not understand the nature of an oath, shall be incompetent witnesses" (Georgia Code Ann. § 24-9-5 [1982]).

Under this approach, the child need not be able to define the term *oath,* or even to give an example of an oath, in order to be judged competent. Consider the case of *State v. Eiler* (Mont. 1988), heard by the Supreme Court of Montana. In this case an eight-year-old sexual abuse victim was judged competent to testify to incidents that occurred four years earlier, although she could not remember where she lived at the time of the alleged abuse or what clothes she and the defendant were wearing when the acts took place. The child's testimony undoubtedly influenced the jurors' verdict of guilt. The defendant appealed the decision partly on the grounds that the child did not appreciate "the duty to tell the truth," a corollary of the oath requirement. In order to show that the girl did not know the difference between the truth and a lie, the appellant (that is, the defendant) quoted a portion of the child witness's deposition:

Q: Is there a reason for telling the truth?
A: Yes.
Q: What's the reason for telling the truth?
A: (No response)
Q: Do you believe in God?
A: Yes.
Q: Okay. And does God have anything to do with you telling the truth?
A: Yes.
Q: What does God have to do with that?
A: I don't know. (762 P.2d 210 [Mont. 1988], p. 214)

In citing this testimony, counsel for the defendant argued that the child did not know what it meant to tell the truth. The appeals court ruled, however, that defense counsel had neglected to call attention to the statements made immediately prior to and immediately following this testimony:

Q: Okay. Now do you know what it means to tell the truth?
A: Yes.
Q: What does it mean to tell the truth?
A: To tell what really happened.

*   *   *

Q: Okay. Does God care if you tell the truth?
A: Yes.
Q: And do you wish to please God?
A: Yes.
Q: Okay. What do you think happens if you don't tell the truth?

A: You won't be resurrected. (762 P.2d 210 [Mont. 1988], p. 214)

* * *

Q: Okay. Do you get in trouble for not telling the truth, not telling the truth at school?
A: Yes.
Q: What happens if you don't tell the truth at school?
A: You have to go to detention.
Q: What is detention?
A: You have to stay in in recess.
Q: And do you ever—would you get in trouble at home for not telling the truth?
A: Yes.
Q: What happens if you don't tell the truth?
A: You have to go to bed. (762 P.2d 210 [Mont. 1988], p. 214)

The appellate court ruled that the child in this case did understand the difference between the truth and a lie, and, having agreed to tell the truth with the understanding that telling a falsehood results in punishment, the child had complied with the spirit of the oath requirement. Similarly, the Texas oath statute was considered fulfilled in *Gonzales v. State* (Tex.App.—Beaumont 1988]) when questions asked by the judge and the prosecutor were sufficient to "impress" witnesses who were minors with their duty to be truthful.

Even a witness who has been "duly impressed" may not be disqualified if he or she has shown some tendency to prevaricate outside the courtroom. The fact that a child has lied previously does not render him or her incompetent. Myers (1987) notes that there are few, if any, witnesses who have not "stretched the truth" (p. 99). Past moral lapses do not relate to competence; rather, such weaknesses speak to the believability of the witness, an attribute which must be assessed by the jury during the course of the trial.

States Following the Federal Rules of Evidence

In recent years, a growing number of states have adopted some version of the Federal Rules of Evidence. Rule 601 of the Federal Rules of Evidence, which became effective in 1975, speaks to the issue of children's competence. It states: "Every person is competent to be a witness except as otherwise provided in these rules." Rule 601 reflects the current trend toward eliminating rules that disqualify witnesses from testifying simply because they belong to

a certain group (Bulkley, 1989). The state of Pennsylvania interpreted this rule literally in *Commonwealth v. Anderson* (Pa.Super.
1988), noting, "Generally, testimony of any person, regardless of
mental condition, is competent evidence, unless it contributes
nothing at all because witness is wholly untrustworthy" (p. 1064).

Experts in the field suggest that Rule 601 is intended to curtail
the need for preliminary inquiry into the witness's competency,
leaving the jury to determine the weight and credibility of the
testimony offered (Myers, 1987). McCormick (Cleary, 1984) notes:

> The major reason for disqualification of (children) to take the stand
> is the judge's distrust of a jury's ability to assay the words of a small
> child. . . . Conceding the jury's deficiencies, the remedy of excluding
> such a witness, who may be the only person available who knows the
> facts, seems inept and primitive. Though the tribunal is unskilled
> and the testimony difficult to weigh, it is better to let the evidence
> come in for what it is worth, with cautionary instructions. (pp. 140-
> 141)

Using the Federal Rules approach, the traditional competency
examination should be unnecessary. In practice, however, despite
the admonition that "every person is competent," trial judges
continue to assess and rule on the competence of children (Myers,
1987). In fact, several states claiming to use the Federal Rules
approach qualify Rule 601 by adding on to it one or more of the
traditional competence qualifications. In Massachusetts, for example, the statute states that "[a]ny person of *sufficient understanding* . . . may testify" (Mass. Gen. Laws Ann. ch. 233, § 20 [West,
1986]). In Kentucky the statute reads in part that "every person is
competent . . . *unless* he be found by the court incapable of understanding the facts concerning which his testimony is offered" (Ky.
Rev. Stat. Ann. § 421.200 [Baldwin, 1981]). Similarly, Graham's
(1981) *Handbook of Federal Evidence* notes that the judge retains
discretion to exclude any individual's testimony if a reasonable
juror could believe that "the witness is so bereft of his powers of
observation, recordation, recollection, and recount as to be so
untrustworthy as a witness as to make his testimony lack relevance" (§ 602.2).

Although Rule 601 (even when amended) clearly paves the way
for more children to testify, other safeguards are built into the
system that prevent improper inclusion of child witnesses. For

example, Rule 603 of the Federal Rules of Evidence states: "[b]efore testifying, every witness shall be required to declare that he will testify truthfully, by oath or affirmation." In order to make a meaningful declaration, of course, the child must be able to distinguish truth from falsity and to appreciate the duty to tell the truth (see examples above). If the court determines that a child lacks either or both of these capabilities, Rule 603 could be invoked to exclude the witness's testimony. Similarly, Rule 403 might be used to exclude testimony of a child witness if she is found to be so marginally competent that the probative value of her testimony would be "substantially outweighed by the danger of unfair prejudice, confusion of the issues, or misleading the jury, or by considerations of undue delay [or] waste of time" (Fed. R. Evid. 403). And, if a prospective child witness's testimony proves unnecessary or merely cumulative, the court could exclude it under Rule 611, which governs the court's broad authority to control the presentation of evidence.

In other words, Rule 601 (and statutes of similar phrasing) provide wide latitude for children to be deemed competent to testify, but the presiding judge still must be the one to decide the probative value of the testimony. In this regard Weinstein and Berger (1987) conclude, "It would, however, in view of the way [Rule 601] is cast, probably be more accurate to say that the court will decide not competency but minimum credibility" (p. 3). The state of Nebraska concurred in *State v. Guy* (Neb. 1988), in which the court opined: "The question as to the competency of a witness must be determined by the court, while the credibility and weight of the testimony are for the jury to determine" (p. 155).

Although some version of Rule 601 has been adopted by several states, there are a relatively small number of legal decisions interpreting it. A review of these decisions suggests that the courts continue to rely on common-law principles of witness competence (Myers, 1987). For example, in *State v. Guy* the state of Nebraska noted:

> In ruling whether or not a child is a competent witness, the trial court must determine whether a child is sufficiently mature to receive correct impressions by his or her senses, whether the child can recollect and narrate intelligently, and whether the child appreciates the moral duty to tell the truth. (p. 155)

With regard to the effect of Rule 601, Myers (1987) concludes:

> The impact of Rule 601 will be felt not so much in the elimination of
> competence as an issue, as in an emphasis on allowing the maximum
> number of individuals to take the stand. In the final analysis, the
> interests of justice are promoted by investing trial judges with
> authority to evaluate and decide upon the competence of child
> witnesses. The trial court is in a unique position to evaluate whether
> a child possesses the minimum capacity needed for meaningful
> testimony. In view of the extraordinary importance of child testimony
> in some kinds of litigation, it is essential that children who are
> incompetent do not take the stand. At the same time, Rule 601
> ensures that in most cases children are permitted to testify. (p. 71)

In other words, while the courts have attempted to separate the
issues of competence and credibility with regard to child witnesses,
in point of fact these issues are inextricably linked in the legal
arena. The argument appears to us to be a circular one: (a)
Competence of the child need not be determined at a preliminary
hearing. (b) Instead, the trier of fact should assess credibility. (c)
In assessing credibility, the judge or jury should rely, in part, on
the competence of the child! Psychological research, on the other
hand, suggests that competence and credibility of the child witness
can, and indeed should, be assessed independently. (See chapter 6.)

States Providing That All Children Are Competent in Sex Offense Cases

The American Bar Association's National Legal Resource Center
for Child Advocacy and Protection recently provided recommendations for improving legal intervention in the sexual abuse of children by members of their own family (Bulkley, 1982). The center
concluded:

> Child victims of sexual abuse should be considered competent
> witnesses and should be allowed to testify without prior qualification
> in any judicial proceeding. The trier of fact should be permitted to
> determine the weight and credibility to be given to the testimony.
> (p. 30)

In the past five years, all jurisdictions have enacted statutes in
accord with the ABA's recommendations (Bulkley, 1989). The Utah
statute is illustrative, reading in part that "[a] child victim of

sexual abuse under the age of ten is a competent witness and shall be allowed to testify without prior qualification in any judicial proceeding" (Utah Code Ann. § 76-5-410 [Supp. 1986]).

Putting aside the particular form of each jurisdiction's child competence statutes, the general trend is to allow more and younger children to testify at trial. Children typically are included as witnesses if (a) they persuade the court that they have personal knowledge of the alleged incidents, and (b) they demonstrate the capacity to observe, sufficient intelligence, adequate memory, the ability to communicate, an awareness of the difference between truth and falsehood, and an appreciation of the obligation to speak the truth.

The Competency Examination

While the vast majority of children are competent to testify, some may be unwilling to do so, and in other cases parents may not allow their children to take the stand, usually because they fear traumatization or retribution. In the McMartin Preschool trial, described in chapter 1, more than 40 children originally were scheduled to be witnesses. After one child was subjected to 16 days on the stand—15-1/2 of them under cross-examination—many parents with children scheduled to be called withdrew permission for them to give testimony.

When a child agrees to provide testimony, the generally accepted rule is that competence is presumed (Haugaard, 1988). Depending upon the statutes operating in a given jurisdiction, however, competence may or may not have to be demonstrated to the court (Melton, 1990). Clearly, in states that presume incompetence below a designated age, competency of the younger child must be proven. In other states the child may or may not be subjected to a competency evaluation prior to being sworn. In any case, the court's more lenient attitude toward competency of children has shifted the burden of proof. Now, as noted earlier, opposing counsel must show that the child is *in*competent rather than the child's counsel having to demonstrate that the witness is competent (Haugaard, 1988; Mahady-Smith, 1985).

The trial judge makes the determination regarding competence of all witnesses including children, and the court has broad discretion in reaching its competency decisions (Myers, 1987). Unless the court abuses its discretion, the judge's determination will be affirmed. Case law provides some interesting examples of abuses by judges in this regard.

In *State v. Cook* (La.Ct.App. 1986), for instance, counsel for the defendant argued that the court endorsed the witness's veracity when the judge rewarded the child with candy in the presence of the jury, following the child's testimony. The appeals court agreed. Similarly, in *State v. R.W.* (N.J. 1986), the appeals court wrote that "the trial judge abused his discretion by promising the child ice cream and in subsequently giving it to her, thereby suggesting to the jury, albeit inadvertently, that the infant had indeed testified truthfully" (p. 1289). However, in *People v. Matthews* (*Ill.* [1959]) the child was judged competent to testify despite the fact that her mother had promised her a paint set if she told the truth. Because the line demarcating abuses is not clear, we believe that the best policy is to avoid making promises of tangible rewards to children called to provide testimony.

The standard procedure for determining whether a particular child is competent to give testimony is to conduct a preliminary or *voir dire* examination before the child is sworn. Whether such an examination is necessary in a given case depends upon the prevailing statutes. Myers (1987) summarizes the situation as follows:

> Such examinations are required for children who are presumed to be incompetent. Preliminary examinations also are common in jurisdictions where an understanding of the oath is required. In states where every person, including children, is deemed competent, preliminary examinations are unnecessary unless the court believes a particular child to be incompetent. As a practical matter, courts in such states frequently conduct competency examinations of younger children. Counsel may request an examination if there is reasonable cause to believe a child lacks competence. In states adopting an absolute rule of competence in sex offense cases, it appears that a preliminary hearing cannot be held. (p. 106)

Any of the legal parties may challenge the competence of the child; however, objections must be timely (Cleary, 1984). *American Jurisprudence* (1960) notes that "Objection to the competency of a witness must be made at the first opportunity and failure to do so precludes further objection on that score" (p. 176).

Timely objection has different implications, depending upon the relevant statutes (Myers, 1987). In jurisdictions requiring competence examinations for certain children, an examination should be requested before the child is sworn and objections raised at the close of the *voir dire* questioning. In jurisdictions following the Federal Rules approach, an examination may be requested by counsel if there are reasonable grounds to question the child's competence. Ideally, the request should be made prior to the child being sworn, but often grounds for incompetence of the witness do not appear until the trial is in progress. Cleary (1984) writes, "After the witness has been sworn, the progress of his direct examination or cross-examination may disclose his incapacity, and then he may be stopped and his preceding testimony ordered expunged" (p. 643). The case of *People v. Murphy* described above is illustrative. Recall that, in this case, the judge rescinded his ruling of competence for a nine-year-old child who decompensated while giving testimony at trial.

The trial judge has a great deal of latitude in conducting the *voir dire* examination of a child. The court may conduct the examination before or during the trial, either in the presence or in the absence of the jury, with or without the participation of counsel (Myers, 1987).

While some argue that it is technically improper for the trial judge to leave the competency examination to counsel (*Sprayberry v. State,* Ga.App. 1985), others suggest that allowing counsel to question prospective child witnesses during *voir dire* assists the court in reaching a fully informed decision (Cleary, 1984).

As a matter of practice, most courts prefer to conduct the competence examination in the absence of the jury. Because the rules of evidence that govern admissibility of testimony at trial do not apply during the competence examination, holding the examination in the presence of the jury might expose jurors to inadmissible evidence.

The factors considered by trial judges in determining competence of a child include the ability to observe, to remember, and to communicate truthfully (Myers, 1987). As discussed in chapters 3 and 4, most children—even those as young as age two or three—possess these abilities, especially if they are asked to describe salient incidents in their lives. Consequently, the vast majority of children are deemed competent to testify. If the child's competence is in doubt, it may be helpful to have the child evaluated by a psychologist or psychiatrist prior to the in-court competency examination.

Myers (1987) notes that "[p]reparing a child for a competency examination is an integral part of preparing the child for testimony at trial. The attorney must ensure that the child possesses—and can demonstrate to the judge—the ability to observe, remember, communicate, differentiate truth from falsehood, and comprehend that punishment follows false testimony" (p. 120). (See chapter 7 for specific suggestions for preparing children for competency examinations.)

When a child successfully completes a competency examination, he or she is judged competent to testify, is sworn as a witness, and is asked to respond to questions from counsel under direct and cross-examination (see chapter 5 for a description of these procedures).

The court's recognition that children can be competent witnesses is an important step. However, as noted earlier in this chapter, the effectiveness of children as legal witnesses depends upon more than their legal competence; also at issue is their credibility. No matter how factually accurate they are, no matter how well they are able to communicate, no matter how resistant they are to suggestion, the question remains: Will they be believed by investigators, attorneys, jurors, and judges?

SUMMARY

Adults generally hold dim views of the capabilities of children as witnesses. A commonly held opinion is that children are poor at remembering the relevant details of an event. On the other hand, adults believe that children generally are honest and therefore are likely to tell the truth as they understand it when they serve as legal witnesses.

If criminal charges are to be filed against a defendant in a child witness case, several players in the legal system will examine critically the veracity of the child's statements—the police, attorneys for the prosecution and defense, and perhaps a therapist. It is asserted commonly that the police and therapists are particularly likely to believe allegations of sexual abuse made by children. Although few empirical studies have been conducted assessing attorneys' views of children as witnesses, those that do exist suggest that, contrary to the commonly held view, neither prosecutors nor defenders are particularly reluctant to bring to trial cases relying on child witnesses. Both groups recognize, however, that special problems are associated with such cases. In addition, lawyers' perceptions are colored to a significant degree by their training and by the type of legal practice they maintain. Prosecutors are far less skeptical about the abilities of children as witnesses than are defense attorneys.

Jurors' perceptions of child witnesses (assessed primarily by means of jury simulation studies) seem to vary, depending upon the circumstances of each case. Generally, jurors appear to be impressed by the honesty of children, especially of young children, and so are likely to find a particular child credible if it is assumed that he or she is too naive to employ ulterior motives. On the other hand, if the credibility of the child witness depends more upon his or her ability to remember, jurors are not likely to perceive the child as believable. The stereotype of children as poor rememberers can be dispelled to some degree if the particular child witness's behaviors violate jurors' expectations—that is, if the child appears confident, alert, articulate, and not confused.

For the majority of legal history, child witnesses have been viewed with suspicion by the judiciary. Recent decisions, however, suggest that this view is changing. Children are appearing as witnesses in increasing numbers of legal cases, and the courts are becoming increasingly amenable to the use of alternative methods for allowing children to testify.

Judges' views of the credibility of child witnesses have been inextricably linked to their definitions of witness competence. In order to be deemed competent to give testimony, potential witnesses of any age must possess certain characteristics—the capacity to observe, sufficient intelligence and adequate memory to store information, the ability to communicate, an awareness of the difference between truth and falsehood, and an appreciation of the obligation to speak truthfully. Historically, children were considered deficient in these abilities and so were excluded from giving testimony at trial. Recent statutes and legal decisions show that the courts now favor the view that a child of any age who possesses the requisite characteristics may testify. Case law and statutory requirements concerning the competence of child witnesses are found in each of the 50 states. Generally, statutes fall into one of four categories: (a) states presuming incapacity below a specified age (a minority), (b) states requiring an understanding of the oath, (c) states following the Federal Rules of Evidence (a growing number), and (d) states providing that all children are competent in sex offense cases (all 50).

Typically, children are included as witnesses if (a) they persuade the court that they have personal knowledge of the alleged incidents, and (b) they demonstrate the requisite characteristics listed above. The trial judge makes the determination regarding competence of all witnesses including children. The trial court has broad discretion in reaching its competency decisions, including ruling on whether a formal competency examination is required or may be waived.

Once the child has been ruled competent to give testimony during the trial, it is left to the jurors to determine the weight to be given to the child's testimony. Thus, even when a witness has been deemed competent, he or she may not be considered credible in the eyes of the triers of fact.

NOTE

1. Of course, others were excluded as well—women, criminals, the mentally deficient, and those unable or unwilllilng to take the oath (Myers, 1987).

3

The Developing Child: A Psycholegal Perspective

Physical and Mental Development

The developing brain

The development of perception

The ordering and interpretation of perceptions

The development of attention

The development of cognition
Mental representations of the world

Cognitive limitations of young children

Emotional and Social Development

Children's psychosocial needs

Morality
Moral reasoning • Moral development

Special Considerations

Traumatized children

Stages of grieving

Working with exceptional children
Retarded children
Disabled children
Children with behavioral or emotional disorders

Summary

The science of children deals with 'average' children. It describes typical behavior at different ages. It invents theories that explain the most common ways of thinking and behaving, the most usual reactions, the most widespread beliefs and attitudes. It deals with what is common, normal, predictable, average.

But there is no average child. The concept is a convenient invention, a necessary creation if we are to speak coherently and meaningfully of all children. We must always keep in mind that each child is a unique individual, that each is different from the 'average' in countless ways, and that no one theory will ever account for all behavior. Children are incredibly more complex than even the most extensive theoretical description of them.

(Guy Lefrancois, Introduction to *Of Children*, 1989, p. 3)

Indeed, children are a fascinating and complex mixture of abilities and shortcomings. Although William James once suggested that infants enter this world in a state of "blooming, buzzing confusion" (1890, p. 488), now it is understood that even infants are governed by finely tuned perceptual and cognitive processes—processes that develop and change in predictable ways over the lifespan (Flavell, 1985).

For several reasons, a working knowledge of the stages and issues of child development is essential to any person who interacts with children in the legal system. First, an understanding of child development helps professionals know what to expect from children of different ages. What can a child of age 10, 7, 4, or 2 understand of complex legal proceedings? Typically, how do such young children react in the courtroom setting? A good understanding of child development helps answer these questions.

Second, such an understanding may be helpful in determining why children sometimes have trouble comprehending questions, recalling information, distinguishing fact from fantasy, or expressing themselves. Young children reason in fundamentally different ways from adults. Those who work with small children must understand these vital differences.

Third, such knowledge assists in accurately determining children's competence to testify and in considering how much weight to give their testimony. As noted in chapter 1, these two issues—competence and credibility—are at the heart of the legal dilemmas associated with children testifying in court. Moreover, as chapter 2 explained, attitudes toward the abilities of children as observers and reporters often are uninformed. If justice is to be served, such attitudes must be based upon a solid understanding of child development.

Finally, understanding child development may be vital to the mechanics of working with children in the legal system. Professionals need to know how to conduct successful interviews, to overcome communication barriers, to deal with problems of factual accuracy, to prepare children for the courtroom experience, to examine and cross-examine children effectively, and to resolve special problems.

For centuries, the competence and credibility of children when testifying have been questioned (Goodman & Helgeson, 1985). Society increasingly is willing to listen to children, although doubts linger concerning children as witnesses, as the reactions of jurors in chapter 2 exemplified. For example, the fact that children sometimes are confused more easily than adults, and consequently may suffer a loss of confidence, places them at a disadvantage within the adversary system because jurors tend to believe witnesses who are confident and do not appear confused (Goodman & Helgeson, 1985). Moreover, children's credibility may suffer because jurors tend to believe witnesses who remember both central and peripheral detail, and children sometimes have difficulty remembering noncentral information (Goodman & Helgeson, 1985; but see Parker, Haverfield, & Baker-Thomas, 1986). Finally, there is a widespread belief that children can be manipulated easily into making false reports (Goodman & Helgeson, 1985). Given the beliefs of society in general and of jurors in particular, it is imperative that those working with children who serve as witnesses be familiar with what is known about the actual capabilities and limitations of young witnesses.

This chapter[1] provides an overview of child development, with a special emphasis on practical implications for those who work with children in legal settings. The chapter is organized into three divisions. The first outlines the stages of child development, including the development of the brain and of perceptual, attentive, and cognitive skills. Part two describes the psychosocial (emotional and social) needs of children and outlines their moral development. Part three addresses special considerations associated with working with child witnesses: understanding their emotional needs in the legal setting, dealing with issues of traumatization and grieving, and working with exceptional children.

PHYSICAL AND MENTAL DEVELOPMENT

The Developing Brain

The human brain processes information, solves problems, makes decisions, and guides behavior—all skills essential to witnessing and reporting events accurately. The brain, however, is immature at birth and requires more than a decade to mature fully. Understanding the intricate process of the brain's development may be helpful to those who work with children, for significant changes occur in a relatively short period of time. These changes dramatically alter children's ability to perceive, attend to, remember, and report events—the precise skills needed for a person to be considered a competent and credible witness.

The human brain is a complex organ composed of approximately 100 billion highly specialized cells that pass chemical and electrical signals across about 100 trillion synapses, or connective spaces between the cells (Hubel, 1979). This amazing mass of tissue, weighing roughly 3 pounds at maturity, consists of three functionally interconnected units that have evolved over the millennia (Maclean, 1970). The first to evolve, the so-called *reptilian* brain, is responsible for such basic life-maintenance functions as breathing, digestion, regulation of metabolism, consciousness, and alertness. The second, or *paleomammalian,* brain is concerned with emotions, scent, taste, sexual behavior, and memory. One part of the paleomammalian brain, the hippocampus, is especially important to memory functions, and matures at about age five (Rose, 1979). When the hippocampus is damaged, the ability to lay down new memories is impaired (Hecaen & Albert, 1978). The third unit, called the *neocortex,* is the seat of language, attention, working memory, spatial understanding, and motor skills. This area of the brain, comprising 99 percent of the two cerebral hemispheres, regulates most of the functions that are of interest to a person working with child witnesses.

At birth, a baby's brain has all the neurons (nerve cells) it will ever have. Neurons destroyed by accidents, aging, or lack of stimulation will not be replaced. Although all of an individual's neurons are present at birth, the size and weight of the newborn's brain is only about 25 percent of what it will be in adulthood. The rapid growth of the baby's brain over the next few years is accomplished primarily through the proliferation of two cerebral components: (a) synaptic connections among neurons, and (b) glial cells. The glial cells do not engage in the "thinking work" done by the neurons of the brain; rather, they are responsible for nourishing the working neurons. They also are responsible for the development of a fatty substance (myelin) that coats and protects the neural fibers, thereby reducing the random spread of impulses from one fiber to another. The myelin sheath is similar to the rubber coating that insulates wires in an electrical cord, keeping them from either losing electrical potential or shorting out. Although most of the myelination of fibers is complete by two years of age, some myelin sheaths continue to develop until the time of adolescence. Because myelination seems to play a role in the ability of the individual to serve as a competent and effective witness, those who work with children may want to understand the process of myelination and how it affects behavior. As neurons become myelinated, they pass impulses more rapidly and efficiently. Initially, efficient functioning occurs only in the primary areas of the cortex. These areas govern motor behavior, primitive sensations, vision, and audition. The cortical association areas, which are responsible for integrating and interpreting the stimuli they encounter, lag behind the corresponding primary areas during the early stages of development. Thus, communication among the various parts of the brain is limited. For example, young children may have difficulty describing their experiences because the impressions they form in memory may not be translated into communications that can be understood by others. As the child grows older, however, the functional parts of the brain become more integrated as myelination progresses.

Improvement in myelination is directly reflected in the abilities of the child. In young infants, for example, the brain's response to a new sight or sound is delayed, likely because nerve impulses travel more slowly over unmyelinated fibers and across immature synapses. The response begins to quicken after babies reach three months of age. By the time the fibers that connect the reptilian cerebellum to the higher functioning cerebral cortex are mature at age four, children respond as rapidly to new sights and sounds as do adults (Yakovlev & Lecours, 1967). Thus, myelination of the neurons of the brain may have some effect on the child's ability to serve as an accurate witness.

One of the last structures to myelinate is the *corpus callosum,* the band of fibers connecting the two hemispheres of the brain. The corpus callosum has two major functions: (a) to keep each half of the brain from interfering with the other's motor control of the opposite side of the body, and (b) to transfer information from one hemisphere to the other. The latter function is particularly important in the case of witnessing an event, because the two sides of the brain must work in concert to translate and transmit information about the event. For most individuals, the right hemisphere of the brain specializes in the perception and analysis of visual patterns, melodies and other nonspeech sounds, faces, spatial locations, and emotions, while the left hemisphere specializes in the production and understanding of language. Thus, to be an effective witness, it is desirable for the individual to be able to do both: (a) to perceive the event accurately (primarily a right-hemisphere function) and (b) to convey information about the perceptions (typically a left-hemisphere function). Communication between the hemispheres of the brain is, therefore, helpful (though not essential) to giving effective testimony.

Myelination of the corpus callosum is not complete until after a child is 10 years old (Galin, Johnstone, Nakell, & Herron, 1979). However, incomplete myelination of the corpus callosum is not sufficient reason to prevent a child from giving testimony. The work of Galin and his associates shows that, although the hemispheres may function autonomously in very young children, communication between them improves greatly by the time the child is 5 years old.

Galin's group wanted to discover how early certain kinds of information are transferred between the hemispheres. They tested three- and five-year-old right-handed girls with tiny pillows of varying textures—e.g., rayon, wool, linen, and denim. With the child's vision blocked, they rubbed a piece of fabric over one of her hands. Next, they rubbed either that same hand or the other hand with either the same or a different fabric. The child was asked to determine whether the two fabrics were the same or not. Three-year-olds did as well as five-year-olds when only a single hand was involved (sending messages to only one side of the brain). However, three-year-olds found the judgment very difficult when both hands were involved (sending messages to both sides of the brain). Five-year-olds, by contrast, made the same number of correct responses whether the fabrics were rubbed on only one hand or on both hands (Galin et al., 1979).

It is important to note that Galin's group tested only a very simple kind of cerebral transfer, the sense of touch. The corpus callosum of most five-year-olds likely is not mature enough for the transfer of more complex information, e.g., that involving complicated decisions and evaluations, such as making inferences and drawing conclusions. Thus, while young children may well be capable of accurately perceiving events and of communicating simple information about those occurrences, they are not able to engage in inferential thinking about the events. It is only as children approach adolescence that their maturing brains permit them to evaluate their perceptions with a degree of sophistication approaching that of adults.

While older children have more mature brains, it is inappropriate to conclude that older children are, a priori, better witnesses. While younger children are sometimes less able to report details about what they have witnessed and to draw conclusions about what they have seen, the clarity of adolescents' and adults' accounts may be clouded by *too much* thinking about the witnessed events. Older witnesses sometimes are less able to separate their *thoughts about* what they perceived from the perceptions themselves. While younger children may commit errors of omission, adolescents and adults may commit errors of commission (Goodman & Helgeson, 1985), i.e., "remembering" details that did not exist or occur.

One example of this phenomenon was provided by an 11-year-old girl. While she and her 9-year-old sister were out for a walk one day, they encountered a young man on a bicycle who yelled to them, calling attention to his exposed penis. The girls provided separate reports of the incident to their mother. Initially, both girls stated that the young man was Caucasian, of college age, shirtless, wore short cutoff jeans, and had exposed his penis through the leg opening of his cutoffs. Later, the older girl changed her report, stating that the exhibitionist had worn not jeans but loose-fitting blue shorts. When the child's mother asked her why she had changed her mind, the girl replied, "He *couldn't* have been wearing jeans, because jeans are tight and he put his penis out through the leg of his shorts. Jeans would be too tight to do that."[2] The culprit never was apprehended, so we cannot know with certainty what he wore. Still, the point remains that the girl's report had changed based upon her thoughts about the memory of her experience.

The Development of Perception

Like adults, children are bombarded continuously by perceptual stimuli. The most basic perceptual processes—those involving the five senses—function at an adult level even during infancy, although some aspects of perception change with age. Specifically, five sorts of changes occur in the development of perceptual abilities (Hall, Lamb, & Perlmutter, 1986):

1. As children mature, their perceptions become more selective and more purposeful.
2. Children become more skillful in discerning the critical information from stimuli.
3. Perception becomes more sensitive as children learn to detect increasingly subtle aspects of stimuli.
4. Children become increasingly aware of the meaning of their perceptions.
5. Children become more proficient at generalizing perceived meanings from one situation to another.

The developmental changes in perceptual ability were demonstrated in an experiment by Zinshensko and Ruzskaya (cited in Zaporzhets, 1965). Three- to six-year-old children were presented with abstract shapes that they were allowed to explore by touch but were prevented from seeing. The children's visual recognition of the objects they had explored with their fingers then was tested. Zinshensko and Ruzskaya obtained results consistent with those of Galin and his colleagues (Galin et al., 1979) who had presented children with the tiny pillows made of different fabrics. At about age five, a sharp improvement in performance occurred, likely as a result of maturing brain structures and functions.

Developing perceptual skills also lead to improved performance in distinguishing among people. Babies as young as five months old are capable of distinguishing between men and women. However, children do not find it easy to recognize unfamiliar people in photographs and short films until they reach adolescence (Hall et al.,1986).

This trend may be accounted for by the fact that young children tend to base their identifications on ephemeral aspects of the person—e.g., hairstyles, accessories, and facial expressions. This phenomenon has been demonstrated in a variety of experiments. Carey and Diamond (1977), for example, showed six- to ten-year-olds color photographs of two women and asked them to identify which woman had been seen in a picture presented a few moments earlier. In the test picture, the original model's dress, expression, or hairstyle had been altered. Younger children (age 6), distracted by the transient details, did poorly on the task. Only older children (age 10) paid attention to the critical stimulus—the configuration of facial features—when judging the photographs.

The finding that young children (i.e., ages three to six) experience difficulty in identifying unfamiliar faces also may be explained in part by the fact that many young children have difficulty integrating the details of a picture into a unified whole. Elkind (1977) demonstrated this lack of perceptual integration by showing children pictures consisting of large figures made up of smaller wholes (such as a child's scooter made from lollipops and candy canes, or a person made from pieces of fruit). When children looked at the pictures, four-year-olds tended to see only the component parts (e.g., candy or fruit) rather than the larger gestalt. Some five- or six-year-olds could see both (components and gestalt), but only one at a time. Nine-year-olds, on the other hand, were likely to describe the pictures as, for example, "a man made out of fruit"; i.e., they were able to integrate their perceptions. This is an important development, as the ability to integrate perceptions may be helpful to children who are called upon to testify.

Although the ability to recognize unfamiliar people may be difficult for younger children, it is important to keep in mind that adults also have problems in this area, as studies of eyewitness accounts have made clear (Loftus, 1979). Moreover, some young children are quite capable of making accurate eyewitness identifications (Perry, Nielsen, Silvius, & Rosenthal, 1986). Research indicates that their performance on eyewitness identification tasks improves when the "culprit" is identified via a live lineup viewed through a screen rather than by selecting from a group of photographs (see generally, Dent & Stephenson, 1979; see also Egan, Pittner, & Goldstein, 1977). This finding has obvious and important implications for practice.

The manner in which children come to understand events also changes with age. During any event, part of the perceptual information changes while the rest remains constant. Our task is to perceive the event as meaningful and unified—as having a distinctive beginning and end, as abiding by certain rules (Hall et al., 1986). For instance, we know that some events are reversible, while others are not. A child may walk from the table to the refrigerator; then the child can retrace the steps and return to the table. This is a reversible event: it makes sense in either sequence. Other events, however, are irreversible. Spilled milk cannot be returned to the glass.

Very young children do not understand the property of reversibility. By age four, however, children can distinguish between reversible and irreversible events. When Megaw-Nyce (1979) showed four-year-olds a film of a reversible event run backward, they accepted it without comment. When the film of an irreversible event (such as the breaking of an egg) was run backward, however, children were aware that the event violated their understanding of the world. Thus, while younger children often are capable of *describing* simple events, they may have difficulty *comprehending* or *interpreting* such events until they are older.

Despite the developmental immaturity of children's perceptual ability, in some respects younger children have more accurate perceptual capabilities than do adults. For example, young children often are more accurate in their estimates of size constancy than are adults.[3] This phenomenon was demonstrated in an experiment by Gibson (1969). Children were asked to estimate the size of a distant object. Five-year-olds erred in their estimates by only 1 percent, while adults were wrong in their estimates by an average of 4 percent. Interestingly, six- to eight-year-olds performed the worst; their estimates were off by as much as 17 percent! Remember that very young children's perceptions are relatively unclouded by thinking about (and therefore transforming) the original perception, so their estimates may be more accurate. The same cannot be said for adults.

As a rule, then, it would be inappropriate to assume that young children, as compared with adults, are less capable of perceiving events accurately. It is true that as they mature their perceptual competence grows, but if children pay attention at the time of an event, they are quite capable of accurately perceiving what transpires. This is particularly true with relatively straightforward, factual occurrences. Because it is about such occurrences that children normally are asked to testify, most youngsters as young as age four (and in some instances as young as age two or three) possess the perceptual skills needed to give accurate testimony.

The Ordering and Interpretation of Perceptions

While most young children have the basic perceptual skills to enable them to give accurate testimony about factual events, it is likely that they may have difficulty in conceptualizing complex events, identifying relationships, recognizing feelings, and attributing intentions (Perry & Teply, 1984-1985). In each of these circumstances, the accuracy of their reporting depends upon their ability to order and interpret perceptions, a gradually acquired attribute that does not reach the standard of adult reliability until about the age of 12 (Collins, Wellman, Keniston, & Westby, 1978; Flapan, 1968).

Flapan (1968) evaluated children's ability (a) to make inferences about feelings, thoughts, and intentions, and (b) to explain sequences of behavior that occur in interpersonal relations. The results indicated that a substantial difference existed between the ability of 6-year-olds and that of older children. Specifically, when shown two movies of factual situations, 6-year-olds were less able to report about the adult's actions, states of mind, and feelings than were the 9- to 12-year-olds. Research on children's ability to accurately understand and interpret events depicted on television corroborates Flapan's finding (Collins et al., 1978). Interpretative ability is not well established until between ages 10 and 13.

Ordering and interpreting perceptions requires an understanding of the concept of time. Although experts disagree about when this concept is mastered (Melton, 1981a), it generally is acknowledged that children under the age of seven or eight have great difficulty in understanding and reporting elapsed time (Piaget, 1969). They are better at reporting events as having occurred in relation to some routine aspect of their daily lives (e.g., "during 'Sesame Street' " or "just before I went to bed"). Without such concrete anchors, the time perceptions of young children may be embellished, diminished, or otherwise distorted.

When distortion occurs in a child's ordering and interpreting of events, the most likely explanation is unconscious error rather than deliberate misstatement. Children have little need to distort their perceptions. On the contrary, they spend many of their waking hours attempting to comprehend what they perceive. Another point to keep in mind is that while young children may have difficulty ordering more complex, less familiar events, misorderings do not necessarily imply that the rest of the report is inaccurate. For example, a child may misorder the sequence of events but still correctly report the details of a sexual assault (Goodman & Helgeson, 1985).

With adults, as well as with children, some distortions in the ordering and interpreting of perceptions are likely to occur. Distortion is especially common with very young children (ages three to six). It is helpful for attorneys and others who work with children to be aware of the types of statements or conclusions that may be beyond the cognitive abilities of a particular child (see "Cognitive Limitations of Young Children" later in this chapter).

The Development of Attention

In order to perceive events, people first must pay attention to them. As children mature, they use their attentive skills more effectively and systematically. The rapidity with which they pick up required information also increases over the span of childhood, likely as a result of improved myelination of the neural fibers. A significant shift in the way children deploy their attending skills occurs between the ages of five and seven. During that time, children begin to attend in a self-controlled, intentional, and systematic manner (Paris & Lindauer, 1982). Their attention broadens, and they become capable of amassing increasing amounts of information from each stimulus. Simultaneously, they develop the ability to focus their attention, calling upon selective attention skills necessary for the successful completion of a task (Hale, 1979). As they mature, children also begin to use a variety of cognitive strategies to help them attend selectively, adapting these skills to the particular task at hand. Children become aware of factors that affect attention, such as motivation and mental effort (Paris & Lindauer, 1982).

There are two basic components to attention: *scanning* and *selectivity*. Laboratory studies have shown that, unless the stimulus they are viewing has a readily recognizable pattern, young children tend to scan unsystematically. While all children tend to scan in a downward fashion, those younger than age five tend to miss information because they often begin their downward scan at the focal point of the picture, thus missing information above that level. Younger children also have a tendency to stop scanning before they have obtained all the relevant information. Judgments they are asked to provide, therefore, may be inaccurate because they are based on only a portion of the available data.

Vurpillot and Ball (1979) demonstrated these points when they asked four- to nine-year-old children to decide whether outline drawings of two houses were the same or different. When the houses were dissimilar, the difference always occurred in one of the windows. When four-year-olds compared the pictures, they did not start at the top and systematically compare each pair of windows, and they did not scan every window. Nearly every one of the oldest (nine-year-old) children, however, scanned systematically and exhaustively.

Moreover, within a given age, some children are much better scanners than others. For example, Vurpillot and Ball (1979) reported that one of the 36 five-year-olds in their study scanned as effectively as a nine-year-old, and nearly half of the six-year-olds tested were as skilled as the older subjects.

Younger children's scanning may be affected in another way as well. Younger children find it difficult to identify figures or patterns in pictures when irrelevant information is added (Day, 1975). Similarly, when they are witnessing an event of legal importance, irrelevant details may distract children from making good identifications or from focusing on vital information. Needless to say, older children and adults also are distracted by irrelevant information. With more mature individuals, however, the capacity to differentiate relevant from irrelevant information is more sophisticated. The simpler the scenarios witnessed, the more likely it is that the child will perceive and recall the incidents with acceptable accuracy (Goodman & Helgeson, 1985).

Children's interests, their expectations about the world, and their strategies for acquiring information also influence their scanning patterns (Day, 1975). Under the right circumstances, therefore, even very young children may scan skillfully. Consider, for example, the card-matching game known as Concentration. Young children are renowned for outperforming older opponents in this scanning/memory game.

Unlike younger children, those above five years usually scan more completely, regardless of where the main point of interest lies (Day, 1975). In witnessing events, then, it might be predicted that older children would be likely to provide more details regarding peripheral information than would younger children (see Wells & Leippe, 1981). Indeed, Parker et al. (1986) found that elementary school children were equally adept at providing information about central and peripheral details of a simulated crime. These researchers did not test younger subjects, however, so we cannot draw developmental conclusions. Still, the ability of older children to provide peripheral information is important because jurors tend to be impressed by witnesses who can provide such detail (see chapter 2).

At the same time, of course, concentrating on the focal point (e.g., the perpetrator's face) has advantages from an evidentiary perspective. Adults in Parker et al.'s study (1986) were far better at reporting central details (descriptions of the perpetrator) than were elementary age children and, as a result, were able to identify accurately the thief from a photo-lineup significantly more often than could the children. In other words, their selective attention made them valuable as witnesses.

In summary, the two basic component skills of attention—scanning and selectivity—improve as children mature. Scanning becomes more efficient and exhaustive; selectivity becomes more refined. These changes notwithstanding, even very young children (ages three to four) have the capacity to attend effectively to the events around them, particularly if those events are relatively straightforward and involve familiar people in familiar surroundings.

The Development of Cognition

One of the major tasks confronting children is understanding the world in which they live. Brain maturation and developing skills in the areas of perception and attention pave the way for such understanding, but cognition entails more than these relatively straightforward processes. Cognition is concerned with the mental activities and behaviors through which knowledge of the world is both attained and processed (Hetherington & Parke, 1986). Cognitive development involves changes in children's intellectual abilities and in their knowledge of the world throughout the course of development.

Two major schools of thought attempt to explain cognitive development. The first, founded by noted developmental psychologist Jean Piaget (see Inhelder & Piaget, 1958),[4] emphasizes developmental changes in the organization or structure of intelligence and how differences in these structures are reflected in the learning of children at different ages. According to the Piagetian model, children progress through four qualitatively different stages on their journey to cognitive maturity. In the *sensory-motor stage,* children from birth to age 2 understand the world primarily through activation of their five senses and through their physical actions on the environment. From ages 2 through 7 children understand the world in a prelogical, intuitive way referred to as *preoperational* thinking. Preoperational children tend to jump from data to conclusions through large, impressionistic leaps. For children of these ages, seeing is believing and magic is reality. By the time children reach age 7 they begin to use logical systems to organize their experiences. At this level, known as *concrete operations,* they use here-and-now, reality-based mental operations to attempt to understand the world. They replace the impressionistic leaps from data to conclusions characteristic of the previous stage with mental strategies that encompass a series of small-scale, reversible steps, each of which may be judged as reasonable or unreasonable. They work hard, for example, to debunk the myths of "magic" and to understand the clever tricks employed by magicians. Their task at this level is to make rational sense of the world around them. Children remain at the concrete operational level until at least age 11. Finally, at the stage of *formal operations,* individuals become capable of complex, abstract reasoning. It is noteworthy, however, that only a portion of adults reach this sophisticated cognitive level (Higgins-Trenk & Gaithe, 1971).

The second model of cognitive development, known as the *information-processing model,* emerged from the experimental laboratory and from a behaviorist approach to psychology (Hall et al., 1986). Rather than focusing on structural changes in intelligence with age, this model explores the role of cognitive operations in processing information. According to this view, children are seen as possessing a variety of cognitive processes and strategies that help them learn about themselves and about objects and events in the world and that facilitate adaptive, intelligent problem-solving. In the next section, these two schools of thought are merged to produce an overview of developmental changes in children's representations of the world.

Mental representations of the world. In order to remember objects, events, and people, humans must store information in memory so that the information can be retrieved at the proper time. We use a variety of means to represent information mentally in memory once the original stimulus disappears. Mental representations are of several types: *enactive* (those that capture knowledge about actions), *imaginal* (those that store mental images), *linguistic* (those that hold verbal or mathematical symbols), *categorical* (those that hold information about concepts), and *operative* (those that involve the interaction of cognition and memory in such a way that stored representations are changed) (Hall et al., 1986). As is the case with perceptions, the use of mental representations changes as children mature. Most adults are capable of using all forms of mental representation; infants and younger children, however, are able to use fewer forms. Each form of representation and the ages during which its use is most salient are described below.

The first form of representation evident in the infant is *enactive.* Through this form, the infant tries to capture knowledge about action in the world. But young babies cannot separate themselves from the world and the objects in it. As a consequence, they do not know where their own bodies end and the environment begins. Therefore, they define events by the actions they evoke (Bruner, 1973). For example, the infant does not understand that a mobile tied to the crib is not an extension of her own body, for every time she thumps her leg on the crib mattress, the mobile shakes. In her mind, presumably, the mobile (environment) simply is an extension of her body (the thumping leg).

During this sensation-bound stage, infants must accomplish a number of tasks. First, they must learn to see themselves as different from the objects around them, thus separating perception from action. Second, they must learn to seek stimulation through their senses and to prolong interesting experiences in the environment through their own actions on it. These interactions with the environment are critical to nourishment of their growing brains as they lead to the development of synaptic connections and glial cells (Lenneberg, 1967). Third, they must learn to define things by manipulating them, and, once defined, to record their existence in memory when the objects no longer are visible.

Children called to testify are unlikely to operate solely at this primitive stage of representation; still, it is important to remember that older children may regress to this sensation-bound level after they have been traumatized severely (see generally Pynoos & Eth, 1984). In such cases it may be helpful to allow children to give their testimony in an enactive way; that is, to permit them to manipulate dolls and other props.

As children outgrow infancy, they begin to rely upon *imaginal representation*. By age two, they use their memories to store mental pictures of what they have encountered. Among some highly skilled adults, this ability is called *photographic memory*. With the advent of this ability during the second year of life, it becomes technically possible for children to serve as witnesses. Assuming they have attended to and perceived an event, children as young as age two or three can store an accurate image of the scene and retain it through adulthood (Inhelder & Piaget, 1958). But two- and three-year-olds (and even some older children) have substantial difficulty in spontaneously offering information about an event through free recall (Marin, Holmes, Guth, & Kovac, 1979). It is, therefore, the interviewer's responsibility to elicit the information through astute questioning. Simple, direct, nonleading questions that tap into the details of the stored mental "snapshot" are most likely to allow very young children to perform at their best (see chapter 4 for research findings that support this contention).

A third form of representation is referred to as *linguistic* because it is based upon the use of words and symbols. For purposes of testifying in court, words and symbols are much more powerful forms of representation than are motor patterns or images. Language is powerful because it allows children not only to represent experiences in memory but also to transform them. With the advent of linguistic representation, children can begin to think about images in such a way that drawing inferences becomes possible. Certainly, this ability is advantageous for children who serve as witnesses. However, precisely because words constitute symbolic representations of an event, object, or person, and as such are one step removed from the vivid mental snapshot of early childhood, they also can distort memory.

The work of Elizabeth Loftus and her colleagues demonstrates the power of language in transforming memory (see Loftus, 1979). In a now classic experiment, Loftus and Palmer (1974) showed that they could introduce a nonexistent object into memory simply by substituting different words into descriptions of an event. Subjects in their experiment viewed a videotape depicting a two-car collision. Loftus and Palmer then divided subjects into five groups and asked them to answer questions about the event, but for each of the groups the collision was described using terms with different connotations: "About how fast were the cars going when they *smashed* into each other?" ". . . when they *collided?*" ". . . when they *bumped?*" ". . . when they *hit?*" or "when they *contacted?*" When asked about their memories again several days later, subjects in the *smashed* condition incorrectly recalled having seen broken glass at the site of the videotaped accident; members of the other groups did not "recall" this [incorrect] piece of information.

Very young children's linguistic representational abilities are rudimentary. Therefore, they may be relatively immune to attempts to distort their memories intentionally (Loftus & Davies, 1984). As children mature, however, they become increasingly susceptible to suggestion that can distort memory.

While the limited linguistic ability of young children may be an asset in preventing memory distortions, the children's immaturity may cause problems in other areas. For example, the early stages of linguistic representation are fraught with possibilities for miscommunication (see "Common Errors in Children's Communications," chapter 4). Recall the dialogue described in chapter 1 in which a young child was questioned regarding sexual assault by her father. Remember that the child clearly differentiated between these statements:

Defense Attorney: And then you said you put your mouth on his penis?
Child: No.

                         *   *   *

Prosecuting Attorney: Did daddy put his penis in your mouth?
Child: Yes.
                            (Berliner & Barbieri, 1984, p.132)

Because such examples are not uncommon when working with children, attorneys and other interviewers must be adept at communicating on the child's level.

The fourth form of representation, *categorical,* allows children to divide the overwhelming diversity of the world into manageable concepts. Conceiving of similar objects as a single concept is efficient and economical. Primitive concepts develop even before babies can talk, suggesting that categorical representation is non-linguistic, at least during early development. Over time, however, concepts become more elaborate and complex and can be communicated to others.

The developing complexity of concepts was illustrated in research by Mandler (1983). Three-year-olds who were asked to put together pictures that are "all the same kind of thing" had little trouble sorting them at a basic level (e.g., cars), but could not sort them at a superordinate level (e.g., transportation). Children one year older, however, were capable of more abstract sorting, understanding that trains and cars were similar in some respects. Goodman and Helgeson (1985) offer a relevant legal example:

> [I]f a child were asked, "Did the man take off his clothes?" he or she might respond, "No," but if asked, "Did the man take off his pants?" he or she might respond "Yes." In the questioner's mind, the first question might subsume the second, but for the child, clothes and pants may be two distinct ideas. Thus, the child's testimony may appear to be inconsistent when it really is not. (pp. 197-198)

How do children discover what objects belong to which category, and how do they place new objects into the correct class? Answers to these psychological questions are important in legal situations. For example, in cases that seek to determine whether a parent has been abusive, the child's rules for categorization may be of primary importance. One child might view two instances of harshness in the last month as grounds for labeling the parent as cruel and unloving. Children are prone to generalize from one or two instances as they build upon emerging concepts (Chase, 1938). A different child, however, might overlook these incidents and view the parent as generally nurturant. In the child's mind, the parent may be quite kind, while on an objective basis the adult has repeatedly demonstrated cruelty (see Rich, 1968). After all, children—especially young ones who have lived in no other home—

have no point of comparison. To them, their family is normal because they have experienced nothing different (see Walsh, 1982). With the child's rules for categorization in mind, an interviewer should take special care to avoid questions that call for a categorized response. For example, the question, "Is your mother kind to you?" calls for an opinion or categorization by the child based upon the mental concepts of "kind" and "unkind." The example in the preceding paragraph illustrates why such a categorization may not be useful. In such a situation it would be better to ask the child simply to describe specific incidents. For instance, in one case, a five-year-old testified at the trial of his mother, who was accused of killing the child's younger brother. The young witness testified as follows: "She always hit him [the brother] on the head with a broom" ("Use of Child Witnesses," Nov. 7, 1983). It was left to the trier of fact to *categorize* the mother's actions.

While categorical representation is efficient, categorization has drawbacks that sometimes lead to inaccurate testimony. Particular problems arise when children oversimplify complex information. Because young children are unskilled at interpreting information, they may be tempted to put data into simplistic, mutually exclusive mental pigeonholes. People may be seen as either wholly good or bad, right or wrong, heroic or evil. The shades of grey that characterize real life often are not perceived by young children (see generally Inhelder & Piaget, 1958).

The interviewer, then, must be careful to assess how simplistic or elaborated are a given child's categorical representations. Skillful questioning about matters unrelated to legal incidents may provide valuable information about the complexity of a particular child's categorical representations. For example, can the child categorize the concrete (e.g., cars, buses, and trains = transportation; apples, oranges, and bananas = fruit)? Is the child able to categorize more abstract concepts (e.g., provisions of food, shelter, and encouragement = nurturance; hitting, burning, and shaking = abuse)? In addition, sometimes it may be helpful for a child psychologist to assess the child and to aid in determining the youngster's cognitive abilities with respect to serving as a witness.

About the time children enter school, qualitative changes in cognitive processes appear. During the years from six until puberty, children increasingly use logic to organize their experiences. Piaget referred to this time as the stage of *concrete opera-*

tions, suggesting that children can use specific mental operations to organize previously stored material (Inhelder & Piaget, 1958).

As comprehension develops, children modify their mental representations to conform to their new understanding. In this sense, memory no longer is passive, simply storing faithful representations of original perceptions (as in imaginal representation). Rather, memories may change as a result of thinking about past events. One advantage of this new understanding is that children may become more skillful at making valid inferences and drawing sound conclusions.

This possibility was demonstrated in research by Furth and colleagues (Furth, Ross, & Youniss, 1974), who showed five- to nine-year-old children a picture of a glass of cola tilted from the horizontal base to a 45-degree angle. The children were asked to draw a picture of the glass "just the way you see it here." The younger children, who did not realize that the level of liquid remains horizontal with respect to the tabletop, drew distorted pictures of the liquid-glass relationship. When asked to draw the tilted glass from memory six months later, 17 percent of the children drew *more* accurate pictures than they had drawn shortly after they saw the picture of the glass. This finding contradicts the commonly held belief that representations either remain the same or else deteriorate over time.

Furth et al. offer a plausible explanation for this surprising finding: they suggest that during the six-month interval, the children acquired a more sophisticated understanding of what happens to the level of contained liquids. As they developed the necessary operative abilities, they reconstructed their representations to reflect more faithfully the original stimulus. Thus, it is possible for children's mental representations actually to improve with the passage of time.

Not all representations improve with time, however; the representative ability of some children does decline. One reason for deterioration in representations during this stage is that children may become susceptible to suggestion and coaching.

Goodman and Helgeson (1985) describe an example of the suggestibility of some young children. Three-year-old twin girls allegedly were abducted. The next day, they were found in a refrigerator. One twin was dead; the living twin (Tina) reported that a blond-haired boy named Jackie was responsible for putting the girls in the refrigerator. Goodman and Helgeson (1985) write:

Even though a boy with blond hair named Jackie lived in the town and other evidence also implicated him in the crime, no line up was attempted. Tina was sent home.

Over the years, Tina was repeatedly interviewed and her story gradually changed. Eventually, she claimed that the murderer was not a boy named Jackie but rather her former babysitter, a mentally-retarded Indian girl also named Jackie. Seven years after the abduction, the babysitter was charged with the crime, and a trial ensued.

At the trial, Tina described in detail what had happened. She testified that Jackie (the babysitter) had come into her grandmother's house, told the sisters to come with her, taken them directly to the abandoned house, and forced them into the refrigerator. The defense argued that family members and the police had coached Tina, and that the years had dampened and distorted her memory. The prosecution argued that memory of traumatic events may be inhibited at first but can become more accurate with time. It was argued further that Tina's current testimony, rather than her original story, was accurate. In the end, some of the jurors believed Tina's testimony, others did not. The trial resulted in a hung jury. (pp. 183-184)

This example clearly demonstrates the importance of quickly obtaining a factual account of a crime. Memory fades over time, and deficits in memory are compounded sometimes by misleading suggestion.

Another point to keep in mind is that while many school age children are capable of reasoning that employs complex logic, typically they only engage in such reasoning when the assumptions underlying the reasoning process are consistent with their personal experience. Generally, such children are not yet able to hypothesize about abstract "what if?" situations outside their experience (hence the label "concrete" thinking).

The important point is that advances in cognitive maturity allow active modifications of children's representations. Sometimes the modifications actually improve the accuracy of stored memories; sometimes not.

Because of the advances in logical reasoning, memory encoding strategies, and communicative skills that occur during the stage of operative representation, six- to twelve-year-old children generally are better witnesses than younger children. Even with these older children, however, limitations exist. Such youngsters are not yet equipped to handle abstract or hypothetical situations that require an assessment of relative ethics. Moreover, at this stage friendships—and even family allegiances —tend to be intense but ephemeral (Selman, 1981). These fair-weather friendships sometimes make children fickle witnesses.

Only at the highest level of cognitive functioning, labeled *formal operations* by Piaget (Inhelder & Piaget, 1958), can children cope effectively with abstractions. At this advanced level children are capable of hypothetic-deductive reasoning. They can analyze "if/then" statements through systematic exploration of logical alternatives. Solutions no longer are reached merely by trial and error, but rather are arrived at by mentally deducing all the possible outcomes, testing the alternatives, and then selecting the best answer.

This stage of formal operations is not attainable until, at the earliest, about age 11 (Harris & Liebert, 1984). Moreover, many adults never achieve the complex reasoning abilities that constitute formal operations (Higgins-Trenk & Gaithe, 1971). Thus, while it is possible that attorneys and clinicians will have the opportunity to work with child witnesses who function at this high cognitive level, most child witnesses will process the world at a preoperational or concrete operational level, so it is advisable that questioning be geared to this level. Remember that even at these relatively early cognitive levels, complicated memory systems are in place to store children's mental representations of the world, and children operating at these levels are capable of providing accurate testimony describing events they have perceived.

Cognitive Limitations of Young Children

As discussed in previous sections, children develop an impressive array of skills to help them perceive, attend to, mentally represent, and understand the world around them. With proper questioning and efforts to alleviate the stress felt by children who give evidence, many children as young as three or four can be competent and effective witnesses. The cognitive abilities of very young children are limited in some ways, however, and persons working with such children should be familiar with these limitations so that appropriate methods may be selected to circumvent potential problems.

Young children (ages three to six) tend to be self-centered. Generally, they have great difficulty adopting another person's viewpoint, either physically or mentally. Thus, they may be unable to re-create or imagine a scene from another person's perspective. Rather than asking the child to do so, the better approach simply is to ask the child to tell what happened from his or her perspective.

Preschool-age children can arrange objects or images in a series, but they cannot draw inferences about nonadjacent components of the series. For example, such children may be able to think about three men—Bill, Tom, and Sam—and conclude that Bill is taller than Tom and Sam is taller than Bill, but without being able to see the men, they are unable to deduce the answer to the question, "Who is the tallest?" (Gander & Gardiner, 1981). The practical implication is that while young children may be able to conjure up a mental image of a perpetrator, they may not be able to compare that person's features with those of familiar individuals. For example, when the attorney asks, "Was he taller than your daddy?" the child may be at a loss about how to answer. It is often better to ask for simple descriptions and to avoid requesting comparisons.

Three- to six-year-old children may be unable to see that objects alike in one respect may differ in other ways. Thus, all four-legged, furry creatures may be referred to as "doggies." A likely explanation for this limitation is that young children tend to focus on the global image, disregarding finer features or details. Thus, although very young children may have exceptionally accurate mental snapshots of a witnessed scene, they typically do not attend to the finer details of the image unless specifically directed to do so. The work of Kosslyn (1983) illustrates this point. Kosslyn asked six- and ten-year-old children to think about an animal. Then he asked them whether the animal possessed a particular feature (such as a hoof or a horn). Next he requested that they form an image of an animal and inspect the image to see if the animal had a specific feature. In response to this request, some of the six-year-olds said, "Oh, you want me to do what I did last time again!"—suggesting that "thinking about" and "forming an image" are identical tasks for children of this age. When asked to visualize the animals, both six- and ten-year-olds could answer questions about large, nonspecific features more quickly than they could identify small features that were specific to a particular animal (e.g., claws on a cat). Kosslyn concluded that most of the youngsters had to "zoom in" on their images to inspect small details, although a few of the older children were able to do so without being instructed. His research led Kosslyn to speculate that detailed information was stored abstractly only for the older children. For them it was easily available when the animal was brought to mind (i.e., through thinking about the image). Presumably, the younger children still were relying primarily on imaginal representation.

Kosslyn's work suggests that interviewers of young children must employ astute questioning. It may be helpful, for example, to ask young children to form an image of the desired object, person, or scene and then to direct them to inspect specified parts of the image (see "Maximizing Children's Memory" in chapter 4).

Young children reason *transductively* (from one specific circumstance to the next), rather than inductively (from the specific to the general) or deductively (from the general to the specific). In the process of reasoning transductively, children sometimes ignore relevant information. For example, a child may reason that because the bathwater goes down the drain and because he or she is sitting in the tub, the child too will disappear into the plumbing when the stopper is removed (Gander & Gardiner, 1981). For this reason, it is usually best not to ask children at this level to provide interpretations of their images. Their reasoning abilities simply are too primitive to enable them to make sense of many events. It is wiser to focus on detailed factual descriptions of their mental images and to let the trier of fact draw the relevant conclusions.

Young children also believe in *animism,* the view that all things (animate or inanimate) are living and endowed with intentions, consciousness, and feelings. One three-year-old, for example, admonished her mother not to cut the girl's hair "because it [the hair] will feel so sad."[5] Thus if young children are asked to speculate on *why* an event occurred in a certain way (i.e., to infer intention), it may be difficult to know whether their responses are valid interpretations of the event or whether they are engaging in animism. Again, it seems prudent to avoid asking for inferences from young children. When young children do reach accurate inferential conclusions, they may not be able to articulate how they did it. Three- to six-year-olds often reach conclusions based upon vague impressions and perceptual judgments that cannot be put into words—the essence of imaginal representation. In part, this difficulty in communicating perceptions is a function of immaturity of the *corpus callosum,* the bundle of brain tissue that connects the two hemispheres of the brain (Roth, 1985). If asked to explain how they reached a particular conclusion, therefore, young children are likely to respond with such statements as "I just know it" or "My teacher said so."

The limitations of the cognitive capacities of children who represent the world imaginally—especially those younger than age four—suggest that caution should be used in employing such children as witnesses. These limitations may be of relatively less concern in cases involving children who have extended contact with an assailant, who are familiar with the assailant, who experienced an event repeatedly, or who give vivid imaginal descriptions of events that remain unwavering over time (see Goodman & Helgeson, 1985; see also Jones & Krugman, 1986). In sum, the developmental immaturity of the youngest children calls for careful evaluation of testimonial competence. Even with their limitations, however, many such children can testify competently about simple factual occurrences.

EMOTIONAL AND SOCIAL DEVELOPMENT

Children's Psychosocial Needs

We humans are a needy bunch. We require more than food, water, and shelter to develop to our fullest potential; we need love, nurturance, and stimulation as well. The latter requirements are referred to as *psychosocial needs*. Children who are deprived of love, nurturance, and stimulation may suffer brain damage, failure to thrive syndrome, emotional disturbance, or even death (see Spitz, 1946).

Even children whose psychosocial needs are met may suffer untoward effects if they experience traumatizing events. Pynoos and Eth (1984) point out that the symptoms that follow trauma frequently include "recurrent and intrusive recollections of the event, traumatic anxiety, dreams, markedly diminished interest in activities, feelings of estrangement and constricted affect, fears of repeated trauma resulting in hypervigilant or avoidant behavior, decline in cognitive performance, and persistent feelings of guilt" (p. 90). Because child witnesses often have experienced such trauma, it is important to understand the basic stages and issues of socioemotional development in children.

Erikson (1963) made important contributions in the area of psychosocial development. He posited eight stages of psychosocial development, each with its own central issue or crisis. Resolution of the central issue allows the individual to progress to the next stage. Failure to resolve the crisis results in the stunting of emotional development. The first five of Erikson's stages are germane to the study of child witnesses.

During the first year of life the central issue is one of *trust versus mistrust*. In order to resolve this issue, babies must come to understand that the world usually is a safe, predictable place and that their needs normally will be met lovingly and consistently. Successful resolution of this crisis is demonstrated by children's firm emotional attachment to their caretakers, which in most cases means their parent(s). Infants who are securely attached to their parents show signs of anxiety or fear if they are separated from them or if a stranger approaches (see Ainsworth, Blehar, Waters, & Wall, 1978). Infants who successfully resolve this issue develop into trusting children. On the other hand, children who have not successfully resolved this issue may have difficulty trusting anyone—attorneys, judges, social workers, and psychologists included. Therefore, they may be especially reluctant witnesses.

From 12 to 24 months the issue to be resolved is one of *autonomy versus shame and doubt*. The need to physically explore the environment blossoms at this point. Although children still use their parents as sources of security, they want to strike out on their own too—to scale the kitchen counter, to attempt such daring new feats as drinking poisonous substances and poking fingers into electrical outlets. Allowing toddlers the freedom to explore in child-proofed surroundings leads to measurably higher levels of social competence at school age (White, 1971). It is essential that toddlers be allowed reasonable amounts of autonomy within safe boundaries. Children who are unsuccessful at resolving this issue or who have been prevented from tackling this issue may not make very good witnesses because they may be uncertain and racked by doubt.

The crisis of the third stage is *initiative versus guilt*. From ages three to five, children want to show that they can initiate their own positive, constructive activities. According to Erikson (1963), harsh parental responses to their initiatives and to their natural sexual overtures can lead to an overdeveloped conscience that always may plague them with guilt. Older children who are stuck at this

psychosocial level may be difficult for attorneys to work with
because their overactive sense of guilt may make them reluctant
to talk, even about innocuous subjects. Such children may feel
responsible for a variety of occurrences, many of which they could
not possibly have influenced. For example, a child who operates at
this level may feel responsible for a grandparent's death, and as a
result may not want to discuss anything regarding the grandparent; or children at this level who have been sexually abused may
remain convinced that the transgressions were their fault. On the
other hand, precisely because such children have well-developed
consciences, they tend to make credible witnesses. The fourth stage
is a decisive one in preparing children to assume effective adult
roles. About the time they enter school, children begin to deal with
the issue of *industry versus inferiority*. They must learn to gain
recognition by becoming good workers. If children at this level are
not praised honestly for their accomplishments, they are likely to
develop a sense of inferiority or inadequacy. Children with strong
feelings of inadequacy, like those who have not achieved a sense of
autonomy, may make poor witnesses. They may be unwilling to
commit to a public stance, offering either no opinion or one that is
wishy-washy. If such children are vital witnesses, care must be
taken to build their confidence before taking the stand because
witness confidence directly affects credibility (Goodman & Helgeson, 1985; Nigro et al., 1989; Ross et al., 1989).

During adolescence, the resolution of previous crises is questioned as teens attempt to forge a unique *identity*. In their search
for personal congruity, teens must refight the battles of their
earlier years and question their parents' ideas and values. Sometimes it happens that this search, instead of resulting in a coherent
personality, ends in *role confusion;* that is, adolescents may experience prolonged confusion about who they are, what they want
from life, and what they expect to contribute to the world. Adolescents experiencing this kind of pervasive confusion may be particularly reluctant to take the stand because they may feel inferior or
exceptionally anxious. On the other hand, adolescents who are
forging an identity successfully may make particularly strong
witnesses because they appear confident and self-assured.

The changes associated with children's emotional development
also affect their approaches to morality. How do children determine
what is "right" to do? Under what circumstances will they obey
rules? If the rules are broken, what makes children tell the truth

or speak lies? The section below reviews changes in children's moral reasoning and behavior.

Morality

Moral reasoning. Moral reasoning is concerned with what individuals think about situations in which some transgression of rules has occurred or in which a moral dilemma is posed. For example, in the classic moral dilemma proposed by Lawrence Kohlberg, people are asked to judge whether the financially strapped man, "Heinz," acted properly or immorally when he stole a medication to save his wife's life after the drug's developer refused to reduce his clearly exorbitant price for the substance (Kohlberg, 1963). Faced with such an example, individuals often are able to reason at relatively high levels of morality. The problem, of course, is that frequently differences occur between what children and adults *say* is right on tests of moral reasoning and what they *do* in practice (Mischel & Mischel, 1976). The problem is compounded further by the fact that normal children sometimes display immoral behavior (e.g., cheating) in one situation but not in another. In fact, inconsistencies in children's moral reasoning and behavior are common (Hartshorne & May, 1928). Over time, however, individuals learn to be either relatively consistent or relatively inconsistent in their honesty (Burton, 1976). Yet, as Hall et al. (1986) note, even when a child develops a general tendency to resist or to succumb to temptation, the conditions surrounding each moral choice will have a strong effect on the child's final decision. Thus, although moral reasoning becomes increasingly unified and consistent as children develop, their day-to-day behavior often turns on situational constraints. Of course, the same is true of adults.

Practically speaking, therefore, child witnesses may or may not act in an objectively ethical manner. The likelihood of their acting morally depends, in part, on the expectations placed on them, their histories, and their level of moral development.

Moral development. The qualitative changes that take place in moral development closely parallel those of cognition. Three of the pioneers in this field, Jean Piaget (see 1932/1965), Lawrence Kohlberg (1963), and Carol Gilligan (1982), suggest that individuals progress through several stages of moral development, with each succeeding stage consisting of a more complex and balanced approach to the moral-social world. Building on the work of Piaget and Kohlberg, Thomas Lickona (1983) outlined six stages of moral reasoning, each with its definition of what is "right" in the eyes of the individual, and with its unique motivation to "be good."

Stage 1 children (ages four and younger) generally believe that it is "right" to get their own way. At this stage, the primary motivation for good behavior is either to obtain rewards or to avoid punishments. Thus, children in Stage 1 may tell the truth because they believe the judge will punish them for lying. On the other hand, children at this stage may be susceptible to bribes or threats offered by adults who have a vested interest in litigation. A child may be persuaded to tell a little lie in exchange for promised goods (including parental love) or in order to avoid unpleasant consequences (e.g., a spanking). Special care must be taken with Stage 1 children to prepare them for the necessity of giving valid testimony.

Stage 2 usually occurs at kindergarten age. Children at this stage tend to feel that they should do what they are told. Being good, then, rests upon obedience to authority. Some children at this level are susceptible to coaching by authority figures. Moreover, a bribe or threat no longer is needed. The adult's wish alone is perceived as a command. Also at Stage 2, children usually evaluate the morality of an act based upon its magnitude rather than upon intentions. Thus, the child who breaks ten teacups while helping wash them is judged more severely than the child who breaks only one teacup in the process of stealing from the cookie jar (Piaget, 1932/1965). Stage 2 children should be encouraged simply to report their observations rather than to evaluate them in moralistic terms.

As children move into the cognitive stage of concrete operations during the elementary school years, their conception of what is right changes. At Stage 3, children continue to look out for themselves, but they also want to be fair to those who are fair with them. Thus, being good hinges upon "what's-in-it-for-me? fairness" and a type of "you scratch my back and I'll scratch yours" philosophy. Children at this level may be quite willing to help an attorney if they see that something may be gained in the process. It may be helpful, therefore, to outline for such children the advantages of testifying truthfully.

During the middle to upper elementary grades, morality is synonymous with niceness; that is, with living up to the expectations of important adults. Children at Stage 4 are eager to please, sometimes even at the expense of conventional ethics. Thus, gaining approval from authority figures may be more important than stating objective truths. This is not to say that these children lack understanding of the difference between truth and falsehood. On the contrary, children as young as three comprehend this distinction. Rather, the point is that circumstances may arise in which Stage 4 children stray from the truth in order to please others (e.g., parents, therapists, attorneys, judges). Unlike children at Stage 2, elementary school youngsters are not so interested in following the dictates of authority figures simply for the sake of being obedient. Rather, they want to be perceived as being nice, as being worthy of approval. Interviewers can appeal to this need in order to gain the cooperation of children at this stage.

Many adolescents begin to move into the fifth stage of moral development. Teenagers begin to develop a sense of responsibility to the social system as a whole. Individuals in Stage 5 believe that they must be good in order to keep the system from disintegrating and in order to maintain self-respect by meeting personal obligations. Explanations of our system of justice are useful with children at this stage.

It is only during Stage 6 that the individual acts in accordance with principled conscience: that is, with respect for the rights and dignity of every individual person in support of a system that protects human rights. Unfortunately, Kohlberg (1976) has estimated that only about 10 percent of the adults in America reach this level of moral reasoning.

SPECIAL CONSIDERATIONS

Traumatized Children

Many children who are called upon to give testimony have been traumatized to some degree, often severely. Such children may have experienced personal harm—physically, psychologically, or sexually—or they may have watched a parent, friend, or other loved one being tortured or murdered.

Severely or chronically traumatized children are likely to regress emotionally; that is, they are likely to function at a less mature psychosocial level than one might predict, given their age (Pynoos & Eth, 1984). Also, like adults, children can experience the clinical syndrome known as *posttraumatic stress disorder* (see American Psychiatric Association, *Diagnostic and Statistical Manual of Mental Disorders,* 1980). This cluster of symptoms includes intrusive and recurrent recollections of the event, dreams filled with anxiety, fear of repeated trauma resulting in avoidant or hypervigilant behavior, decline in cognitive performance, lack of interest in activities, constricted affect and estrangement, and persistent feeling of guilt (Horowitz, Wilner, Kultreider, & Alvarez, 1980). Among children in particular, several additional symptoms are common, including increased misperceptions of the duration and sequencing of events; unconscious reenactments (i.e., unknowing, sometimes dangerous performance of acts similar to the traumatic event); repetitive, unsatisfying play concentrated on traumatic themes; pessimistic expectations for the future; and significant personality alterations (Pynoos & Eth, 1984). Recall that Susie, introduced in chapter 1, experienced most of these symptoms following her abduction, sexual assault, and attempted murder.

Pynoos and Eth (1984) studied children who had experienced severe traumas. Their work suggests that characteristic developmental differences in behavior appear after children experience severe trauma. Preschoolers are likely to appear withdrawn, subdued, or even mute. They commonly react to parental homicide, for example, with anxious attachment behavior, signaling a regression to Erikson's (1963) first psychosocial stage, *trust versus mistrust.* They are likely to engage in reenactments and play centering on traumatic themes.

School-age children may exhibit greater diversity of behavioral aberrations. They are more aware of internal body sensations, and therefore are more likely to complain of stomachaches, headaches, and other somatic discomforts. They find it harder to control their behavior, reminiscent of the difficult-to-control *autonomy versus shame and doubt* stage described by Erikson (1963) as typical of two-year-olds. Moreover, they tend to become less trusting of adult restraint if they have experienced or witnessed a serious breach of restraint on the part of an adult. Usually, such children show marked declines in school performance. The reactions of adolescents begin to resemble those of adults with posttraumatic stress disorder. Initially, such adolescents express rage, shame, and betrayal. Their behavior then becomes rebellious, typically including antisocial acts, use of illicit drugs, and/or strong urges to enter prematurely into adulthood by dropping out of school, leaving home, or getting married. Furthermore, Pynoos and Eth (1984) note that "the adolescent is more likely to experience a major life-threatening loss of impulse control. Because of teens' access to automobiles and weapons, reenactment behavior can be particularly dangerous" (p. 93). Moreover, in the interview situation, adolescents may seem uncooperative, suspicious, and guarded. When they are willing to talk, they sometimes focus on judging themselves and others (symptomatic of a return to Erikson's guilt stage), rather than on giving objective details.

Case studies indicate that traumatic events, particularly ones that result in the death of children's parents, represent exceedingly painful, disruptive events that *must* be managed as noted above. Such events are likely to stimulate destructive and aggressive urges in children. In addition, traumatized children often experience feelings of loss and abandonment, as well as a lack of trust in others (Pynoos & Eth, 1984; see also Santostefano, 1967).

Children of different ages also react to death in characteristic ways. Preschool-age children, for example, tend to view death as a disappearance or as "going to sleep," a view that implies reversibility (Kastenbaum, 1967). During the early elementary school years, however, children gradually accommodate themselves to the proposition that "death is final, inevitable, universal, and personal" (Kastenbaum, 1967, p.101) After the age of 10, children usually understand fully the permanence of death, although even more mature children may not be able to accept the finality of death (Kastenbaum, 1967).

Stages of Grieving

One of the ways in which people give closure to traumatic events in their lives is through the process of grieving, particularly if the trauma resulted in the death of a loved one. It is important to note, however, that grieving also occurs in the absence of death. After severe trauma, children may grieve over lost innocence, abusive incidents, lack of action on their part in preventing a traumatic event, and so forth. Based upon the pioneering work of Elisabeth

Kübler-Ross (1969), Kalish (1981) outlined five stages in the process of grieving. It is helpful for professionals who plan to interview grieving children to understand the unique characteristics of each stage.

The first stage in the process of grieving is called *denial and isolation.* During this stage children do not believe the reality of the trauma. They may feel numb (Kalish, 1981), or they may actively deny the trauma. This stage is similar to the physiological shock that envelopes a person following serious injury. Attempting to interview children at this point may be counterproductive because sensations, perceptions, and memories may be blunted.

During the second stage, grieving children experience *anger,* including rage and resentment. Adults in this stage often are able to verbalize these feelings in such comments as, "Why me?" Young children, however, do not have this level of sophistication. Instead, children who are suffering from these intense feelings may act out their anger, becoming belligerent, unruly, or temperamental (Pynoos & Eth, 1984). Children in this stage may be difficult clients or witnesses. In some cases, anger may be displaced directly onto the interviewer. Whenever possible, therefore, it is advisable to proceed with legal action after children have overcome these intense feelings of anger and resentment. As Pynoos and Eth (1984) suggest, it may be particularly helpful for such children to be assigned to a therapist who is an expert in childhood trauma.

Bargaining is the third stage in the grieving process. During this phase children are likely overtly or covertly to promise good behavior in the hope that this bargain will restore magically the status quo; that is, will remove or undo the traumatic circumstance. During this stage children experience "a restless kind of searching, accompanied by preoccupation with thoughts of the dead person" (Kalish, 1981, p. 222) or traumatic event. In cases involving the death of a parent, guilt also is evoked because, in the child's mind: (a) the child was not better behaved while the parent was alive, (b) the "bad" child was allowed to live while the "good" parent had to die, (c) the child previously felt intense anger toward the dead parent, or (d) the child had unconscious (or even conscious) death wishes directed toward the dead parent. The latter source of guilt is especially potent for young children, who engage in "magical thinking" (Piaget, 1952), the belief that thoughts *cause* actions in the external world.

Children in the bargaining stage may experience intense grieving and, therefore, must be dealt with carefully. At the same time, however, children in this stage of grieving may be quite cooperative in interviews and during legal proceedings in the mistaken belief that legal proceedings somehow will bring about the status quo ante. When it becomes obvious that bargaining is not going to work, bereaved children enter the stage of *depression,* at which time the feelings of loss become overwhelming. Unlike depressed adults, who typically display symptoms of sadness, despondency, poor appetite, and lethargy, depressed children may exhibit restlessness, irritability, sulkiness, or pouting (Wenar, 1982). Eventually most grieving children overcome the acute sense of loss or trauma, complete their mourning, and arrive at the stage of *acceptance.* This stage is characterized by detachment from the lost parent or traumatic incident and a willingness to cope with life once again. While this stage may be the most appropriate time psychologically to work with child witnesses, often it is not reached for years. Moreover, recent evidence suggests that a favorable legal outcome, while unable to restore the status quo ante, may serve a healing function (Pynoos & Eth, 1984).

While all children are likely to pass through these stages of grieving, it is important to keep in mind that each child reacts somewhat differently. The variations in response result from a variety of factors. How children cope in specific instances of trauma, violence, or murder is dependent upon such factors as their age, their concept of the traumatic event, who was harmed in the incident, the emotional states of the people around them, the home situation before the traumatic event occurred, the relationships the children have or had with their parents, what kind of traumatic event was witnessed or experienced, whether the children get counseling, what type of therapy they receive and for how long, their ability to build new relationships, and where they are placed after the incident (home, foster care, close family member's home) (Pynoos & Eth, 1984).

From their long-term study of traumatized children, Pynoos and Eth (1984) concluded that children's efforts at mastering trauma can be either impeded or enhanced by involvement in judicial proceedings. For example, children who see an assailant go free may feel betrayed by the legal system and by previously trusted adults. Among such children this feeling is likely to hinder mastery of the trauma. On the other hand, children who have less stressful court appearances and who see justice served as they hoped it would be, may progress more quickly and easily through the stages of grieving. Regardless of the particular behavioral outcomes of the traumatic occurrence, children of all ages must be given a chance to explore their recollections fully. Such exploration facilitates recovery and allows them to discuss more neutral memories associated with the event. If children feel unable to cope with the emotional distress associated with traumatic memories, then recall may remain a threat. For such children testifying may be impeded (Folkman & Lazarus, 1985).

Pynoos and Eth (1984) suggest several strategies for helping the traumatized child, strategies that should improve recall, reduce anxiety, relieve symptoms, and allow for better testimony. They recommend that police officers and judicial officials be educated about the special needs of child witnesses and that a guardian, advocate, or trusted adult participate in the initial interrogation. They also suggest that an expert in childhood trauma serve a special role in assisting children and that children be specially prepared for the courtroom experience. Finally, whether they testify or not, children need to be informed of the judicial outcome of the case. Like adults, children have a need to give closure to the traumatic events in their lives. (Chapters 5 and 7 discuss procedures designed to reduce the traumatization of child witnesses.)

Working With Exceptional Children

Sometimes attorneys work with children referred to as "exceptional," a term denoting that such children are in some way different from "normal" youngsters. Some exceptional children are retarded in functioning, while others are disabled or exhibit symptoms of emotional or behavioral disorders. Whenever an attorney works with exceptional children, it is advisable to consult with a specialist such as a child psychologist, child psychiatrist, or social worker experienced in working with children who have the same condition as the client.

Retarded Children

Retardation may be caused by a variety of factors, including chromosomal aberrations, malnutrition, deprivation, and illness during gestation (Erickson, 1987). Generally speaking, the cause of retardation is of less concern to the court than is an understanding of the child's capabilities. By definition, any retarded child functions at a level—cognitively, socially, and/or emotionally—lower than would be predicted on the basis of chronological age alone.

Within the general group of mentally retarded persons, four classifications are recognized by the American Association on Mental Deficiency (AAMD): mild, moderate, severe, and profound (Erickson, 1987; see also American Psychiatric Association, *Diagnostic and Statistical Manual of Mental Disorders,* 1980). While the normal IQ range is 85 to 115, *mildly retarded* individuals typically score in the 50-70 range on intelligence tests. Approximately 80 percent of retarded individuals are grouped in this category. Generally, as adults, the mildly retarded are capable of mastering simple educational tasks and of living semi-independently. *Moderately retarded* people, comprising 10 percent of the retarded population, have intelligence quotients in the 35-49 range. They typically require supervised living conditions but often can work in sheltered workshops. Approximately 3 to 4 percent of the retarded are classified as *severely retarded.* Most people in this range of intelligence (IQ of 20-34) can be toilet trained and can learn personal care skills. *Profoundly retarded* persons, with IQs in the 0-19 range, usually require full-time care.

The fact that a child is retarded does not necessarily disqualify the child from testifying. Many retarded children, especially those with milder conditions, have the capacity to serve as witnesses. However, it is necessary to convince the trier of fact that the child is competent and credible. Jurors tend to believe witnesses who appear mature and confident and who are not easily confused (see generally Goodman et al., 1984). Because many individuals hold preconceived notions regarding the limitations of the retarded, special care must be taken to discuss or demonstrate the particular capabilities of the retarded child who is testifying. It may be helpful, for example, to educate the trier of fact regarding the difference between chronological and mental age. The chronological age of the child is calculated as years and months since birth. Mental age, on the other hand, is determined by assessing the child's intellectual level of functioning. Thus, a retarded child may have a chronological age of 8-10 (8 years and 10 months) but a mental age of 5-10 (5 years and 10 months). In such a case, it would be reasonable to assume that the child's capabilities in giving evidence would resemble those of a 5-year-old, not those of an 8-year-old.

Disabled Children

There are many types of handicaps, including visual and hearing impairments, other physically disabling conditions, and chronic medical conditions (e.g., diabetes, heart conditions, asthma) (Erickson, 1987). If a disabled child's mental functioning has not been adversely affected, there is no reason to believe that the child cannot give effective testimony. In some cases the disabled child may be an exceptionally helpful witness. For example, a visually impaired child may be able to identify important sounds that might be missed by a sighted person. Likewise, a deaf child may be able to give more complete descriptions of visual details than would a hearing child.

Perhaps the most difficult aspect of working with a disabled child is communication. In some cases interpreters or special communication devices may be required. Under such conditions it may be more difficult to assess whether the child understands questions and explanations. Moreover, use of an interpreter introduces the risk that information may be lost in translation. These obstacles, however, are not insurmountable. (See chapter 5 for a description of legal standards associated with using an interpreter in the courtroom.)

Children With Behavioral or Emotional Disorders

Behavioral disorders of childhood include such conditions as hyperactivity, poor impulse control, difficulties with conduct, substance abuse, and delinquency (Erickson, 1987). Emotional disorders include, for example, excessive fears and anxieties, school phobia, clinical depression, and pervasive developmental disorders (e.g., autism and childhood schizophrenia) (Erickson, 1987).

Multiple problems are associated with these conditions. For example, poor attention span and perceptual difficulties are common among behaviorally disordered children (Erickson, 1987). Some emotionally disordered children have difficulty in separating fact from fantasy (Erickson, 1987). With any of these conditions, communication may be difficult, and in rare cases, impossible (e.g., some cases of autism). In addition, special risks are likely to be associated with stress and traumatization of such children. The myriad problems associated with working with behaviorally or emotionally disordered children suggest that such children typically should not testify. Certainly there are occasions on which exceptional children perform adequately. Because of their unique behavioral difficulties, however, the attorney must take special care when calling such children to the stand.

SUMMARY

A working knowledge of the stages and issues of child development is essential to any person who interacts with children in the legal system. With such knowledge, the professional can have reasonable expectations of children, can understand the difficulties children are likely to have when they interact with the legal system, and can help determine the child's competency to testify.

As children develop, their brains mature. One important development is myelination of the neural fibers, which makes transmission of information more efficient within the brain. As children mature, their perceptions also become more selective and more purposeful. Their attention improves as well. They develop the ability to scan an event visually and to select the important information to be reported. Moreover, they become better at explaining sequences of behavior and making inferences about feelings, thoughts, and intentions.

However, while older children have more mature brains and more sophisticated perceptual, attentive, and inferential abilities, it is inappropriate to conclude that they are a priori better witnesses. Sometimes older witnesses are not able to separate their thoughts about what they perceived from the perceptions themselves, leading to false conclusions.

One of the major tasks confronting children is to understand the world in which they live, a cognitive process. In order to remember objects, events, and people, humans must store information in memory so that the information can be retrieved at the proper time.

Humans use several types of mental representations. Enactive representation captures knowledge about sensations and actions. This is a primitive form, probably rarely used by children who serve as witnesses. As children outgrow infancy, they begin to rely upon imaginal representation, the ability to store information in memory as mental "snapshots." A third form of representation is referred to as linguistic, for it relies upon the use of words and symbols. With the advent of linguistic representation, children can begin to think about images in such a way that drawing inferences becomes possible. A fourth form of representation, categorical, allows children to divide the overwhelming diversity of the world into manageable concepts. While categorical representation is efficient, problems may arise when children oversimplify complex information.

As comprehension develops, children modify their mental representations to conform to their new understanding. Thus, memories may change as a result of thinking about past events. Sometimes these modifications improve the accuracy of stored memories, sometimes not.

Because of the advances in logical reasoning, memory encoding strategies, and communicative skills that occur over time, 6- to 12-year-old children generally are better witnesses than are younger children. Furthermore, the cognitive abilities of very young children are limited by such factors as egocentrism, transductive reasoning, and animism. The developmental immaturity of the youngest children calls for careful evaluation of testimonial competence. Even with their limitations, however, many such children can testify competently about simple factual occurrences.

Children mature not only cognitively, but also socially and emotionally. During the time from birth through adolescence, emotionally healthy children learn to develop trust, autonomy, initiative, industriousness, and personal identity. If children are confronted with unhealthy environments or if they experience severe or prolonged trauma, their socioemotional development may be stunted.

The qualitative changes that take place in moral development closely parallel those of cognition and emotion. Children's views of what is "right" or moral change in predictable ways. At first, morality is egocentric: What is "right" is that I get my way. Over time, the child comes to understand that morality involves a sense of responsibility to the social system as a whole and commitment to a set of ultimate principles. But the ability to reason morally is not a good predictor of moral action. Therefore, as legal witnesses, children (and adults) may or may not act in an objectively ethical manner. The likelihood of their acting morally depends, in part, upon the expectations placed on them, their histories, and their level of moral development.

Severely or chronically traumatized children may regress cognitively, emotionally, and morally. They even may experience a clinical condition known as *posttraumatic stress disorder.* The cluster of symptoms associated with this disorder includes intrusive and recurrent recollections of the event; dreams filled with anxiety; fear of repeated trauma, resulting in avoidant or hypervigilant behavior; decline in cognitive performance; lack of interest in activities; constricted affect and estrangement; and persistent feeling of guilt.

One of the ways in which people give closure to traumatic events in their lives is through the process of grieving. Kübler-Ross (1969) has outlined five stages in this process: denial and isolation, anger, bargaining, depression, and acceptance. How children cope in specific instances of trauma, violence, or murder is dependent upon a variety of factors: their age, their concept of the traumatic event, who was harmed in the incident, the emotional states of the people around them, the home situation before the traumatic event occurred, the relationships they have or had with their parents, what kind of traumatic event was witnessed or experienced, whether they get counseling, what type of therapy they receive and for how long, their ability to build new relationships, and where they are placed after the incident. Children's efforts at mastering trauma may be either impeded or enhanced by involvement in judicial proceedings.

Sometimes "exceptional" children may be called to testify. Some exceptional children are retarded in functioning, while others are disabled or exhibit symptoms of emotional or behavioral disorders. The variety of problems associated with working with behaviorally or emotionally disordered children in particular suggests that such children typically should not testify. Whenever an attorney works with exceptional children, it is advisable to consult with a specialist experienced in working with children who have the same condition as the client.

NOTES

1. A version of this chapter appeared in *Child Witness Law and Practice* by J.E.B. Myers, 1987, New York: John Wiley.

2. This incident was reported to the first author.

3. *Size constancy* refers to the ability to understand that objects remain the same size regardless of how near or how far away they are (Harris & Liebert, 1987). Interestingly, by the time babies are a few months old, they can accurately judge the sizes of objects in their world (Hall, Lamb, & Perlmutter, 1986).

4. The discussion of Piagetian stages of development in this section is based on Inhelder and Piaget's work.

5. The first author's daughter, at age three, provided this example.

4

Children in Court: Issues of Comprehension, Memory, and Communication

Children's Understanding of Legal Personnel and Proceedings

The concepts of court and courtroom

Personnel

The judge
Attorneys
Witnesses
The jury
Minor court personnel

Procedures

The obligation to tell the truth

Memory

Models of memory

Types of remembering

Recognition memory
Reconstruction memory
Recall memory

Strategies for and deficiencies in remembering

Children's suggestibility

The impact of stress

The impact of inducements to keep secrets

Maximizing children's memory

Language and Communication

Language development

Common errors in children's communications

Overextension
Underextension
Syntactical errors

Avoiding communication errors

Summary

My memory is the thing I forget with.

(a child's definition, cited in Grossberg, 1985, p. 60).

. . . even if children know the information desired by the court, have the capacity to relate this information appropriately to different listeners, and know the relevant social roles played by the legal actor, they may not be able to do all of them simultaneously. Thus children's behavior as witnesses may convey the impression of inaccuracy independent of the maturity of the component skills or even the validity of the child's story.

(Warren-Leubecker, Tate, Hinton, & Ozbek, 1989, p. 175).

CHILDREN'S UNDERSTANDING OF
LEGAL PERSONNEL AND PROCEEDINGS

What do children know about the legal system, and how do they come to know it? Consider this example provided by Saywitz (1989):

A frightened young child sat in the back of the courtroom anxiously awaiting the judge's decision. Will she be allowed to go home, sent to a stranger's house, or sent to a children's hall? She listened intently while a decision was made about where she would be placed for the next six months as the civil and criminal cases unfold. The hearing was over and she was still bewildered. She started to cry. She asked her caseworker where she was going to live. The caseworker responded with a puzzled look "Didn't you listen to what the judge said? He said the minor will live with her grandmother."

The child responded, "I heard him say the minor was gonna live with grandma, but where am *I* gonna live?" . . . Had the judge recognized that many children under ten think of minors as people who dig coal, this child's fear and anxiety about her future could have been reduced. (p. 132)

AUTHORS' NOTE: Parts of this chapter appeared in J.E.B. Myers (1987), *Child Witness: Law and Practice,* New York: Wiley.

As a rule, children understand very little about the legal system—its players, its rules, and its procedures (Flin, Davies, & Stevenson, 1987; Saywitz, 1989; Warren-Leubecker et al., 1989). Not surprisingly, comprehension increases as children get older. Still, children generally see court as a "bad" place filled with "bad" people (Flin et al., 1987; Saywitz, 1989; Warren-Leubecker et al., 1989), in other words, a place to be avoided.

Whitcomb, Shapiro, & Stellwagen (1985) suggest that children may fear many aspects of the legal system simply because of their lack of knowledge about or experience with it. In fact, why *shouldn't* unprepared children be frightened by the courtroom experience? They are asked to enter a formal-looking enclosure, face the American flag and an authority figure in a black gown, and submit themselves to intense and often prolonged questioning from strangers in front of an audience of grown-ups. These circumstances hardly make any of us feel relaxed!

Of course, some young children understand that court is a place to resolve disputes; yet they tend to be in the dark about even the most basic concepts: Who is the judge, and what does he or she do? What is an attorney? What is a jury? How are decisions made?

Not only do young children demonstrate a general paucity of knowledge about the legal system, they also labor under serious misconceptions and inaccuracies. Saywitz (1989) asked young children to define such legal terms as *court, charges,* and *jury.* Some responses reflected an ignorance or misunderstanding that could be humorous in another context, e.g., "Court is a place to play basketball," "Charges is what you do with your credit card," and "Jury is the stuff you wear on your neck and finger like a ring (i.e., jewelry)" (pp. 136, 142).

The limited and distorted nature of children's conceptions of the legal system isn't surprising, given their sources of knowledge about it. Saywitz (1989) argues that the depictions of the court system in school lessons and on television tend to be simplistic, removing the dilemmas and "gray areas" inherent in actual legal cases. Macaulay (1987) suggests that television tends to "misrepresent the nature and amount of crime . . . , the roles of actors in the legal system . . . and present important issues of civil liberties in distorted ways" (pp. 197-198). For example, how often does the actual culprit break down and confess on the witness stand (as

"Perry Mason" would have us believe)? Or, if the child's source of knowledge is "People's Court," why would he or she think that attorneys ever appear in court? Or if "Night Court" is more familiar, why would he or she understand the true roles of (or feel a modicum of respect for) any of the players?

Of course, some children have firsthand experience with courts. It might be reasonable to assume that their knowledge would surpass that of other, less experienced children. Grisso (1981) lays this assumption to rest. In a study of the abilities of 600 wards of the juvenile court to comprehend the Miranda warnings and their implications, Grisso found that the majority did not understand either the warnings or their implications. Comprehension (or lack of it) was not related to the children's amount of prior experience with the courts or police or to their race or their socioeconomic status.

Saywitz (1989) argues that direct experience with court may in fact reduce comprehension of the legal system because it presents more complex information in a more confusing context. In other words, it may be difficult for children to understand the legal proceedings and the roles of the various players because the system does not operate in a straightforward, textbook-like fashion. Instead, the process is fraught with motions, delays, continuances, objections, and other obfuscations.

It is safe to assume, then, that most youngsters know precious little about courtroom personnel and procedures. Moreover, they do not always develop legal concepts in a logical fashion. Rather, they may move from complete lack of knowledge to incorrect perceptions and assumptions before they finally achieve accurate comprehension (Warren-Leubecker et al., 1989). In the next section, we explore this developmental journey into children's understanding of the participants, procedures, and issues associated with the legal system.[1]

The Concepts of Court and Courtroom

Warren-Leubecker et al. (1989) assessed children's understanding of the legal system. Only 18 percent of the three-year-olds in their sample knew what a courtroom was, whereas approximately 40 percent of six-year-olds, 85 percent of seven-year-olds, and more than 90 percent of all groups over the age of nine were familiar with the concept of a courtroom. In another study of children's conceptions of the legal system, Saywitz (1989) discovered that very young children tend to understand the observable characteristics of the legal system, but not the defining features. For example, four- to seven-year-olds tend to describe legal personnel by their dress and everyday behavior (e.g., sitting, talking, and helping), rather than in terms that differentiate among their judicial roles. By contrast, most teens can describe the court as a subsystem of an overarching government and can accurately describe the function of all players, including the jury and minor court personnel.

Personnel

In general, children tend to develop the concept of *judge* before that of lawyer. *Jury* is one of the last concepts they comprehend.

The judge. Ninety-one percent of the three-year-olds in Warren-Leubecker et al.'s (1989) study did not know anything at all about a judge, let alone other court personnel. By age four, children began noting that a judge "dresses in black" (p. 166), but often added such irrelevant details as having white or gray hair, being old, or wearing glasses. Saywitz (1989) also found that the judge is likely to be described by young children in terms of the judicial black robe and "hammer," rather than as someone who is in charge of the courtroom and who determines sentences. By third grade (ages eight to nine), the judge's role in determining guilt or innocence and in deciding appropriate punishments began to emerge. By adolescence, the concept of the judge was well established.

Attorneys. Warren-Leubecker et al. (1989) found that children under the age of seven have no idea what a lawyer does. Those children who venture to guess are likely to say that an attorney " 'loans money,' 'writes down everybody who's bad,' . . . 'plays golf,' 'lies,' and 'sits around' " (p. 168). Not until the age of ten do children understand that an attorney prosecutes or defends people accused of crimes. However, most children of this age believe that trial lawyers' only purpose is to defend criminals. Warren-Leubecker et al. (1989) note, "In fact, many children used the term 'lawyer' exclusively for defense functions, and 'attorney' for prosecution," so that when asked, "Who is in a courtroom?" several children listed both lawyers and attorneys (p. 174). The specific duties of the lawyer are not well elaborated until adolescence.

Witnesses. Saywitz (1989) found that the majority of four- to seven-year-olds lack any understanding of the role of witnesses at trial. Although they may know that the goal of the court is to accomplish some act (e.g., deciding where the child will live or punishing a "bad" person), they do not understand that evidence must be collected, presented, and evaluated. Saywitz notes that the young children in her sample had "a naive view, assuming that the evidence almost magically presented itself and was, of course, true and believed" (p. 148). In other words, many four- to seven-year-olds operate under the myth that all witnesses tell the truth and that they invariably are believed. Older children begin to see that a witness's credibility must be assessed; they become cognizant of factors that a judge or jury could use in determining the credibility of a given witness.

The jury. Some legal roles are completely foreign to young children. The concept of *jury*, for example, is beyond the comprehension of most four- to seven-year-olds. Even at ages eight to nine, the concept remains elusive, but by ages ten to twelve the concept tends to emerge. Children at these older ages are aware that the court is a fact-finding body that seeks to uncover the truth. Still, they do not understand that sometimes the truth (reality) differs from the judge's or jury's decision about what happened (Saywitz, 1989). Indeed, many children of these ages do not realize that the jury is an impartial body, thinking instead that "victims, witnesses, and defendants ask their friends to come be on the jury" (Saywitz, 1989, p. 151). Twelve- to fourteen-year-olds begin to become aware of the true function of the jury. They understand that decisions may in fact be based on inaccurate information, that witnesses may perjure themselves, and that winning the case is not always synonymous with discovering the truth. However, only the three oldest children in Saywitz's sample understood that the judge and jury make independent decisions. Therefore, most children who testify may be oblivious to the need to convey their message to the jury, as well as to the judge.

Minor court personnel. Such legal players as the bailiff, court reporter, and court clerk typically are not mentioned until at least age six (Warren-Leubecker et al., 1989). Even among the oldest children, these personnel receive short shrift. Only 15 percent of Warren-Leubecker et al.'s sample ever mentioned the court reporter—perhaps not a surprising finding when we consider the fact that only 40 percent of the oldest group even mentioned the jury or attorneys!

Procedures

Very young children have no concept of the court and, therefore, cannot comprehend legal procedures. Those children who are developing a concept of the court tend to know that it is a place to "settle arguments or solve problems" (Warren-Leubecker et al., 1989, p. 169). Still, most young children believe that the court is a "bad" place and that only "bad" people go to court (Flin et al., 1987; Warren-Leubecker et al., 1989). Clearly, this notion must be corrected before a young child is asked to take the stand. Children in middle childhood (ages 9 to 11) are more likely to say that the court is neither good nor bad, and by adolescence their perceptions of the court tend to shift to the positive. Still, their understanding of the specific procedures and actions involved in a court case remains hazy, tainted perhaps by the distorted "lessons" television has offered them regarding the law (Macaulay, 1987).

The Obligation to Tell the Truth

Children who are called to testify need to understand more than simply the roles of the players and the procedures involved in a legal case. They also need to know that as witnesses they must be judged both competent and credible. In order to be found competent as witnesses, children must possess a sense of the obligation to tell the truth. The requirement to testify truthfully is relatively straightforward for adults. For children, however, the truthfulness requirement presents interesting issues.

The great majority of children, even at the tender age of three, have a grasp of the difference between truth and falsehood, and of the duty to tell the truth in court (Johnson & Foley, 1984). Despite this basic fact, however, it is important to consider each child's age and stage of moral development when assessing the youngster's comprehension of the obligation to be truthful. Review of Lickona's (1983) six stages of moral reasoning (described in chapter 3) suggests that when children are asked to speak *truthfully* about events, their responses sometimes depend upon their age and moral frame of reference. Children in Stage 1 of moral development (ages four and younger) tend to believe that it is right that they get their own way. They are motivated by rewards and punishments. Their concepts of good and bad are not yet well defined, and they may be persuaded more easily to stray from the truth, believing, perhaps, that such action fits as easily into the "good" as the "bad" category. At this level, truth may mean what is most advantageous for the child. The court must encourage the child to tell about events as they really happened. Questions that ask for simple descriptions of specific actions—not conclusions or inferences—should help avoid pitfalls lurking at this stage.

At Stage 2 of moral development (generally kindergarten age), being good (and, therefore, truthful) rests upon obedience to authority. With children at this level, descriptions of the truth may change, depending upon the child's allegiances. This potential problem is of particular importance in cases involving incest or child custody. Which parent does the child want to live with? A child who is ambivalent, may appear fickle. If a child has some understanding that a parent may be sent to prison on the basis of his or her testimony, he or she may be reluctant to speak the truth. If this problem arises, it may be helpful to impress upon the child that the judge is the authority who must be obeyed and that the judge wants to know how things really happened.

From ages six through eight or nine, children operating at Stage 3 tend to believe in a "you scratch my back and I'll scratch yours" philosophy of reciprocal benefit. At this stage children need to understand what they have to gain by testifying truthfully. Because they are not at the level of principled conscience, they may be convinced or frightened out of testifying truthfully if they believe that they may be harmed more than helped by telling what actually happened. (Indeed, this problem may arise for adults who have been threatened or intimidated.) With youngsters at Stage 3, it is important to explain in simple terms how testifying truthfully will serve justice and benefit the child as well. It may be helpful to refer to other incidents from the child's personal experience that show how justice was served when the child spoke truthfully.

Children at Stage 4 are eager to please others and to be seen as nice. This stage typically encompasses the middle to upper elementary grades (ages 9 through 12). Children at this level usually want to say whatever pleases important adults. As their ability to make inferences improves, they become adept at reading the intentions and desires of adults. Testifying truthfully can become confused with saying what an important adult wants to hear. Those in authority should impress upon the child that what the judge wants to hear is what actually happened, no matter how unpleasant the events may have been and no matter how much distaste others' expressions may show.

Adolescents at Stage 5 usually want to keep social systems operating smoothly. They understand the need to meet personal obligations, including the need to testify truthfully. At this stage explanations of our system of justice are helpful.

Keep in mind, however, that some children (and adults) never progress beyond the rudimentary levels of moral reasoning (Kohlberg, 1963). Moreover, if the child has been traumatized or threatened, the result may be regression to an earlier level of functioning (see generally Pynoos & Eth, 1984). In such a case, use of instructions and techniques associated with earlier levels of functioning (described above) may prove beneficial.

Children are no more prone to lying than are adults. Most children, even those who have regressed morally, want to be truthful. Children in Warren-Leubecker et al.'s (1989) sample insisted that they would tell the truth even if someone they knew (including their parents) broke the law. Of course, moral behavior does not always follow from moral intention or reasoning (see Burton, 1976), but generally, children have little to gain from being deceitful (see Faller, 1984). If speaking truthfully is defined for them and if the obligation to tell the truth is impressed upon them, most children speak the truth as they understand it.[2]

MEMORY

Models of Memory

Memory involves the acquisition, storage, and retrieval of information. Each of these plays a separate role in understanding children's memory abilities. Two major schools of thought have developed to explain memory in children. According to the Piaget-ian view (Inhelder & Piaget, 1958), memory cannot be separated from intelligence. Therefore, the way to understand memory is to become familiar with how children in general develop cognition (see chapter 3).

From an information-processing point of view—the other major approach—memory primarily is concerned with the *transfer* of information within the brain. Information-processing theorists often use a computer analogy to divide memory into "hardware" and "software" components (Atkinson & Shiffrin, 1968). According to this view, the "hardware" of memory is composed of three parts: (a) *sensory registers,* which record information for a brief three- to five-second period; (b) *short-term store,* a temporary, working mem-ory that allows us to remember active, conscious material; and (c) *long-term store,* where information is held permanently. The "soft-ware" of memory is composed of the various strategies or control processes we use to help us remember and transfer information among the various "hardware" components. Developmental differ-ences in memory result from age-related changes in the ability to use memory strategies.

Regardless of the model employed to explain the development of memory, research studies of memory duration suggest that the ability to store information does not change greatly with age. Once a piece of information is stored successfully in memory, a pre-schooler probably will remember it as well as an adult (Werner & Perlmutter, 1979). Why is it, then, that young children sometimes have trouble remembering information accurately? Two factors account for this phenomenon. First, it is difficult for youngsters to *encode* information; that is, to get the material from working memory into long-term storage. Second, retrieving the information from long-term storage and putting it back into working memory sometimes is troublesome. Both problems seem to result from the fact that most of the space allotted to control processes in children's active, working memory is filled by the instructions for encoding and retrieving information; that is, the child still is mastering the task of remembering. Over time, children become more efficient at processing information because the instructions become auto-matic. This efficiency allows them to store more raw data and to transform it so that it can be comprehended. As Hall et al.(1986) explain, "[i]f less space is needed for carrying out basic processes, then more room will be available to hold information and manipulate it in complex ways. This allows children to develop increasingly sophisticated programs for encoding and retrieval" (p. 255).

Types of Remembering

The first steps in remembering an event are (a) to perceive it and (b) to pay attention to it. Children may be very effective witnesses because they tend to concentrate on observing, rather than on observing *and* interpreting their observations, as adults are likely to do. However, children sometimes fail to note some peripheral elements because such elements may lack significance in their experience. At the same time, other extraneous elements may be given exaggerated importance because of their transitory relevance to the child (see *American Jurisprudence Trials, 1966*). For example, some children may be unable to describe the clothes a person was wearing because they have not learned to be conscious of detail in appearance or dress. In contrast, other children who are preoccupied with fashion may be able to describe the clothes in great detail (*American Jurisprudence Trials, 1966*).

In addition to the initial perception of events, children must have sufficient ability to remember and report information. Recall that younger children's brains are not fully developed. In particular, the corpus callosum, the bundle of fibers that provides communication between the two hemispheres of the brain, continues to mature during the first decade of life. Thus, while children may be able to perceive an event accurately, they may have difficulty translating their perceptions into words. The event may be safely stored in memory in some representational form (enactive, imaginal, etc.), but the child may have difficulty effectively communicating the existence or content of the memory.

No matter how or in what form information is stored, in order to be effective witnesses, children must be able to demonstrate their retention of material by one of three means: recognition, reconstruction, or recall.

Recognition memory. Recognition is the simplest form of remembering because it requires only that we perceive an object as something that was perceived previously. Because recognition is based upon perception and on patterns of simple motor responses, it is within the capacity of very young infants. (In fact, this primitive memory process occurs in many lower animals [see

Piaget & Inhelder, 1973]). For example, within the first week of life, newborns can recognize the smell of their own mothers' breast milk and prefer it to the smell of milk provided by other lactating mothers (Macfarlane, 1977).

Studies generally have found that recognition improves rapidly as children mature. For example, one study found that two-year-olds were correct in their recognition judgments on 81 percent of the objects presented and that four-year-olds were correct 92 percent of the time (Myers & Perlmutter, 1978). Still, children under 10 have difficulty identifying those faces that are observed briefly, are disguised, or are unfamiliar. Recognition memory is of relatively little help in such cases. Skill in making such identifications increases with age (see generally Ceci, Toglia, & Ross, 1987a; Chance & Goldstein, 1984). Also, younger children, when given the task of identifying a face from a set of them, may not concentrate as much. They sometimes need to be encouraged to pay attention.

Some studies indicate that recognition memory is better during the early elementary school years than at other times. For example, two different studies report the curious finding that face recognition memory improves steadily from 6 to 10 years, declines from 11 to 12 years, and then improves from age 13 on (see, e.g., Carey, 1978). Other researchers found that on a photo recognition task, 6-years-olds had higher mean identification accuracy (M = .95) than either adults (M = .74) or 3-year-olds (M = .38) (Goodman & Reed, 1986). The varying accuracy rates obtained in these studies suggest that additional questions must be answered if the face-recognition literature is to be clarified. For example: Was the observer likely to be aware of the event at the time it was taking place? Did the central character of the incident command attention? Could the culprit's face be seen clearly? For how long? These factors are likely to have strong bearing on recognition memory (Goodman & Reed, 1986).

In general, it is reasonable to conclude that by the time children enter school, their recognition memory is very good, at least for simple stimuli. Anyone who has played the memory game Concentration with a young child can attest to this fact! Indeed, five-year-olds are as proficient as adults in recognizing pictures of commonplace objects (Nelson & Kosslyn, 1976). However, children generally do not do so well with more complex stimuli, those requiring skilled scanning and registration of information (Perlmutter, 1984). This limitation is important in the legal context, for witnesses typically are asked to testify regarding complex events.

Reconstruction memory. Reconstruction memory is a specialized method of retrieving material from storage (Piaget & Inhelder, 1973), which involves reproducing the form of information that was seen in the past. Reconstructing the scene of a crime is an example. Goodman and Hahn (1987) note:

> The extent to which the retrieval environment matches the encoding situation is an important determinant of a person's ability to provide accurate and complete eyewitness testimony. The more cues shared at acquisition and retrieval, the better retrieval will be. (p. 271)

Piaget suggested that children's reconstructive memory is superior to their free recall because when children manipulate concrete objects, they intentionally repeat the natural order of events (Piaget & Inhelder, 1973). Watching a group of children play "house" or "cops-and-robbers" will provide support for Piaget's observation. Even two- and three-year-olds demonstrate up to 75 percent accuracy on simple reconstructions (Cohen, Perlmutter, & Myers, 1977; Perry, Nielsen, Burns, Cunningham, & Jenkins, 1987).

In some cases it may be possible to reconstruct the sequence of events in a legal case by returning to the scene of the alleged crime and reexperiencing contextual cues. At other times, of course, it is impossible to do so, often because the exact location is unknown. In such circumstances, two recently developed techniques may prove helpful.

Using *context reinstatement* (Fisher, Amador, & Geiselman, 1989; Fisher, Geiselman, Raymond, Jurkevich, & Warhaftig, 1987; Geiselman, Fisher, Cohen, Holland, & Surtes, 1986; Geiselman et al., 1984; Geiselman, Fisher, MacKinnon, & Holland, 1985), witnesses participate in interviews in which they are encouraged to re-create the scene mentally and to report everything they can remember. The interviewer may ask them, for example, to focus on the surroundings, the smells and sounds, the temperature, the location of the furniture, or anything else about the event that may elicit memories they could not otherwise recall. These activities are intended to help reinstate the context in which the crime occurred. Recent evidence suggests that this type of "cognitive" or "context reinstatement" interview leads to recall of more details than does a standard interview, with fewer confabulations than in such other procedures as hypnosis (Fisher & Quigley, 1989; Perry et al., 1987).

A second reconstructive memory technique is described by Hall (1989). This approach

> allows the child to draw or to direct the interviewer to draw a large sketch (floor plan) of his house and to use the family dolls or dolls made from clay to suit the design of the child to act out the events of a typical or a remembered day in the child's life. "Where does everyone sleep?" "Who wakes you in the morning?" "Dresses you?" "Bathes you?" "Puts you to bed?" The child's actions and descriptions as the story unfolds are spontaneous, and the stimulus materials are sufficiently nonspecific to minimize the probability that the child's response is due to negative coercion or a positive attempt to conform. The freedom encouraged in this form of play-interview allows the child to supply the underlying information about the crucial relationships in his or her life. Expanding the "game," with large sheets of newsprint spread across the floor, allows exploration of neighborhood and day-care or school areas, with a "child's-eye view" of the safe and the dangerous places and people in their significant life-space. (p. 461)

Use of such techniques in the investigation of sexual abuse may help a young child to respond to reconstructive memory cues and provide information necessary to the investigation. Alternatively, anatomically correct dolls may be used to assist in the reconstruction of an act (but see the caveats discussed in chapter 6). Even very young children may perform adequately on such tasks. Not surprisingly, however, on such complex tasks as reconstructing a crime from photographs, the performance of most young children is not impressive.

Recall memory. Recall is the most complex form of retention test. It requires that previously observed events be retrieved from storage with few or no prompts. It also is the form of retrieval most often required of witnesses. Unlike the simpler forms of memory retrieval, recall ability is strongly age-related. For instance, in one study subjects ranging in age from five years to young adulthood observed an unexpected, staged incident in which a person interrupted a presentation and complained angrily about the use of the room. Subjects then were asked to use recall memory to relate what they could remember about the incident. A number of the younger subjects volunteered no information. On the average, kindergartners and first graders recalled about one correct item per subject, third and fourth graders about three, seventh and eighth graders about six, and college students between seven and eight (Marin et al., 1979). It is important to note, however, that although the youngest (kindergarten-first grade) were able to recall less, what they did say tended to be correct (only 3 percent error). In contrast, the other age groups had error rates of 12, 8, and 10 percent, respectively (Marin et al., 1979).

In addition to describing what they saw, subjects answered 20 simple questions about the incident. In a recognition task, the youngsters also were asked to select the man they had seen from an array of six similarly lit photographs of men with beards, glasses, medium-length brown hair and wearing the same shirt (Marin et al., 1979). The results indicated that children of all ages were as capable as adults of answering simple, direct questions about the incident and that children were as adept as adults at selecting the person they had seen from the photo array.

Perry and Teply (1984-1985) draw the following conclusions regarding this research:

> In the context of a legal interview or examination, this research suggests that when children are simply asked to tell what they can remember about an event, the quality of the narrative of older children will be better than that of younger ones, but neither will give as full a narrative as an adult. It also suggests, however, that even young children (kindergarten-first grade) have sufficiently developed ability to remember past events and that simple, direct (nonleading) questions or recognition recall [i.e., cued recall] appear to be viable means of finding out factual information from them. Using those methods, their answers apparently are no less credible than those of an adult, absent other influences. (p. 1389)

Still, it is important to keep in mind that certain trends are evident in the development of recall ability. Generally speaking, infants are poor at recall.[3] Although preschoolers begin to organize their memories around concepts, even their recall memory is poorly developed. Several factors explain the limited recall of these children:

Their incompetence at recall may be due to a number of factors that affect memory. Preschoolers appear to be ignorant of strategies (such as rehearsal or clustering) that help register information in memory. They may be limited by their inappropriate research tendencies (such as their propensity to recall the last object shown). They may have difficulty in internally generating material. Finally, their limited verbal ability may limit their production of available information. (Hall et al., 1986, p. 257)

If the material to be recalled is part of young children's pattern of daily life, their recall improves. For example, when three- and four-year-olds were studied in their own homes, they showed an amazing amount of recall about their experiences (Todd & Perlmutter, 1980). They recalled information well, both spontaneously and in response to an adult's questions. Sequences of actions, however, still were poorly recalled.

When children enter school (at the time their operational representation abilities are developing), their recall improves. For example, when six- or seven-year-olds recall a story, they recall it much as an adult would (Kail & Hagen, 1977) Typically, however, holes remain in their versions of the story. While most of the important features are recalled, the incidental facts may be forgotten or not reported. As with adults, children also tend to recall the meaning of the sentences they have heard, but not their exact phrasing. Also, they sometimes "recall" information that was not actually part of the story, but that is consistent in meaning with what they were told—a phenomenon referred to by developmental psychologists as *elaborated recall*.

The problems of missing information and elaborated recall can be troublesome when a child takes the stand. Of course, adults too experience these problems. In fact, among older children and adults, elaborated recall may be an even greater problem, as these individuals tend to draw inferences from what they experience. As a result, they sometimes "remember" details that never occurred. For example, adults are more likely than young children to recall that a room "became dark" when they are told that a light switch was turned off (Hall et al., 1986).

It would be erroneous to assume that younger children necessarily have poorer recall than do older children or adults. In some cases, younger children can provide *more* accurate information.

The important point is that because of their limited ability to use memory strategies, children often know more than they can freely recall. When children begin to use memory strategies efficiently, however, their ability to transfer material through the memory system improves dramatically.

Strategies for and Deficiencies in Remembering

When adults are asked to remember information—whether it is as simple as a telephone number or as complex as a lengthy poem—they use various memory strategies either at the time they encode the material or at the time they retrieve it or both. These strategies may include repeatedly rehearsing the material, creating mnemonic rhymes, or putting small bits of information into larger chunks that can be remembered easily. Young children (under age six) typically have not developed memory strategies. Without such strategies at their disposal, children under age six experience difficulty in recalling events, and it is only where such strategies are not needed that these children perform as well as older children or adults (Brown, Bransford, Ferrara, & Campione, 1983).

The use of *rehearsal* as a memory strategy is almost automatic for adults. We use it whenever we repeat information to ourselves in order to remember a telephone number or the items on a short grocery list. Ten-year-olds, too, almost always use this technique. Young children, however, have not mastered this technique (Harris & Liebert, 1987).

As children mature, their rehearsal techniques become more effective (Ornstein & Naus, 1978). For example, if third-graders are given a list of words to remember, they tend to repeat each new word over and over without rehearsing previous words, resulting in limited recall. Older children who are given the same task mix the words they rehearse so that they learn the entire list. Older children also use more rehearsal time than do younger children, and test themselves repeatedly.

Another memory strategy is *imagery,* which involves (a) mentally picturing a person, place, or object; or (b) visually associating two or more things that must be remembered. Children discover this strategy much later than they do other mnemonics, and some people never learn this technique (Flavell, 1977). Like other memory strategies, imagery can be used by young children if they are instructed in its use. Because young children's imaginal representation is so strong, instruction in the use of imagery may be a worthwhile expenditure of time for those who work with child witnesses.

One of the most effective memory strategies is *organization,* the grouping of items around some common element or theme. Preschoolers do not spontaneously organize material as well as older children do. When items are presented to young children in small blocks, one category at a time, they can remember the categories (e.g., fruits, toys, colors). However, if the individual items are presented randomly, most six-year-olds do not organize the material well, even when there are only a few items in each category (Furth & Milgram, 1973).

While children as young as five can sort items into categories, they do not use the categories to help them remember (Moely, 1977). For example, when presented with a list of random words and asked to "put together the words that go together," most five-year-olds can categorize animal-words, food-words, color-words, and so forth. After completing such a task, however, most young children fail to use the organizational information as cues to help remember the words on the list.

Another technique that can aid recall is the use of *external cues,* such as string tied around the finger to remind a child to call home after school. In one study designed to investigate the use of external cues to improve memory, children saw 24 pictures selected from eight categories, plus one cue card for each category (Kobasigawa, 1974). For example, three animal pictures were cued by a picture of a zoo. When the children were allowed to use the cue cards by themselves during the recall period, only one-third of the six-year-olds decided to use them, and when they did, they used them poorly. When the experimenter showed the children each cue card and specifically asked them to recall all three items, six-year-olds were as proficient as eleven-year-olds. This finding suggests that although a memory strategy may not be used spontaneously by a child, it may be employed by a knowledgeable adult to aid a child in recalling events—certainly a useful piece of information for preparing a child to give effective testimony at trial.

People also use *internal cues* (that is, imagined ones) to assist memory. An interesting experiment by Salatas and Flavell (1976) examined children's use of internal cues for remembering. The children learned a list of words by category and then were tested repeatedly until they could recall every item in each category. Next, the investigators asked the children such questions as "Which ones [items] are small enough to fit in this box?" In order to answer the question, children had to complete several mental steps: (a) go through the items, (b) decide which objects would fit, and then (c) list them aloud. Only 1 of the 36 six-year-olds could handle this complicated task. Nine of the 32 nine-year-olds could do it, and most of a group of college students automatically produced the requested items (Salatas & Flavell, 1976). When given specific instructions on how to conduct the mental search, more than half the nine-year-olds could answer the question, but few of the six-year-olds could. Apparently, most six-year-olds and many nine-year-olds are incapable of using internal cues to conduct systematic searches of memory (Kobasigawa, 1974, 1977).

Although children unquestionably have techniques less sophisticated than adults have for recalling information, on some tasks young children perform as well as older children and adults. This is particularly true when children know more about a subject than their more mature counterparts. For example, one study demonstrated that older children learned word lists much more efficiently than younger children learned the same lists. But when the lists were varied so that each group memorized words that were meaningful to them, younger children recalled as many words as did older children (Richman, Nida, & Pittman, 1976). In a similar study, when words on a list were grouped by general category (e.g., teacher's names, books on the class reading list, television shows), younger children performed as well as older children did (Linberg, 1980). Even very young children can demonstrate impressive memory skills when they have a substantial knowledge base. For example, a four-year-old boy who had become fascinated with dinosaurs was studied over six sessions. He was able to recall the names and characteristics of no less than 46 types of dinosaurs (Chi & Koeske, 1983), a feat that many college professors wish they could replicate in their students!

Thus, child witnesses may be able to demonstrate adequate or even superior memories if they are questioned about elements of their daily life or about subjects in which they have a sizeable knowledge base. Their memory performance declines, however, when they are asked to use internal cues that require systematic searches of memory and the reporting of only those items that fit specific criteria; that is, when they are asked to make judgments about their memories.

Children's Suggestibility

It is commonly believed that children are more suggestible than adults (see Goodman et al., 1984). Certainly children, like adults, are subject to suggestion, but psychological research discloses that children are not as suggestible as many adults believe them to be (see Duncan, Whitney, & Kunen, 1982).

Studies of suggestibility among children and adults offer mixed findings. Some studies support the conclusion that young children are no more suggestible than adults. That is, a number of studies have demonstrated that children as young as five years of age can answer objective questions concerning simple events as well as adults can (see generally Goodman & Helgeson, 1985). For instance, Duncan et al. (1982) presented a series of slides to six-, eight-, and ten-year-olds, and to college students. One set of slides dealt with the caveman Krog who, with his friends, was attacked by a bear. The subjects were asked three types of information questions: (a) "When the bear appeared, where did it chase the men?" (no information question): (b) "After the bear appeared and broke the man's spear, where did it chase the men?" (correct information question); and (c) "After the bear appeared and broke the man's fishing pole, where did it chase the men?" (misleading information question). The subjects then were asked follow-up questions to examine whether the information questions influenced the subjects' memory of the depicted visual events (e.g., "Were the men hunting when the bear appeared?" or "Were the men fishing when the bear appeared?"). The results demonstrated that children and adults were influenced equally by the questions that were asked after the slide presentation. A second analysis, based upon only those instances in which there was correct memory of the visual sequence, showed that the younger subjects appeared to be *less* influenced than the older subjects! A follow-up experiment in which memory change was evaluated by a slide recognition task obtained a similar pattern of results.

In another study, previously described in the section on recall memory, subjects from kindergarten to college age observed an unexpected, staged incident—an interruption in which a person complained angrily about the use of the room (Marin et al., 1979). After 20 objective questions had been asked of the subjects, they were asked two misleading questions ("Did the man slam the door as he closed it?" and "Was the package the man carried small?"). The impact of these questions was assessed at a second testing session two weeks later, when the subjects were asked about the incident. The results indicated that children were not more easily swayed into incorrect answers by the use of misleading questions than were adults (Marin et al., 1979).

In contrast, some studies have found that under certain circumstances, children may be more suggestible than adults. For example, in one study, films portraying two crimes—shoplifting, and failure to return to its known owner a purse left on a bus—were shown to three groups: third-graders, sixth-graders, and college-age adults (Cohen & Harnick, 1980). Half the observers were asked questions in a nonsuggestive form (e.g., "What was the young woman carrying when she entered the bus?"). The other observers were asked questions in a suggestive and misleading form (e.g., "The young woman was carrying a newspaper when she entered the bus, wasn't she?"). In actuality, the woman had a shopping bag. The results showed that the third-graders gave a poorer memory performance than the older groups and that the grade-schoolers had a greater tendency than the older group to accept false suggestions, although all three groups were influenced to some extent.

One week later, a different interrogator asked all the observers for the same information, using a multiple-choice (recognition) format (e.g., "Which of the following was the young woman carrying when she got on the bus? (a) an umbrella, (b) a shopping bag, (c) a newspaper, (d) a hatbox") (Cohen & Harnick, 1980). Again, the results showed that the third-graders had poorer memories than the older subjects for the relevant events. Moreover, almost all observers chose either a correct response or one suggested during the previous session, with the youngest group choosing the greatest number of suggestive responses in comparison with the other groups. It is important to note that the analysis of results attributed the youngest group's inferior performance on suggestive items mainly to their inferior encoding of the film in memory. The effect of suggestion upon the material that had been encoded well was *not* significantly different for the three age groups (Cohen & Harnick, 1980).

In another experiment, Goodman and Reed (1986) found that, in general, adults were more likely to answer suggestive questions correctly than were six-year-olds and that six-year-olds were better than three-year-olds. When asked accurate but leading questions, however, the six-year-olds answered with the *greatest* accuracy (followed by the three-year-olds and then the adults). Moreover, adults made more intrusion errors than did either three- or six-year-olds. That is, adults tended to let inaccurate information intrude on their memory of the event. While three- and six-year-olds tended to be somewhat more suggestible than adults overall, this finding did not hold true for central information that had been encoded properly in memory.

In light of these complex results, what conclusions may be drawn regarding children's susceptibility to the effects of suggestion? A review of these and other studies of suggestibility of children led two commentators to conclude:

> Taken together, the results of these studies support the conclusion that adults spontaneously recall more about events they have witnessed than do children, but not the simple notion that children are always more suggestible than adults.
>
> Probably no single factor can by itself explain the discrepant findings of these studies. This points to a possible resolution of the discrepancy. Perhaps age alone is the wrong focus for these studies. Whether children are more susceptible to suggestive information than adults probably depends on the interaction of age with other factors. If an event is understandable and interesting to both children and adults, and if their memory for it is still equally strong, age differences in suggestibility may not be found. But if the event is not encoded well to begin with, or if a delay weakens the child's memory relative to an adult's, then age differences may emerge. In this case the fragments of the event that remain in the child's memory may not be sufficient to serve as a barrier against suggestion, especially from authoritative others. Of course, if the child's grasp of the language is so weak as to make him or her oblivious to the subtle implications in the suggestive information, then the child may be immune to the manipulation regardless of the interest value or memorability of the stimuli, or the loss of an accurate memory record. (Loftus & Davies, 1984, p. 63)

Thus, several specific factors seem to interact with age in influencing a person's response to suggestion. These factors include degree of suggestion, centrality of the information to be remembered, strength of the memory, linguistics, the questioner's status, and intimidation of the witness. These factors are discussed in greater detail in chapter 6.

The Impact of Stress

Psychological research has shown that intimidation and stress can decrease a person's willingness and ability to retrieve information from memory (see, e.g., Goodman & Helgeson, 1985). This phenomenon occurs with some frequency in the classroom, when students suffer from test anxiety and are not able to summon information they have studied well. A similar kind of anxiety may inhibit some victimized children from telling their stories accurately under difficult circumstances, for example, when the defendant is in the courtroom. In a study of age differences in eyewitness testimony, Goodman and Reed (1986) found that the performance of three-year-olds was inferior in almost every way to that of six-year-olds and adults. They cited evidence suggesting that the three-year-olds seemed to be more threatened by the research experience than were older subjects, and conjectured that this increased stress led to declines in performance.

Because children generally are more easily intimidated than are adults, it is especially important to limit as much as possible the ill effects of intimidation. In this way, suggestibility is reduced.

The Impact of Inducements to Keep Secrets

As described above, memory is influenced by developmental factors, as well as situational factors. One factor that seems to influence the accuracy and completeness of children's reports is incentives for secret-keeping. Particularly in cases of sexual abuse, children may be motivated to keep secrets. Incentives for keeping secrets might include (a) physical threats to the child or to loved ones, (b) telling the child that the perpetrator will get in trouble if the child discloses the secret (which may lead to disruption of the family unit, the child's main source of support), and (c) promises of tangible rewards if the child keeps quiet (Bottoms, Goodman, Schwartz-Kenney, Sachsenmaier, & Thomas, 1990).

Even young children have some knowledge of secrets (Marvin, Greenberg, & Mossler, 1976) and will keep secrets when given only moderate motivation. For example, Clarke-Stewart, Thompson, &

Lepore (1989) asked five- and six-year-old children to observe a confederate posing as a janitor. He played roughly with a doll and then told the children to keep his activities a secret so that he would not get in trouble. He also promised them candy if they would keep the secret. The janitor's "boss" (actually a confederate of the research study) then questioned the children about their experience using one of two interview formats. In the biased interview condition, when the adult suggested to the children that the janitor was guilty of the doll play, all children agreed that he had played with the doll; in other words, they betrayed the janitor's secret. Of those children who participated in a nonleading interview, only 39 percent disclosed the janitor's secret. Clarke-Stewart et al. (1989) note that those children who kept the secret tended to be less socially mature and lower in moral reasoning, more withdrawn and more anxious than those children who did not keep the secret. These results have led some to suggest that leading questions may, in fact, be *necessary* to accurate fact finding when interrogating children regarding alleged sexual abuse (see generally MacFarlane).

In another laboratory study, Wilson and Pipe (1990) found that children who kept a confederate's secret were not less accurate in other respects than children who mentioned the secret. Moreover, errors that the children made were ones of omission (i.e., omitting actions that actually had occurred), rather than errors of commission (i.e., actively falsifying information).

Finally, Bottoms et al. (1990) explored children's accuracy in reporting events that their own mothers told them to keep secret. They found that younger children (ages three and four) tended to disclose the secret, whereas five- and six-year-olds generally kept the secret, "omitting information about the most salient activities of the session" (p. 9). As in the Wilson and Pipe (1990) study, children's memory errors were ones of omission rather than commission. In contrast to the Clarke-Stewart et al. (1989) study, however, even a completely leading interview did not result in the children telling the secret. They were equally likely to keep the secret when given the leading or the specific interview. Bottoms et al. (1990) suggest that, in their study, the children might have been more highly motivated to keep the secret because they were protecting their own mothers; alternatively, the interview used by Clarke-Stewart et al. (1989) might have been more leading and accusatory. Bottoms et al. (1990) conclude:

We can speculate that if a child will keep a secret about an innocuous, nonthreatening act in our laboratory for the reward of a toy and so as not to get the parent in trouble, we should not automatically discount the testimony of a child who delays in disclosing a crime—that child may be responding quite understandably to pressure from a trusted person to keep the event a secret. (p. 10)

Thus, a variety of factors may influence a child's memory. These include developmental sophistication of the child, salience of the events and details to be remembered, the child's use of memory strategies, the stress associated with the events and postevent interviews, and inducements not to disclose information about the events in question.

Maximizing Children's Memory

In addition to guarding against suggestibility and reducing stress, adults may take several steps to improve the reporting of children's memories. First, the interview should take place as soon as possible following the event. Although the stress level may be high and the effects of traumatization serious at this point, memory still is strongest (and often most nearly accurate) at the time of the first interview (see Lipton, 1977). In addition, the interview should be conducted by an unbiased person. Dent (1982) found that regardless of an interviewer's experience with children, the least accurate reports were obtained from child witnesses when the interviewer held preconceived notions about what had happened.

Second, following the opening, rapport-building part of the interview, allow the child to provide a free narrative account of the event. Unstructured statements tend to be somewhat incomplete. However, the narrative format usually elicits accurate information (Lipton, 1977).

Third, help the child organize the information to be remembered. For example, in a case that involves repeated abuse over a period of months, the child may organize the memories according to what happened during each season or at the time of significant events (e.g., school starting, holidays, birthdays, etc.). The same technique may be used to help the child remember the sequence of each incident. For example, the interviewer may ask the child to outline what happened when the assailant and the child met that day (i.e., what activities they were engaging in), what happened during the time of the assault, and what happened after the assailant and child parted.

Fourth, help the child rehearse the order of events. In this regard, the child must be taught how to use the memory device of rehearsal. It may help to explain that "it is easier to remember something if you say it out loud over and over again." The caveat here, of course, is that the child should rehearse only the *sequence* of major events. If the entire testimony is rehearsed, the child is likely to appear to have been coached, rendering the child's testimony unconvincing.

In some cases it is helpful to ask the child to "picture in your head what happened," thereby tapping into the child's natural tendency to use imagery. If the interviewer has established comfortable rapport with the child, it may be helpful to suggest that the child close his or her eyes while picturing what happened. If the child is uneasy with the interviewer, however, requiring closed eyes may cause additional stress (Perry et al., 1987), since the child may fear that something bad will happen while his or her eyes are closed. After asking the child to picture the event, the questioner should ask the child to inspect specific details of the image (or series of images). This step is important because children are likely to report only the central feature of the image, not the peripheral details (Kosslyn, 1983). Start by asking open-ended questions (e.g., "Do you see anything else?" or "Do you hear anything else?"), and then proceed to more structured questions, using such indefinite articles as *a* (e.g., "Do you see *a* car?" or "Did you hear *a* car?"). If affirmative responses are given, ask about the details of the image (e.g., "What color is the car?"). Inspecting the images in this way should provide more and better information about the event.

With some children it is helpful to use external cues, such as props. It is preferable to use props only after other techniques have been explored so that memories are not unwittingly altered. In the case of an automobile accident, for example, the child may be given a set of toy cars to use in depicting the event. If the set offered does not contain a car of the correct color, the child may select a car of the wrong color and, after playing with it, "remember" that the original car was the color of the toy car selected.

Depending upon the circumstances of the case, potentially useful props might include a set of anatomically correct dolls (including all family members); a generic toy room that might be used to represent a home, school, or other building; and toy cars, trucks, bicycles, and tricycles.

It is important to keep in mind that the usefulness of these techniques varies depending upon the age, maturity, intelligence, and cooperativeness of the child. Older, brighter children are likely to have more success using these techniques than are younger, less intelligent, or more reticent children.

LANGUAGE AND COMMUNICATION

In addition to helping children remember events, interviewers must be able to communicate effectively with them. Knowledge of the stages of language development and of common errors children make in the use of language aids communication.

Language Development

Children in virtually all cultures progress through the stages of language development in the same basic order. Even newborn babies are capable of communicating with their caretakers by means of the first stage of language development, crying. Schaffer (1971) identified three distinct patterns of crying: (a) a low intensity, arrhythmic cry that gradually becomes louder and more rhythmic, often suggesting hunger; (b) the enraged cry, characterized by the cry-rest-inspiration-rest pattern; and (c) the pain cry, which starts suddenly, is piercing in intensity, and consists of a long cry followed by a long silence (breath holding) and then by a series of short gasping inhalations (cited in Hall et al., 1986).

Over the course of the next year, babies develop a variety of communication skills. First, they learn to coo, which allows them to initiate, prolong, or end social interactions. As Hall et al. (1986) note, "A smile and a coo will often keep an adult near; by falling silent and turning away, a baby can shut off communication" (p. 377). Even nonlanguage forms of communication, therefore, can be powerful means of shaping the behavior of others, a fact that can be all too apparent in court.

Before most babies reach the age of one year, they are capable of babbling, expressive jargon (nonsense words uttered with sentence-like intonation), and one-word utterances. In the next year, toddlers progress from two-word utterances to telegraphic speech (only essential words strung together). In the third year, vocabulary increases exponentially, and children can produce complex

Box 4.1

Age Norms for Understanding Questions

2 years
Yes—No questions

2½ years
What
What do
Where

3 years
Who
Whose
Why
How many

3½ years
How

4 years
How much
How long (duration)

4½ years
How far

5 years
How often

5½ years
How long (time)
When

SOURCE: Adapted from Bloom and Lahey, 1978.

sentences. Although different children progress through these stages at different rates, most children are capable of uttering simple sentences by the time they are three years of age (see Hall et al., 1986), rendering them more likely as candidates to provide testimony at trial. Some precocious children are capable of communicating at this level by age two. Of course, the ability to understand and produce complex sentences continues to increase into adulthood.

In addition, there are developmental trends in children's mastery of the various question forms used in the English language. Bloom and Lahey (1978), in studies of normal children's language development, have derived age norms for understanding questions (see Box 4.1). Most children master comprehension of the various question types by age 5-1/2. Delays may be caused by language handicaps, learning disabilities, mental retardation, and hearing impairment. Moreover, older children who are experiencing stress or trauma may have difficulty interpreting questions that, under normal circumstances, they could handle with finesse.

While the course of completing the amazing feat of learning a culture's language system generally progresses in a straightforward manner, it is not without its bumps. Children make several characteristic errors on this journey, including overextension and underextension of words, and syntactical errors.

Common Errors in Children's Communications

Overextension. Youngsters sometimes extend the meaning of a word in their small vocabularies to encompass actions or objects for which they have no word. Such use of a word is known as *overextension*. Overextension occurs in from one-fifth to one-third of the communications of young children (Hall et al., 1986). While overextension violates adult rules of language, children use the device in logical ways. From the child's perspective it makes good sense to apply one word to objects that resemble one another (Clark, 1983). For example, all four-legged, furry animals may be referred to as "doggies." Moreover, it has been suggested that children's overextensions may not signify a true need to communicate (see Whitehurst, 1982). Children who overextend words in their own speech often understand the same words in a much more restricted fashion when spoken to. The courts, then, must be careful to decipher the specific meanings of words used by young children. Careful questioning about the similarities and differences between words used to describe perceptions may be necessary.

Underextension. Children also tend to *underextend* the meanings of words: they attribute to a word only part of the meaning the term has for adults. Underextension occurs when children come upon a poor example of a term, an example that is far removed from the central meaning they have for the word (see Anglin, 1977). For example, young children may not categorize ketchup, cookies, and lollipops as "food," perhaps because these substances typically are not labeled by adults as "things to eat that are good for you." This type of error in communication may have particular significance in litigation. For instance, if the attorney is attempting to establish whether a parent was abusive to the child, the child may have a very limited understanding of the term *abusive.*

Syntactical errors. Another potential source of error in communication is *syntax,* the juxtaposition of words to convey meaning. In English, as in many other languages, the order in which words are spoken partially determines their meaning. English sentences typically follow a subject-verb-object sequence. Because understanding of this general concept of word order does not develop until children are at least preschool age (three to four years old), many misunderstandings may develop when communicating with young children. Consider this example of early linguistic miscommunication provided by a two-year-old who typically liked to have her lunchtime sandwich cut into pieces to resemble a jigsaw puzzle:

Mother:	Do you want your sandwich cut?
Child:	Yes.
Mother:	(Begins to cut sandwich.)
Child:	(Getting upset.) No! No!
Mother:	Don't you want it cut?
Child:	Yes. I want it cut!
Mother:	(Begins to cut sandwich again.)
Child:	(Getting very upset.) No! No!
Mother:	I don't understand you. *Show* me what you want.
Child:	(Taking knife from mother and cutting the sandwich) *I* want it cut! (Translation: *I* want *to* cut it.)[4]

As this example illustrates, avoiding syntactical miscommunication often involves asking children to *show* adults what they mean, rather than asking them to explain themselves.

Avoiding Communication Errors

Although a lawyer's well-honed verbal skills are valuable for many legal purposes, these skills sometimes present a significant barrier to communication with children (or even adults). For this reason, when lawyers or other adults work with children, they must choose their words with great care. This is true whether the adult is asking questions or explaining matters. Being cognizant of several points may aid the communication process.

Because words do not always mean the same thing to children as they do to adults, the adult must be careful to define terms. For example, it would be virtually useless to give explanations to a child that include such words as *abuse, negligence, verdict, trier of fact, presumption,* or *compensate.* Terms must be translated for the child. For example, *abuse* might be defined as "someone hitting you, or burning you or touching you where it doesn't feel good to you." Similarly, *negligence* might be explained as "when something bad happens and it's someone's fault." Use of simple words and sentences illustrated by examples is the best practice.

Active-voice sentences (e.g., "Karen *spilled* the milk" or "The red car *hit* the blue car") tend to be understood, whereas passive-voice sentences (e.g., "The milk *was spilled by* Karen" or "The red car *was hit by* the blue car") are more difficult for children to comprehend and should be avoided. It also is well to avoid double negatives, such as "Is it not true that your mother was not at home?" A better approach is, "Was your mother at home?"

Adults should not expect children to be able to answer questions about abstractions, especially concerning a subject they have not previously considered (Freeman & Weihofen, 1972). Nor should a child be expected to fully understand evaluative questions, such as, "Do you get along well with your father?"

Finally, avoid summarizing the child's testimony and then asking for a general confirmation of its accuracy. Because children tend to put information into extreme categories (e.g., "truth" versus "lie"), if the statement is *generally* correct, the child may say that the statement is correct, perhaps leading the court to conclude that there are no errors in the summary. Conversely, if there is even *one* error in the summary, the child may deem the account incorrect. It is better, therefore, to check the veracity of each point in the testimony.

As a general rule, adults should use simply phrased, active-voice sentences with only a few modifying words (i.e., adjectives and adverbs) when talking with child witnesses. Also, when the meaning of children's sentences is unclear, it is better to ask them to "say it in another way" than to attempt to rephrase the sentence for them. Children are too likely to agree with the authority figure's version of the statement. Because of young children's strong need for acceptance from adults, they may be willing to sacrifice linguistic accuracy for approval.

SUMMARY

As a rule, children understand precious little about the legal system—its players, its rules, and its procedures. Those legal concepts with which children are familiar may have distorted or inaccurate meanings. Most children move from complete lack of knowledge about legal personnel and procedures to a phase of incorrect perceptions and assumptions before they finally achieve accurate comprehension. Developmentally, children acquire the concept of *judge* before that of either *attorney* or *jury*.

The great majority of children, even as young as age three, understand the difference between truth and falsehood and appreciate their duty to tell the truth in court. Still, moral behavior does not always follow directly from moral reasoning, so judges must take care to explain to children the importance of relating the facts as they actually happened.

The reporting of past events depends upon the witness's ability to demonstrate retention of the relevant material. There are three means of remembering such material: recognition, reconstruction, and recall. Recognition is the simplest form and the one most readily accessible to young children. Recall is the most difficult to demonstrate. It would be erroneous to assume, however, that younger children necessarily have poorer recall than do older children or adults; in some cases younger children can provide more accurate information than their elders. The important point is that because of their limited ability to use memory strategies, children often know more than they can recall freely. When children begin to use memory strategies efficiently, however, their ability to transfer material through the memory system improves dramatically.

It is commonly believed that children are more suggestible than adults. Certainly, children, like adults, are prone to suggestion. Psychological research discloses, however, that children are not as suggestible as many adults believe, especially when they are questioned about salient events in their lives. Moreover, several specific factors seem to interact with age in influencing a person's response to suggestion: degree of suggestion, centrality of the information to be remembered, strength of the memory, linguistics, the questioner's status, intimidation of the witness, and so forth.

In addition to helping children remember events, interviewers must be able to communicate effectively with them. It is important for those who question children to be knowledgeable about the stages of language development and of common errors in language usage, such as overextension and underextension of words and syntactical errors. It is best for adults to use simply phrased, active-voice sentences with few modifying words when talking with child witnesses. Also, it is vital to ask frequently for confirmation of the interviewer's summary of the child's statements.

The accuracy and credibility of children's testimony can be increased by helping young witnesses understand legal proceedings and the roles played by each actor in the system, by giving them strategies for remembering information and reporting it, and by avoiding common errors in communication.

NOTES

1. Indeed, the same can be said of adults in similar situations—for instance, how much more frightening is childbirth without education about it and previous experience with it?

2. In fact, among some psychologists, it is common practice to ask children between the ages of three and five what is happening in their family, for very young children are the most likely source of uncensored information.

3. Several developmental researchers have provided evidence that infants can discriminate novel stimuli from previously experienced stimuli. Fantz (1965, 1966), for example, demonstrated this phenomenon in neonatal vision by measuring differential sucking responses of infants exposed to novel and repeated visual stimuli. It should be noted, however, that cognitive psychologists would not be likely to call the processes used by neonates "recall" (R. Belli, personal communication 1990); rather, they would be more likely to refer to the phenomenon as "recognition."

4. This example was provided by the first author's daughter.

5

With Liberty and Justice for All: Protecting the Rights of Child Witnesses, Defendants, and the Public

Protecting Children From Traumatization

Protecting Defendants From False Charges

Protecting Defendants' Constitutional Rights

The right to a public trial

The right to confront accusatory witnesses

Examination of Children as Witnesses in Court

Direct examination of the child witness

Use of leading questions • Use of demonstrative evidence

Cross-examination of the child witness

Procedures Designed to Reduce Traumatization of Child Witnesses

Preparation of the child witness

Alteration of the courtroom

Rearranging courtroom furnishings • Use of screens

Alteration of standard courtroom procedures

Recesses and postponements
Providing support persons for child witnesses
Excluding witnesses from the courtroom
Novel approaches to obtaining testimony

Use of a neutral questioner • In camera *testimony*
Videotaped testimony
Testimony videotaped during the criminal investigation
Use of videotaped testimony when the child is ruled "unavailable"
Use of previously recorded videotaped testimony
The hearsay rule and its exceptions
Use of an interpreter

Summary

Nobody wants to victimize the victim again. But we can't allow emotion to take over, either. Just the stigma of being charged is so great that the defense must have a real chance.

(San Francisco Judge Robert Dossee, quoted in *Newsweek,* May 14, 1984)[1]

The criminal justice system was designed for adults. It expects victims to undergo multiple interviews and court appearances, expects testimony to be detailed and articulate, and provides opportunity for a cross-examination that may confuse even the most sophisticated of witnesses. It is not surprising, therefore, that introducing children into the criminal justice system as key witnesses in criminal and civil procedures has been fraught with difficulties. In this process, courts have been required to tackle a number of questions: Who has the right to be present at the proceedings, to observe the witnesses, and to hear the testimony offered? How should child witnesses be questioned under both direct and cross-examination? What are the parameters of confrontation in cases involving children as witnesses? What forms of confrontation are legally acceptable, and how vigorous may the confrontation be? What specific procedures should the court allow to protect those most likely to be harmed by the experience of testifying—the child witnesses?

How has the judicial system responded to these dilemmas? Many courts have instituted innovative procedures:

In Massachusetts, judges bring in pint-size witness chairs so youngsters' feet won't dangle. In Maryland, children who have trouble speaking may draw what happened. In Minnesota, a child frozen with fear was permitted to testify from under the prosecutor's table. And from Manhattan Beach, Calif., to Brooklyn, N.Y., children in court use dolls to describe crimes whose names they don't know. . . . In Texas, victims' statements are videotaped early in investigations and can even be introduced at trial—so long as the child is available for cross-examination. In Colorado, courts are experimenting with funneling lawyers' questions through a friendly therapist. In Wash-

ington and Colorado, state laws permit a counselor to tell the jury
what a young child told him, even though it's hearsay that can't be
cross-examined. (King, McDaniel, Sandza, & Doherty, 1984, p. 32)

Child advocates hail such reforms, noting that they make the
courtroom experience more humane for children. Moreover, some
researchers claim that interventions designed to reduce ambiguity
about the experience (e.g., visiting the courtroom prior to giving
testimony) and the scariness of testifying (e.g., a friendly word from
the judge) actually may improve the quality of children's testimony
(Melton, 1984a).

But constitutional scholars and defense attorneys generally
have another view of such innovative practices. For example, a
Denver judge's practices—stepping down from the bench to greet
young witnesses at the courtroom door and walking them to a
special seat with its back to the defendant—were struck down
when challenged. A Colorado appeals court ruled that the judge's
methods breached her duty to maintain an impartial posture
toward all witnesses (Wiehl, 1990). In 1984 Melton (1984a)
remarked that such proposals raise serious constitutional issues:

> These proposals all raise serious constitutional issues. Each arguably
> invades one or more of the following fundamental rights: the
> defendant's [S]ixth [A]mendment rights to a public trial and to
> confrontation of witnesses and the public's [F]irst [A]mendment
> right, through the press, to access to the trial process. (p. 6)[2]

In child witness cases, therefore, courts often are caught on the
horns of a dilemma. On the one hand, they must ensure that justice
is served by using every legal and ethical means available to
discover the truth of the matter and to protect the rights of the
accused. On the other hand, it is incumbent upon courts to protect
victims from further traumatization, badgering, and harassment.
"In short," comments Melton (1981b), "society's interest in punishing child molesters may come into conflict with its obligation as
parens patriae to protect dependent minors" (p. 184). We do not
mean to imply that the search for truth is compromised by a desire
to protect children. On the contrary, we intend to show that the
search for truth is aided by special treatment of child witnesses.
Thus, in cases involving children as witnesses, legal procedures
need to be examined in the light of balancing three important

objectives: (a) protecting children from traumatization, (b) protecting defendants from false charges, and (c) protecting defendants' constitutional rights. In this chapter we address each of these complex issues. Of course, given the 300-year history of the Anglo-American legal system and the 200-year analysis of the U. S. Constitution, "an entire room could be filled up with scholarship" on these topics (L. McGough, personal communication, 1990). Our review, therefore, cannot be exhaustive, but rather is intended to heighten awareness.[3] This chapter concludes by analyzing a number of innovative procedures recently introduced to reduce the distress of children who testify.

PROTECTING CHILDREN FROM TRAUMATIZATION

It is widely held that children experience emotional trauma as a result of repeated questioning by police and attorneys and of repeated court appearances (e.g., Goodman, 1984b; Goodman et al., 1990; Katz & Mazur, 1979; Parker, 1982). Berliner and Barbieri (1984) note:

> One major barrier to prosecution of child sexual-assault cases is the fear that the child will be further traumatized by involvement in the legal process. . . . [T]he victims and their families may be reluctant to report the crime to authorities because of the fear that the child will be subjected to further trauma by the criminal-justice process. It can be lengthy and requires the child to repeatedly face traumatic memories: The victims and their families can have no guarantee that the child will not encounter untrained or insensitive personnel. (p. 128)

Even defense attorneys acknowledge that involvement in legal proceedings can be devastating to children (Heeney, 1985). This view was shared by U.S. Supreme Court Justices Burger and Rehnquist, who commented that the traumatic impact of trial procedures on children certainly must be greater than the impact on adults in similar kinds of proceedings (*Globe Newspaper Co. v. Superior Court,* 1982). Furthermore, Melton (1981b) notes:

> Children are less likely than adults to have the cognitive and emotional resources for understanding the experience, and legal author-

ities not used to communicating with children may find it difficult to allay their concerns. (pp. 8-9)

The emotional trauma experienced by children who are involved in giving legal evidence takes many forms. Fear is a common symptom. In a comprehensive study of the emotional reactions of child sexual assault victims, 65 percent of the children observed were rated as experiencing "some distress" or as being "very distressed" (Goodman et al., 1990, p. 83). The researchers note:

> Even though the experience of testifying was less aversive than initially feared by the children we interviewed, many children still found the event upsetting. One child told us that it was "worse than I thought—like a nightmare." Another stated, "[I felt] scared, really upset, and I just couldn't remember that many things." And, even though the defense attorneys' popularity improved, they were still unpopular. One teenager commented, for example, "I can't stand him. He made me mad. He kept trying to, he'd say "Didn't you say this?", and I didn't. He kept trying to make me lie. (p. 71)

The most striking finding, according to Goodman and colleagues, concerned the children's negative attitudes toward facing the defendant. Several children stated that they could not look at the defendant because they were so frightened (typically because they or their families had been threatened); other witnesses avoided eye contact with the defendant because they were angry.

Other researchers have studied children's symptoms outside the courtroom setting. They note that children may experience nightmares; unconscious reenactments (unknowing, sometimes dangerous, performance of acts similar to the original traumatic occurrence); repetitive, unsatisfying play around traumatic themes; pessimistic expectations for the future, including the prospect of dying; and pronounced, perhaps fixed, personality alterations (Pynoos & Eth, 1984).

The case of eight-year-old "Jeanette" (reported by Margo Harakas, Sunrise, Florida) is illustrative. The child was sexually assaulted on repeated occasions by her neighbor. In agreeing to testify against her assailant, "Jeanette" said, "I want (him) to go to jail so he won't do what he did to me to anybody else." But "Jeanette's" bravery belies her traumatization. It took the installation of a security system, participation in karate lessons, and the purchase of a Doberman watchdog to vanquish Jeanette's nightmares and to make her feel secure again in her own home. While the specific symptoms vary on a case-by-case basis, Pynoos and Eth (1984) discuss some typical emotional patterns for children who testify in court:

> Previous clinical reports have neglected to consider correlations between children's symptoms and the ongoing criminal proceedings. For instance, prompt arrest can alleviate the initial fear, while trial postponement may result in prolonged anxiety. We have observed several cases in which specific symptoms, such as unconscious reenactment behavior or traumatic dreams, have reappeared at critical junctures during the proceedings. (p. 96)

Although ample anecdotal evidence exists to suggest that children are traumatized by giving testimony in court, good empirical research on this topic is scanty (Goodman, 1984b, Goodman et al., 1990). In 1963, Gibbens and Prince reported that child sex victims who were involved in court proceedings experienced greater distress than those who did not appear in court. The researchers cautioned, however, that it was likely that only the more severe cases of abuse resulted in court appearances for child victims, so the research sample was biased. DeFrancis's (1969) study of nearly 200 child sexual assault cases in the New York courts led to the conclusion that involvement in the legal process was stressful for children and families. However, DeFrancis did not study a comparison group of sexually assaulted children whose cases were *not* brought to trial, so there is no way of knowing whether the trauma reported by the children resulted from the experience of testifying or from the assaults they had endured.

On this point, Goodman and Michelli (1981) asked Judge Orrelle Weeks of Denver juvenile court how children fared in the courtroom. She replied:

> The only time that children seem to be traumatized by serving as witnesses is when they have to recount in detail foul events to which they themselves have been the victim. This is most pronounced for cases involving sexual molestation. Often the law requires that the specifics of the sexual act must be stated. We try to be as gentle and

understanding as possible. If the child is testifying about an event that is not so personal, the child does not seem to be adversely affected by the experience. (p. 90)

Some experts even have suggested that the experience of testifying in court actually may be beneficial for some children. Melton (1984a) states the case as follows:

> [P]articularly for young children, it is equally plausible that children's responses are *less* severe on average than those of adults. Provided that parents and others do not overreact and that they are supportive of the child during the legal process, it may well be that the trial experience will cause little trauma. At least for some child victims, the experience may be cathartic; it provides an opportunity for taking control of the situation, achieving vindication, and symbolically putting an end to the episode. (p. 8, footnote omitted)

Pynoos and Eth (1984) echo this view, suggesting that involvement in legal activities can, in itself, be a coping strategy. In cases of a parent being killed in front of a child, for example, the opportunity afforded the child witness to speak on behalf of the deceased parent is often of paramount importance. Pynoos and Eth report that "[o]lder children not called to the witness stand have described feeling they had again failed to come to the aid of their slain relative" (p. 101). Similarly, victimized children may feel that providing testimony in court helps bring the defendant to justice, a sentiment voiced by "Jeanette" above.

Thus, social science experts disagree over whether the courtroom experience is consistently traumatizing or cathartic for child witnesses. To be sure, the specific reactions of a particular child witness depend in large measure upon the personality of the child, the nature of the trial, the way in which the child witness and courtroom personnel have been prepared, and the procedures allowed by the trial court. Yet most experts agree that even when the end result is satisfying to the child, the experience of testifying is emotionally distressing. Therefore, it is argued, the courtroom and its standard procedures should be altered to accommodate child witnesses (see for example, Goodman et al., 1990). We agree with this view. Even if the courtroom experience is not as bad for children as we generally think it may be, some changes can be made easily without encroaching upon the defendant's constitutional rights (see chapter 6).

PROTECTING DEFENDANTS FROM FALSE CHARGES

Children are not the only ones who may suffer in child witness cases, however. At times, defendants also are victimized. It is true that even public defenders acknowledge that charges of child sexual assault rightfully are upheld in the majority of cases that go to trial (Howson, 1985). But such a statement is misleading because only a fraction of cases end in trial; for a substantial number either the charges are dropped (for lack of sufficient evidence) or the defendant pleads guilty, sometimes to a lesser charge. As Whitcomb et al. (1985) report, plea rates are quite variable:

> In Orlando, one judge estimated that more than 80 percent of child sexual abuse cases are settled by guilty plea; one prosecutor had not seen a case go to trial in her two and one-half year tenure with the State's Attorney's Office. In Des Moines, however, only seven of 22 defendants (19%) whose cases were disposed in 1983 pleaded guilty; nine (41%) went to trial. (Four cases were dismissed and two cases were revoked on other charges.) In Ventura, there were 82 filings and 26 trials in 1983, for a trial rate of 32 percent. (p. 7)

Typically, prosecutors take child victim cases to trial when the evidence is strong, conviction is likely, and the defendant refuses to plea bargain. Thus, the statistics on successful conviction rates must be interpreted with caution.

Moreover, false accusations do occur. Sometimes they are the result of mistaken beliefs, while at other times they stem from outright maliciousness. Victims of Child Abuse Laws (VOCAL), a national organization formed to assist those who believe they have been falsely accused, gets 35 to 100 complaints every day. VOCAL estimates that 60 percent of these allegations stem from divorce-custody situations and that 80 percent of the accusations are made by mothers against fathers (Hopkins, 1988).

The cost of litigating these cases can be staggering, both financially and emotionally. Hopkins (1988) reports that "[s]ome cases have cost upwards of $200,000" (p. 49), and many of the accused go bankrupt defending themselves.

But the emotional costs are far more impressive. Levy (1989) comments:

[A] parent labelled an abuser suffers substantial stigma. Children have been removed from their parents without any hearing; parents and children have been denied any contact whatever for lengthy periods. Juvenile court "termination of parental rights" proceedings have often followed the initial adjudication [that is, at a time when the defendant still is presumed innocent]. Although the "penalty" imposed in neglect proceedings may not be a deprivation of freedom as it is in criminal cases, it does involve a deprivation of family autonomy from government interference. . . . (p. 386)

Consider the words of exonerated defendant "Roy":

I thought in a court of law the policeman would say, "Here's the gun, here's the body, here's the witness." But where's the evidence here? Guess what? You don't need any. I don't think I'll ever be normal again. To be on your guard at all times because anything you might say or do could someday be twisted against you. . . . How is a father supposed to have a relationship with his child if he's not allowed to bathe her, tickle her, kiss her, take care of her? For the past two years, I haven't spoken to a child other than [my child]. Because whenever I see a kid, I'm thinking, "If your mother only knew you were talking to an accused child molester."

And even though I was found innocent, the damage is done. You know how people think, "Okay, so maybe you didn't do anything as bad as they said you did. But Roy, you must have done *something* for this to go on for two years." And what about Lucy? What have they done to my child? (Hopkins, 1988, p. 49)

As Roy's case demonstrates, great care must be taken to avoid false accusations. Because these accusations are more likely in cases of civil custody disputes and of criminal charges that erupt from disagreements over visitation rights, such cases should be scrutinized with particular care. Partly for this reason, the judicial system has developed a number of safeguards to protect the defendant in criminal and civil trials.

PROTECTING DEFENDANTS' CONSTITUTIONAL RIGHTS

Unfortunately, those courtroom practices that accommodate child witnesses may violate defendants' rights under the First and

Sixth Amendments (Melton, 1984c). These amendments guarantee the defendant's right to a public trial in which accusatory witnesses can be confronted.

The Right to a Public Trial

The defendant's protection is facilitated by a trial in which persons may be informed by the media even if they cannot attend the trial in person. The First Amendment states in part, "Congress shall make no law . . . abridging the freedom . . . of the press . . . " (Amendment I, the Constitution of the United States), while the Sixth Amendment states in part that "[i]n all criminal prosecutions, the accused shall enjoy the right to a . . . public trial" (Amendment VI, the Constitution of the United States). In other words, the defendant has the right to a public hearing of the charges against him or her. However, should the defendant prefer privacy, he or she may not demand secrecy. The Court has defended staunchly its preference for open proceedings.

The press and the public do not share the defendant's unconditional right to an open trial under the Sixth Amendment, but the First Amendment guarantees them limited access to criminal trials. In *Globe Newspaper Co. v. Superior Court* (1982) the court held:

> [T]he right of access to criminal trials plays a particularly significant role in the functioning of the judicial process and the government as a whole. Public scrutiny of a criminal trial enhances the quality and safeguards the integrity of the fact finding process, with benefits to both the defendant and to society as a whole. Moreover, public access to the criminal trial fosters an appearance of fairness, thereby heightening public respect for the judicial process. And in the broadest terms, public access to criminal trials permits the public to participate in and serve as a check upon the judicial process—an essential component in our structure of self-government. In sum, the institutional value of open criminal trials is recognized in both logic and experience. (pp. 606-607)

For both First and Sixth Amendment reasons, the Court is clear in advocating public trials. For example, in the opinion for the Court in *Richmond Newspapers, Inc. v. Virginia* (1980), then Chief Justice Warren Burger relied heavily on common-law precedent that dates back to before the Norman conquest, stating: "What is significant is that throughout its evolution, the trial has been open to all who cared to observe" (p. 2830).

While the right to a public trial is vital, it is not absolute (Myers, 1987). In compelling cases of competing interest, the right yields. The Supreme Court has held, however, that denial of the right to a public trial must be the exception to the general rule and has offered these guidelines to invoking the exception:

> [T]he party seeking to close the hearing must advance an overriding interest that is likely to be prejudiced, the closure must be no broader than necessary to protect that interest, the trial court must consider reasonable alternatives to closing the proceeding, and it must make findings adequate to support the closure. (*Waller v. Georgia*, 1983, p. 48).

Although convincing reasons for closing proceedings may be advanced in a variety of cases, it is relatively common to do so in cases that involve child witnesses, particularly those who allegedly have suffered sexual abuse. Indeed, in the *Globe* decision, the Court held that the state has a compelling interest in protecting children who are victims of sex crimes from further trauma and embarrassment, even when to do so overrides the First Amendment right of the media and the public to attend criminal trials. The Supreme Court has approved closure where necessary to protect a child, provided that necessity is demonstrated in the particular case.

Still, the desire to protect child witnesses from embarrassment and trauma does not justify a closed trial in every case. The *Globe* decision established that trial judges must determine on a case-by-case basis whether barring public and press is necessary to protect the welfare of a young victim. The opinion held:

> Among the factors to be weighed are the minor victim's age, psychological maturity and understanding, the nature of the crime, the desires of the victim, and the interests of parents and relatives. (pp. 608-609)

Thus, whether a given trial will remain open or will be closed rests squarely in the hands of the presiding judge and the attorney (usually prosecuting) who must argue that the interests of the particular child are compelling enough for the judge to close the trial to the press and public.

While *Globe* suggests that trial courts should be sympathetic to the needs of child witnesses, it also indicates that the broader procedural reforms designed to protect youngsters who take the stand are unlikely to pass constitutional muster. Indeed, the more recent decision in *Maryland v. Craig* (1990) gave weight to this implication. Writing for the majority, Justice O'Connor affirmed the specificity requirement:

> [T]he right to confront accusatory witnesses may be satisfied absent a physical, face-to-face confrontation at trial only where denial of such confrontation is necessary to further an important public policy and only where the testimony's reliability is otherwise assured. . . . The requisite necessity finding must be case specific. (p. 673)

The Right to Confront Accusatory Witnesses

In addition to guaranteeing that trials are public, the Sixth Amendment also states in part, "In all criminal prosecutions, the accused shall enjoy the right . . . to be confronted with the witnesses against him . . ." (Amendment VI, the Constitution of the United States). As noted above, this clause implies that confrontation shall be face-to-face. In Anglo-American law, this right stems from the trial of Sir Walter Raleigh, in which the defendant was convicted of treason after a trial by affidavit. Raleigh never was able to confront his accusers or to summon witnesses on his own behalf. The framers of the Constitution responded to this type of abuse with the Confrontation and the Compulsory Process Clauses of the Sixth Amendment (Graham, 1985).

But the right to confrontation predates American law; indeed, it is a tradition with ancient roots. Justice Scalia, writing a literary opinion for the majority in *Coy v. Iowa* (1988), traced the history of the face-to-face confrontation requirement.[4] Quoting the Bible (Acts 26:16), he noted that such a requirement existed even under Roman law:

> The Roman Governor Festus, discussing the proper treatment of his prisoner, Paul, stated: "It is not the manner of the Romans to deliver any man up to die before the accused has met his accusers face to face, and has been given a chance to defend himself against the charges." (p. 2800)

Scalia also quoted Shakespearean verse to emphasize the English common-law tradition of face-to-face confrontation:

Then call them to our presence—face to face, and frowning brow to brow, ourselves will hear the accuser and the accused freely speak. . . . (Richard II in *Richard II,* act I, scene 1)

Scalia then cited turn-of-the-century American legal precedent from *Kirby v. United States* (1899):

[A] fact which can be primarily established only by witnesses cannot be proved against an accused . . . except by witnesses who confront him at the trial, upon whom he can look while being tried, whom he is entitled to cross-examine, and whose testimony he may impeach in every mode authorized by the established rules governing the trial or conduct of criminal cases. (p. 2800-2801)

He continued,

More recently, we have described the "literal right to 'confront' the witness at the time of trial" as forming the "core of the values furthered by the Confrontation Clause". (p. 2801, citing *California v. Green,* 1970)

Justice Scalia concluded, "We have never doubted, therefore, that the Confrontation Clause guarantees the defendant a face-to-face meeting with witnesses appearing before the trier of fact" (p. 2800).

Judicial interpretation of the Confrontation Clause has been troublesome in child witness cases, however. Under what specific circumstances is the defendant's right to face-to-face confrontation abused? For example, must the child physically face the defendant in open court during formal proceedings? Or is it permissible for the child to confront the defendant at preliminary hearing instead? May the child provide testimony *in camera* (i.e., in the judge's chamber) rather than in open court? Is previously videotaped testimony, introduced as evidence at trial in lieu of *viva voce* (i.e., live) testimony, violative of the defendant's Sixth Amendment right to confrontation? Is simultaneous broadcasting of the child's testimony that is being videotaped outside the presence of the defendant permissible?

Melton (1981b) notes that the scope of the First and Sixth Amendment rights of the defendant (whose liberty is at stake in criminal proceedings) and their implications for special procedures in cases involving child witnesses are not yet settled in law. Moreover, sometimes the means used to protect the defendant's constitutional rights (e.g., vigorous cross-examination in settings designed for adults) serve to traumatize child witnesses—who, interestingly, have no constitutional rights to protection during the investigation of a crime or during the trial (Goodman, 1984a; Parker, 1982). Although case law still is evolving relative to child witnesses, it is helpful to understand trial procedure and to be familiar with current legal opinions in this area. Box 5.1 describes the circumstances of two recent Supreme Court decisions that are referred to at several points in this chapter.

EXAMINATION OF CHILDREN AS WITNESSES IN COURT

Like other witnesses who take the stand, child witnesses can expect to undergo both direct and cross-examination.[5]

Direct Examination of the Child Witness

The purpose of direct examination is to get the witness's story into the official record of the court. In theory, competence of the witness no longer is at issue; however, the reality in cases employing children as witnesses is that the prosecuting attorney often may harbor doubts that the jury will see the child as believable (Myers, 1987). Some legal experts suggest, therefore, that prosecutors use a portion of the direct examination to ask questions directed at convincing the jury of the child's competence (see McGough, 1989).

Use of leading questions. Because testifying is a stress-inducing experience for most witnesses and especially for children, recollection on the stand may not be optimal. For this reason, it is tempting for counsel to refresh the reluctant witness's memory by using leading questions. All jurisdictions however, limit the use of leading questions during direct examination (Myers, 1987). Rule 611(c) of the Federal Rules of Evidence states:

> Leading questions should not be used on direct examination of a witness except as may be necessary to develop his testimony. Ordinarily leading questions should be permitted on cross-examination. When a party calls a hostile witness, an adverse party, or a witness identified with an adverse party, interrogation may be by leading questions.

Box 5.1

Fact Summaries and Background in
Two Recent Supreme Court Decisions

Chapter 5 discusses the implications of two recent Supreme Court decisions involving innovative ways to present the testimony of children in order to reduce the likelihood that their testimony will induce further emotional distress. The facts in these two trials and their appeals are presented here, as background.

Coy v. Iowa, decided by the Supreme Court in 1988, involved two 13-year-old girls who had been sexually assaulted while sleeping in a backyard tent. John Avery Coy, a neighbor, was arrested, tried, and convicted of the assault even though the victims could not positively identify him because the assailant had worn a stocking over his head during the attack. Although the girls' testimony did not include an identification of the defendant as their attacker, the court authorities assumed that merely seeing the defendant in court would retraumatize the children. (An Iowa state law presumed that children under age 14 would be so affected.) Thus, the presiding judge approved the placement of a large, semitransparent screen around the defendant; he could see the witnesses dimly, but they could not see him. Use of the screen required darkening the room and turning bright lights onto the screen.

After his conviction, Coy appealed on two grounds. First, he asserted that the screen's presence denied him due process because it led the jury to infer that he was guilty. The Supreme Court rejected this claim. Second, he contended that the use of the screen deprived him of his Sixth Amendment right to be confronted with the witnesses against him. The majority of the Supreme Court agreed with Coy on this point. A 6-2 vote overturned his conviction and sent the case back to Iowa for retrial.

Maryland v. Craig, decided by the Supreme Court during its 1989-1990 term, concerned defendant Sandra Ann Craig, who owned a child-care facility in Howard County, Maryland (between Washington, DC, and Baltimore). She was convicted of sexually abusing children under her care. The trial judge, invoking a 1985 state law, permitted four young children (ages four to seven) to give their testimony over closed-circuit television, a procedure allowed by statute in 32 states (Greenhouse, 1990).

A Maryland state appeals court dismissed the abuse conviction, stating that the trial judge, before allowing the closed-circuit testimony, first should have questioned the witnesses about their ability to testify. Thus, just five weeks after the *Coy* decision was announced, this state court interpreted that Supreme Court ruling as requiring a face-to-face confrontation at some point, either at the preliminary hearing or at the trial. But the U.S. Supreme Court (by a 5-4 vote) reversed the Maryland court's action and upheld the conviction of Craig. They ruled that although the confrontation between defendant and accusers was not "face-to-face," the constitutionally protected rights of the defendant had not been abridged using the disputed procedure.

Myers (1987) notes that there are several exceptions to the rule against use of leading questions on direct examination: establishing preliminary and undisputed matters; introducing topics for further inquiry; refreshing a witness's recollection; and dealing with hostile, biased, or unwilling witnesses. But, in fact, courts frequently permit leading questions during the direct examination of children who experience difficulty testifying because of embarrassment, fear, or reluctance. Generally, the preferred practice is to begin the direct examination with nonleading questions but to permit limited use of leading questions if the child appears unable to proceed (Myers, 1987).

The trial judge is responsible for determining the appropriateness of leading questions and has the authority to determine when the use of such questions should cease. For example, if the witness is completely reluctant, the court may rule that the attorney's questions are so leading that counsel is attempting to "tell the story" for the witness. In *State v. Orona* (1979), for example, the New Mexico Supreme Court wrote:

> Developing testimony by the use of leading questions must be distinguished from substituting the words of the prosecutor for the testimony of the witness. Here, the trial court, in permitting every word describing the alleged offense to come from the prosecuting attorney rather than from the witness, abused its discretion in such a manner as to violate principles of fundamental fairness. (p. 1045)

Generally speaking, direct examination of the child witness should proceed in a supportive but factual manner. Legal precedent suggests that leading questions should be restricted; instead, children should be encouraged to describe the alleged incidents in their own words.

Use of demonstrative evidence. An alternative to leading the witness during direct examination is to use demonstrative evidence. According to *The Plain-Language Law Dictionary*, demonstrative evidence is "evidence that appeals directly to the senses" or "evidence which does not depend upon testimony" (Rothenberg, 1981, p. 93). In other words, demonstrative evidence consists of things, as distinguished from the assertions of witnesses about things (McCormick, cited in Cleary, 1984, p. 663).

Demonstrative evidence falls into two general classes: (a) *real* evidence (i.e., objects that played an actual part in the matter being litigated, such as weapons), and (b) evidence designed to illustrate or aid testimony (e.g., anatomical dolls, drawings, etc.). The latter class of demonstrative evidence often is used in trials involving children as witnesses (Myers, 1987).

As with the competency examination, use of demonstrative evidence lies within the discretion of the trial judge. McCormick (Cleary, 1984) notes, "Whether the admission of a particular exhibit will in fact be helpful, or will instead tend to confuse or mislead the trier, is a matter commonly viewed to be within the sound discretion of the trial court" (p. 669). Elaborating on this point, Imwinkelried (1980) suggests that "[t]he only limits on the use of demonstrative evidence are the trial judge's discretion and the trial attorney's imagination" (p. 78).

Case law suggests that attorneys are not required to show that the witness will be completely unable to testify without the assistance of the proposed demonstrative aid. Rather, "the test is whether or not the testimonial aid will likely assist the jury in understanding the witness's testimony" (*State v. Eggert,* Minn. Ct. App. 1984, p. 161). Under this ruling, a young sex abuse victim in *State v. Eggert* was allowed to illustrate her testimony using dolls, despite the defendant's objection that the demonstrative evidence was unnecessary because the child was able to tell her story without the use of the aids.

Particularly in sexual abuse litigation, young children often use drawings and/or so-called "anatomical dolls" to illustrate their testimony. These dolls, constructed to include parts that represent genitalia and body orifices, have been referred to by several labels—anatomically correct dolls, sexually anatomically correct dolls, anatomically detailed dolls, and simply anatomical dolls (Freeman & Estrada-Mullaney, 1988). While the particular label used may seem trivial, the name employed for these devices has not escaped the attention of the court.

In *Cleaveland v. State* (Ind. Ct. App. 1986), the Indiana Court of Appeals ruled that the fact that a doll is not completely "anatomically correct" does not mean it cannot be used as demonstrative evidence. In its opinion, the court described how the young witness used a male doll and a female doll to demonstrate that the defendant had pulled down her pants and underwear and put his hand between her legs, touching an area indicated in pink on the female doll. The defendant's lawyer argued that because the pink area between the doll's legs did not accurately represent the human vagina, the child should not have been allowed to use the doll during her testimony. The trial judge disagreed, noting that the doll used by the witness had sufficient anatomical detail to help the jury.

The Texas Court of Appeals ruled in 1986 that "[t]he use of dolls is often critical when the complainant witness is very young" (*Vera v. State,* Tex. Ct. App. 1986, p. 686). Others, too, have cited the advantages of using anatomical dolls at trial. Freeman and Estrada-Mullaney (1988) suggest that the dolls aid in establishing rapport and reducing stress, as well as assisting communication and even establishing competency. On the other hand, critics have argued that anatomical dolls impede the fact-finding process for two reasons: (a) dolls suggest fantasy to children, encouraging them to fabricate stories, and (b) exaggerated doll genitalia suggest sexual impropriety (Freeman & Estrada-Mullaney, 1988).

In this regard, Levy (1989) traces the history of the use of anatomical dolls:

> Dolls were "discovered"in 1976 and first manufactured for general use in child sexual abuse investigations in 1980, and the first appellate decision following a trial in which an expert testified about anatomically correct dolls occurred in 1982. By the time the first study of any kind was publicized, 129 civil and criminal appellate cases reflecting the use of anatomically correct dolls at trial had been reported. Even now little effort has been devoted to obtaining standardized baseline data—that is, some criterion measure of how children generally relate to the dolls so that satisfactory comparisons can be made between the reactions of children who have not been and children who may have been sexually abused. (p. 400)

Recently, one study of children's use of anatomical dolls was conducted by Goodman and Aman (in press). Eighty three- and five-year-olds experienced a social interaction with a male confederate and later were tested under one of four recall conditions: reenactment with anatomical dolls, reenactment with regular dolls, free recall with visual cues, or free recall without visual cues. Goodman and Aman (in press) found:

Overall, our findings support the view that anatomically detailed dolls do not in and of themselves lead "nonabused" children to make false reports of sexual abuse. The number of commission errors on the specific and misleading abuse questions did not vary as a function of doll condition. These errors are considered particularly dangerous as they might lead to the false arrest of an innocent person. In addition, children did not provide spontaneous reports of sexual abuse in free recall, despite the presence of anatomically detailed dolls. Finally, children demonstrated little in the way of sexually related behaviors except to manipulate the dolls' genitalia (p. 19). . . . Our study is most relevant to the claim that anatomically detailed dolls promote false reports of abuse when no abuse has occurred. Overall, our findings indicate that the use of anatomically detailed dolls in and of itself does not lead children to make false reports of abuse even under conditions of suggestive questioning. (p. 24)

Still, attorneys, as well as other professionals who interview alleged child victims, must be cautious in their use of anatomical dolls. Both prosecutors and police officers have been subjected to civil rights lawsuits alleging in part that anatomical dolls were misused during interviews with victims and that as a result of this misuse, criminal charges were initiated improperly (Freeman & Estrada-Mullaney, 1988). For example, in *Higgs v. District Court* (Colo. 1985), the court cautioned prosecutors that if they engage in investigatory activities usually assigned to the police, those functions must be completed correctly or else prosecutors could face financial penalties:

The court held that prosecutors have absolute immunity from civil damages *only* when performing an "advocatory" function. When they perform an "investigative" function or an "administrative" function, they are only qualifiedly immune and could thus be *successfully sued* for damages. (Freeman & Estrada-Mullaney, 1988, p. 2.)

Police officers conducting investigations through the use of anatomical dolls also must proceed with caution. A Fairfax County, Virginia, police officer was required to pay damages of $55,000 to a man who previously had been arrested and accused of sexually abusing his ten-year-old daughter. The daughter later alleged that the officer had forced her into incriminating her father on charges of photographing and molesting her.

Anatomical dolls usually are packaged with an instruction manual. Prudent advice is to follow the manufacturer's instructions carefully. Freeman and Estrada-Mullaney (1988) note:

> Enterprising critics might try to introduce these manuals into evidence and claim that since you did not follow the instructions, the results are invalid. As an alternative attack, an expert might testify that standard techniques for the use of dolls exist and you did not follow them. (p. 4)

However, we are not aware of any standard protocol for using anatomical dolls. Indeed, Levy (1989) claims:

> [I]n 1987 there were fifteen doll manufacturers, but a large proportion of professional users (more than half of North Carolina users in 1985) may rely upon homemade dolls. Nor does anyone know the impact of the diversity on sexual abuse evaluations and judicial proceedings in which the dolls are used. (p. 397)

Because of the difficulties inherent in using anatomical dolls effectively in court, some attorneys prefer to use the child witness's drawings as demonstrative evidence. This technique may be problematic as well, however. Brooks and Milchman (1990) note that there is very little empirical research that identifies unambiguous signs of sexual abuse in a drawing produced by a child. Moreover, they state, "the lack of signs of abuse in a drawing cannot be used to conclude that there was no abuse. It may mean that the child chose to conceal the abuse, lacked the skills to represent his experience through drawings, or resisted communicating with that evaluator" (p. 9).

Use of demonstrative evidence may be beneficial in many cases, and even critical in some, but care should be taken that illustrative aids have been obtained without tainting the evidence.

Cross-Examination of the Child Witness

The right to cross-examine witnesses is a vital piece of the Sixth Amendment right to confront accusatory witnesses. The classic legal reference, *McCormick on Evidence,* (Cleary, 1984) states:

> For two centuries, common law judges and lawyers have regarded the opportunity for cross-examination as an essential safeguard of the accuracy and completeness of testimony, and they have insisted that the opportunity is a right and not a mere privilege. (p. 47)

Defendants, therefore, have a constitutional right to confront even the youngest of accusers.

The purposes of cross-examination of any witness are twofold: (a) to elicit testimony favorable to the cross-examiner's theory of the case, and (b) to undermine direct testimony by challenging the witness's credibility and/or statements under direct questioning (Myers, 1987). The specific goals of cross-examination vary from one witness to the next; however, several basic objectives underlie most cross-examinations of children:

> Counsel may commit the child to a specific version of the facts so that the child can be impeached with prior inconsistent statements or contradicted by extrinsic evidence. The examiner may spotlight inconsistencies in the child's testimony. Such inconsistencies may indicate that the testimony is mistaken or deliberately falsified, or that the child is confused, uncertain, highly suggestible, or lacking in personal knowledge of the facts. The examiner may hope to show that the child was coached, or that the direct testimony was memorized. Finally, cross-examination may demonstrate that the child lacks the capacity to observe, remember, or communicate. (Myers, 1987, pp. 182-183, footnotes omitted)

Defense attorneys have developed some specific means for achieving the ends described by Myers. Heeney (1985) suggests one strategy:

> A criminal defense attorney should strive to develop evidence of the behavior of the child complainant and the defendant himself that is inconsistent with abuse. The concept is that a complaint by a child of prolonged, repeated, horrifying sexual and physical abuse is unworthy of belief in the face of an apparently normal and happy existence. To this end, subpoenaed school records, teachers, counselors, and

family members may demonstrate good grades, excellent school attendance, lack of disciplinary problems, no emotional, behavior, or learning disorders. Otherwise adverse family members can be helpful to show the absence of bad dreams, depression, unexplainable tears, and general unhappiness. (p. 14)

Although cross-examination is a right of constitutional magnitude, the right is not unlimited, and trial judges have discretion to control the scope of such examination (Myers, 1987). Rule 611(a) of the Federal Rules of Evidence states:

> The court shall exercise reasonable control over the mode and order of interrogating witnesses and presenting evidence so as to (1) make the interrogation and presentation effective for the ascertainment of the truth, (2) avoid needless consumption of time, and (3) protect witnesses from harassment or undue embarrassment.

Specifically, the trial judge may limit or refuse to permit cross-examination in the following areas:

1. Embarrassing questions
2. Irrelevant or collateral matters
3. Questions that are unduly time consuming
4. Questions that assume facts not in evidence
5. Confusing, misleading, ambiguous, unintelligible, or compound questions
6. Harassment or annoyance of the witness
7. Undue prejudice
8. Questions designed to elicit inadmissible evidence
9. Questions that are improper because they violate a rape shield law. (Myers, 1987)

Note that the court *may* limit or refuse to allow cross-examination in the above areas; however, it is not required to do so. Myers (1987) notes that the overriding importance of cross-examination sometimes impels courts to permit questioning at the boundary of propriety, particularly when the defendant is charged with the sexual assault of a child.

Cross-examination is an art that requires finesse under any circumstances, but especially when the witness is a child. Indeed, there is a very fine line between successfully discrediting the

testimony of a child and appearing to badger the young witness.
Juries tend to sympathize with child witnesses and so are especially wary of attorneys who play the bully (Heeney, 1985). For this
reason, many trial lawyers have developed more subtle ways of
challenging child witnesses during their cross-examination.

Myers (1987) describes one such tactic:

> After a friendly rapport is established, [cross-examining] counsel may
> ask a series of innocuous questions to which the child will agree.
> Counsel demonstrates approval and pleasure with the answers, thus
> reinforcing the likelihood of further agreement. Once the child is in
> the groove of agreeing to neutral questions, counsel moves subtly into
> questions designed to elicit favorable information. The attorney con-
> tinues speaking in the same friendly, upbeat tone of voice, and the
> same nods of approval follow favorable answers. When this technique
> works, the child may agree to a version of the facts that is favorable
> to the cross-examiner or that is inconsistent with the direct testi-
> mony. (p. 198)

Heeney (1985) recommends another strategy, in which the defendant is portrayed as someone who has had direct and open contact
with the police and other authority figures:

> These contacts emphasize that the defendant is not a person with
> something to hide or who is the type that avoids drawing attention
> to himself. This type of evidence has the benefit of indirectly "black-
> ening" the child complainant in the eyes of the jury, and renders her
> credibility suspect. The tactic avoids the harshly received frontal
> assault on the child as a person, which is a consequence of an
> aggressive cross-examination on the child complainant. (p. 16)

Sometimes these subtle approaches are sufficient to achieve the
goals of cross-examination. At other times, opposing counsel may
find it necessary to induce in the child a belief that disagreeing
with the cross-examiner may lead to unpleasantness. For example,
by having the child witness describe what happens when she lies
at home or at school, or when she disagrees with important authority figures in her life, the cross-examiner may plant the suggestion
that it would be wise to agree with the questioner. In this way, the
child may be trapped into impeaching her direct testimony.
Because of the inherent risk of alienating the jurors, however,
questions designed to impeach or discredit the child usually are

held in abeyance until the opposing attorney has capitalized on the subtler, more positive approaches described above (Heeney, 1985; Myers, 1987).

Regardless of the particular methods employed during cross-examination, we argue that its historic purposes often are not served when children are the targets. We are more likely to safeguard the accuracy and completeness of children's testimony if cross-examination is limited (see chapter 6).

PROCEDURES DESIGNED TO REDUCE TRAUMATIZATION OF CHILD WITNESSES

As noted above, even under the gentlest of examinations, child witnesses may experience severe emotional upheaval. Several innovative approaches have been suggested to reduce the traumatization likely to be experienced by children who undergo direct and cross-examination on the witness stand, and some have been subjected to legal test.

In dealing with child witnesses, the court must consider several intriguing questions: Should the courtroom itself be altered to accommodate the needs of young witnesses? Should the child witness be shielded from the defendant? Who should be allowed in the courtroom when the child testifies? Should standard procedures be altered when a child is the witness? Where and by what means should testimony be obtained from a child?

Jurisdictions across the United States have tested methods that address these questions. Generally, innovative procedures fall into three categories: (a) preparation of the child witness for the courtroom experience, (b) alteration of the courtroom, and (c) alteration of standard courtroom practice.

Preparation of the Child Witness

Children tend to view the courtroom as a threatening place, a place in which "if the witness gives the wrong answer, he'll go to jail" (Saywitz, 1989, p. 150). When asked, "Do you know what a courtroom is?" only 18 percent of the three-year-olds surveyed in one study replied in the affirmative. The percentage increased steadily with age, however, with approximately 40 percent of the six-year-olds, 85 percent of the seven-year-olds, and over 90 percent of the those over age nine indicating that they knew what a courtroom was (Warren-Leubecker et al., 1989). At best, then, the courtroom is viewed by children as an unfamiliar place, and at worst as a forbidding environment.

The child witness may be prepared in a number of ways for the experience of testifying. First, the child needs to understand the purpose of litigation and the roles of the various people who interact with the legal system. It is helpful to spend some time educating the witness in these areas.

Second, the child needs to be familiarized with the courtroom itself. A "field trip" can be useful in pointing out the judge's bench, the witness stand, the tables where attorneys and defendant will sit, the jury box, and seats for the audience. The child may be allowed to physically explore the surroundings and to ask questions about the setting.

When the child seems relatively comfortable, the legal process may be explained. It may be particularly helpful to enlist the aid of others who can play the roles of the various professionals in the courtroom, thereby simulating what the actual courtroom experience will be like.

These methods of preparing the child witness for giving testimony at trial have not been subjected to legal test, for they do not infringe upon the defendant's rights in any way. Indeed, the defendant has the right to experience the same kind of preparation. Generally, the more preparation the child witness can be given, the better.

Alteration of the Courtroom

In many jurisdictions, efforts are being made to reduce the threatening appearance of the courtroom when children will be taking the stand. Two innovative procedures have undergone judicial scrutiny: (a) rearranging courtroom furnishings, and (b) use of a screen to shield the child witness's view of the defendant. While these efforts are applauded by child advocates, sometimes novel alterations of the courtroom run afoul of the defendant's Sixth Amendment right to face-to-face confrontation with the accuser.

Rearranging courtroom furnishings. One means for making the courtroom a less intimidating place is to rearrange the furnishings. Some states have offered statutory suggestions to this effect. The

California Legislature, for example, enacted a statute that provides that "[i]n the judge's discretion the judge, witnesses, support persons, and court personnel may be relocated within the courtroom to facilitate a more comfortable and personal environment for the child witness" (Cal. Penal Code § 868.8(c)). Under this provision, the court may seat the parties and their attorneys, the judge, and the child around a table rather than isolating the child on the witness stand (Myers, 1987). Another California statute permits removal of the judicial robe "if the judge believes that this formal attire intimidates the minor" (Cal. Penal Code § 868.8(b)).

The informality introduced by these procedures meets with little legal resistance. As Myers (1987) notes: "Defendants in criminal cases will be hard pressed to argue that such minor tinkering with traditional trial practice violates the due process clause" (p. 423). Indeed, under Rule 611(a) of the Federal Rules of Evidence, trial courts have considerable discretion to control the mode and order of the proceedings.

Use of screens. The use of screens at trial is another matter entirely, however, for placing a barrier between defendant and accuser directly defies the Sixth Amendment Confrontation Clause of the Constitution (but see *Maryland v. Craig* [1990]). For nearly a century, the courts have rejected prosecutors' attempts to shield alleged victims from defendants at trial. In 1899, for example, a six-year-old child claimed that she had been sexually abused by her father. At trial the judge turned the child's chair toward the jury and ordered the defendant to sit behind the child, in a distant corner of the courtroom. The defendant could not hear the child's testimony, see her face, or confer with his attorney. In this case, *State v. Mannion* (1899), the Utah Supreme Court held that the procedure violated the defendant's constitutional right to confrontation of his accuser. A similar conclusion was reached nearly 100 years later in the case of *Herbert v. Superior Court* (1981), in which a five-year-old victim of alleged sexual abuse professed difficulty testifying at the preliminary hearing. In an effort to relieve the child's discomfort, the magistrate turned her chair away from the defendant. In this case, the defendant could hear (but not see) the child and could consult with his attorney. Still, the appellate court held that this procedure violated the defendant's right to face-to-face confrontation, noting that "[a] witness's reluctance to face the accused may be the product of fabrication rather than fear or embarrassment" (p. 855).

More recently, a U.S. Supreme Court case in 1988 (*Coy v. Iowa*) spoke directly to the issue of using physical shields to alleviate traumatization of the child witness. In Coy's trial, courtroom lighting was adjusted and a screen was placed between the defendant and the children when they testified. The screen permitted the defendant to perceive the witnesses without the witnesses being able to see him. The defendant argued that this procedure, authorized by an Iowa statute, violated his Sixth Amendment right to confront the witnesses against him. He further contended that his right to due process was violated because the procedure would make him appear guilty and thus erode the presumption of innocence. The Supreme Court ruled in favor of the defendant, noting that face-to-face confrontation helps ensure integrity of the fact-finding process by making it more difficult for witnesses to fabricate testimony. Justice Scalia, writing for the majority, said:

> The State can hardly gainsay the profound effect upon a witness of standing in the presence of the person the witness accuses, since that is the very phenomenon it relies upon to establish the potential "trauma" that allegedly justified the extraordinary procedure in the present case. That face-to-face presence may, unfortunately, upset the truthful rape victim or abused child; but by the same token it may confound and undo the false accuser, or reveal the child coached by a malevolent adult. It is a truism that constitutional protections have costs. (p. 2802)

Coy was granted a new trial, with the understanding that no screen could be used. Yet the Justices did not close the door on creative means for shielding child witnesses from trauma. Justice Scalia noted that because there were no individualized findings that the particular child witnesses in Coy needed special protection, "the judgment here could not be sustained by any conceivable exception" (p. 2803). In a concurring opinion, Justice O'Connor stated:

> I agree with the Court that appellant's rights under the Confrontation Clause were violated in this case. I write separately only to note my view that those rights are not absolute but rather may give way in an appropriate case to other competing interests so as to permit the use of certain procedural devices designed to shield a child witness from the trauma of courtroom testimony. . . . I wish to make

clear that nothing in today's decision necessarily dooms such efforts by state legislatures to protect child witnesses. (*Coy v. Iowa,* 1988, pp. 2803-2804)

More recently, the Supreme Court's 1990 decision in *Maryland v. Craig* carved out a constitutional exception permitting states to create special procedures to protect child witnesses when there are case-specific findings of need. In this regard, L. McGough (personal communication, 1990) notes, "*Craig* strongly indicates that even screens would now be permitted if the required specific showing of need were demonstrated." As yet, however, this assertion is untested in the courts.

Still, some attorneys have developed creative means for upholding the letter of the law in *Coy* while simultaneously protecting the child witness. A Washington state prosecutor, for example, advocates that the examining attorney stand between child and defendant while the youngster is testifying, thereby creating a human "shield" (V. Bones, personal communication, 1990).

Alteration of Standard Courtroom Procedures

In addition to changing the physical characteristics of the courtroom, some jurisdictions have attempted to assist child witnesses by altering standard courtroom practices. Five such procedural changes are discussed below: (a) recesses and postponements, (b) barring the press and the public from the courtroom, (c) excluding witnesses from the courtroom, (d) providing support persons for child witnesses, and (e) using novel approaches to obtain testimony.

Recesses and Postponements

Because young witnesses tend to have short attention spans and seem particularly traumatized by the courtroom experience, it generally is counterproductive to keep them on the stand for extended periods of time. On the other hand, lengthy postponements and continuances may prolong anxiety and may cause memory deterioration (Melton, 1981b). The court, therefore, must weigh carefully any adverse impact caused by a postponement against the need for delay. Trial courts have broad authority in this regard. Indeed, several states have enacted statutes expressly providing that the examination may be interrupted briefly to

provide the child relief from the pressures of the courtroom. Section
868.8 of the California Penal Code, for example, states:

> In the court's discretion, the witness may be allowed reasonable
> periods of relief from examination and cross-examination during
> which he or she may retire from the courtroom. . . .

Myers (1987) notes that recesses during direct examination are
unlikely to pose significant problems, whereas interruption of
cross-examination may raise constitutional issues. Typically, during cross-examination the child witness is the most uncomfortable
and the most in need of respite. In fact, opposing counsel's express
purpose may be to force the child to experience anxiety or discomfort in an effort to make the child uncertain about the statements
expressed under direct examination (Heeney, 1985). Interruption
at this point, therefore, may clash with the defendant's Sixth
Amendment right to confront accusatory witnesses. Defendants
may argue that frequent interference with the right to develop a
line of cross-examination squelches their right to confrontation. On
this point Myers (1987) concludes:

> The need to protect the child must be balanced against the right of
> the defendant to vigorously cross-examine the witness. In general,
> the greater the importance of the child's testimony for the state, the
> greater the need to thoroughly cross-examine. In the final analysis,
> the matter should be left to the sound discretion of the judge. (p. 126)

Providing Support Persons for Child Witnesses

Because testifying in court can be such a traumatic experience
for children, many jurisdictions are inclined to allow support
persons to be present in the courtroom while young witnesses
testify. Sometimes the support person is a parent or other relative;
at other times, the support person is a professionally trained
victim/witness aide. For instance, one national program, called
CASA (Court Appointed Special Advocates), recruits and trains
volunteers for this express purpose.[6]

While it is acceptable for the support person to offer emotional
assistance to the child witness, the legal boundaries of "support"
are not entirely clear. For example, in some cases it is appropriate
to let the support person stand next to the testifying child. On rare
occasions it may be allowable for the child to sit in the lap of the

supporting adult. Myers (1987) cautions, however, that such practices likely will be considered objectionable "when the adult coaches or prompts the child or when the arrangement causes the jury to feel overly protective or sorry for the youngster" (p. 422).

On the other hand, one practice that might seem to fly directly in the face of the defendant's right to confront the accusatory witness has passed judicial scrutiny, at least at the state level. In *Parisi v. Superior Court* (1983), the California Supreme Court ruled that the defendant's confrontation rights were not violated when a magistrate listened to the whispered testimony of a frightened child victim and repeated it aloud for the record. This case has no precedential value, however, as the California Supreme Court ordered that *Parisi* not be officially reported (Myers, 1987). Moreover, it is unclear what the court's posture might be if the child were to whisper in the ear of a support person other than the judge. Until there is further opinion from the court, the discretion of the trial judge prevails in cases involving support persons for child witnesses.

To help unmuddy the waters in this area, some states are enacting statutes designed to address the issue of support persons for child witnesses. For example, part of California Penal Code \sec 868.5(c) reads:

> Notwithstanding any other provision of law, a prosecuting witness 16 years of age or under in a [sex offense case] shall be entitled for support to the attendance of up to two family members of his or her own choosing, one of whom may be a witness, at the preliminary hearing and at the trial, during the testimony of the prosecuting witness. Only one of those support persons may accompany the witness to the witness stand, although the other may remain in the courtroom during the witness's testimony (West 1986 Supp.).

As such statutes show, the state is beginning to realize that young victims should not have to experience retraumatization when they testify. As Myers (1987) aptly notes:

> Authorizing the presence of a support person is an appropriate antidote to the sometimes disabling fear engendered by the courtroom. We do not expect young children to go to the doctor's or dentist's office alone. We should not ask them to go to court alone either. (p. 423)

Excluding Witnesses From the Courtroom

Allowing children to be aided by support persons during legal proceedings is commendable; however, this policy may, in another respect, fly in the face of long-established courtroom practice. Under Rule 615 of the Federal Rules of Evidence, the court is required to exclude witnesses from the courtroom on the request of a party. Myers (1987) notes that "[T]he purpose of the exclusionary rule is to prevent witnesses from consciously or unconsciously shaping their testimony in light of the testimony of other witnesses" (p. 418). What happens, then, when a person who is a witness in a case—and therefore typically would be excluded from the courtroom under Rule 615—needs to be present to support a child who also is a witness in the case? This dilemma has several possible resolutions. First, counsel may argue that presence of the support person/witness is vital to the child witness's ability to testify, thus establishing a compelling reason to override Rule 615. Indeed, the rule "does not authorize exclusion of . . . a person whose presence is shown by a party to be essential to the presentation of his cause" (Fed. R. Evid. 615(3)). This tactic may be successful in jurisdictions in which the trial judge has discretion to authorize witnesses to remain in the courtroom as, for example, provided for by statute. In such a case, *Commonwealth v. Berry* (1986), the Pennsylvania appeals court noted that it was appropriate for a 15-year-old rape victim's mother to remain in the courtroom, stating:

> [w]here . . . there is minimal risk that subsequent witnesses will merely echo preceding witnesses, the court may allow those witnesses to remain, with good cause, despite a sequestration order. (p. 243)

Alternatively, if the only available support person is also a witness, the testimony of the support person may be taken before that of the child, as provided for by California statute. While this approach is preferable, it is not without its shortcomings. Opposing counsel may well object on the grounds that the adult may need to be recalled to the stand after the child has testified. On this point, esteemed evidentiary scholar Wigmore (Cleary, 1984) notes that the exclusionary rule "continues for each witness after he has left the stand, because it is frequently necessary to recall a witness in consequence of a later witness's testimony" (p. 470). This point notwithstanding, Rule 615 clearly allows for the presence of a support person/witness when it has been established that the child witness will be unable to proceed if the adult is excluded. A third—and preferable—approach is to arrange for the presence of a support person who is not a witness (e.g., a CASA). As soon as it is determined that the child likely will take the stand, the aide may be contacted, introduced to the child, and allowed to establish rapport with the young witness. Care must be taken that the aide not serve as a paralegal; rather, the role of the aide simply is to provide emotional support to the child so that the witness can testify at trial.

Novel Approaches to Obtaining Testimony

When child witnesses—especially the very young—offer evidence, it may be necessary to use novel procedures to obtain their testimony. In some cases, the adversarial process played out in the standard way is either too confusing or too intimidating for the young witness. In such cases, the court may allow a neutral person to question the child, testimony may be obtained in chambers rather than in open court, videotaped testimony may be admitted into evidence, and/or special hearsay exceptions may be invoked. At other times, the language of the child may be immature or incomprehensible to the court, and so an interpreter may be necessary.

Use of a neutral questioner. In some cases the court has allowed a neutral questioner to examine a child witness (see for example Jones & Krugman, 1986). Although case law is scant in this area, it is certain that if such a procedure is used, the defendant's constitutional rights must be safeguarded. For example, counsel for the defendant should be present during the questioning, or at least should be able (a) to hear the interchange between examiner and child, (b) to object to the examiner's questions, and (c) to transmit questions to the interviewer during the examination of the child.

In camera testimony. Several states have held that it is permissible in child custody proceedings to have some form of *in camera* testimony in which the child is interviewed privately by the judge to determine the child's preference. In 1984, Melton (1984b) criticized this procedure, noting:

[I]n criminal proceedings in which the defendant's liberty interest is at stake, testimony in chambers would clearly violate constitutional guarantees of due process if the defendant insisted on invoking his or her right to confront witnesses and to be present at trial. . . . Moreover, *in camera* testimony may also conflict with the fundamental constitutional principle of open trials. The general issue therefore is the degree to which the courtroom can be closed without violating either the defendant's or the public's constitutional rights. (p. 186)

More recently, case law has spoken to this issue. Specifically, in *Maryland v. Craig* (1990) the Supreme Court ruled that *in camera* testimony, broadcast via videotape to the courtroom where the trial is occurring, is permissible when it has been demonstrated to the court that the child witness would be unduly traumatized by giving testimony publicly. (See also discussion of exceptions to the hearsay rule, discussed later in this chapter.)

In another recent case, *Kentucky v. Stincer* (1987), the Supreme Court ruled that a defendant's rights to confrontation and to be present during critical stages of the trial had not been violated although he had been excluded from a preliminary hearing regarding the competency of the child witness. The Court's opinion noted that the "exclusion did not interfere with the defendant's opportunity for effective cross-examination at trial" and "there was no indication that the defendant could have done anything had he been at the hearing, nor would he have gained anything by attending" (p. 632). Thus, there is precedent for conducting preliminary hearings concerning child witnesses in chambers. The jury still is out, however, concerning the specific circumstances under which a child may testify *in camera* during the trial itself.

Videotaped testimony. A videotaped interview, especially when obtained soon after the alleged incident, has the potential for serving several important functions. First, it may reduce the number of pretrial interviews required of the child, which in turn may lessen the chance of revictimizing the child. Second, it offers the opportunity to observe the gestures and facial expressions accompanying the child's initial statement of allegation that often signal the veracity of the child's account. Third, a videotaped interview ruled admissible at trial may prompt a guilty plea by the defendant, thereby eliminating the need for the child to appear as a witness in court (Landwirth, 1987). Fourth, as *State v. Sheppard*

(1984) documented, with some children, videotaping actually may increase the accuracy of testimony. In *Sheppard,* the Court relied upon the testimony of forensic psychiatrist Robert L. Sadoff, who noted:

> [For the child who testifies] there is guilt as well as satisfaction in the prospect of sending the abuser to prison. These mixed feelings, accompanied by the fear, guilt, and anxiety, mitigate the truth, producing inaccurate testimony. The video arrangement, because it avoids courtroom stress, relieves these feelings, thereby improving the accuracy of the testimony. (p. 1332)

Opponents of the technique argue, however, that use of video testimony raises serious constitutional issues. Graham (1985) states that traditionally the Court has "relied on confrontation of the accusers by the accused as some assurance of reliability" (p. 18). Moreover, as noted above, confrontation generally has been construed as meaning a *face-to-face* encounter between defendant and accuser.

The defendant's right of confrontation generally excludes as "hearsay," statements that are made out of court, not under oath, and without opportunity for cross-examination. Certainly, video statements may fall under these exclusions. Because such "hearsay" statements may be crucial in a case involving a child witness, Landwirth (1987) notes that "the law has developed a number of specific exceptions and criteria by which they may be admitted into evidence" (p. 587). Such rules are outlined in state statutes, most of which follow guidelines articulated by the U.S. Supreme Court. Landwirth (1987) summarizes these guidelines as follows:

> As applied to child sexual abuse cases, they are generally interpreted to provide that, if the child will appear in court and be available for cross-examination, prior interview statements may be admitted on the theory that the child's courtroom presence will meet the confrontation requirement. However, if the child's earlier statements are being offered in lieu of court appearance to spare the child that experience, additional criteria must be met. The child must be "unavailable" for a court appearance and the nature of the statement in question must either correspond to one of the recognized [*sic*] exceptions to the rule against hearsay or be accompanied by particular indicators of trustworthiness. Compelling public policy interests

and special necessities of the case may on occasion justify admission of out of court statements even if the child is available to appear. (p. 587)

Although these guidelines seem reasonable, case law still is evolving in this area, and some state statutes have not yet been tested. Legal experts, however, have identified several requirements likely to be held essential (Landwirth, 1987). These requirements are concerned with the issues of videotaped testimony (a) during the criminal investigation, and (b) at times when the child is deemed "unavailable" to provide testimony at trial.

Testimony videotaped during the criminal investigation: The police are trained to conduct criminal investigations with vigor, sometimes including interrogating witnesses using manipulative techniques (Wald, Ayres, Hess, Schantz, & Whitebread, 1967). In the case of a child witness, information usually is gathered by either a police officer or a child protection worker who may ask leading questions in order to elicit information from the often reluctant accuser. Such videotaped interviews probably will be excluded from evidence at trial, however, because leading questions generally are inadmissible. Professionals who interview children during a criminal investigation, therefore, require special training in videotape interviewing techniques suitable for use in the courtroom (Landwirth, 1987; see suggestions provided in chapter 7).

Use of videotaped testimony when the child is ruled "unavailable": In some cases, the court may determine that a given child is "unavailable" to provide testimony at trial because the procedure would induce excessive trauma in the child. In such a case, videotaped testimony may be presented during the trial via simultaneous broadcasting of the child's testimony from a room outside the courtroom.

In 1990 the Supreme Court upheld the simultaneous broadcasting procedure in *Maryland v. Craig,* ruling that people charged with child abuse are not always entitled to a face-to face confrontation with their young accusers. (See Box 5.1.) The Court held that the Constitution allows for exceptions to such potentially traumatic confrontations when competing interests of the state are overriding. Justice O'Connor wrote the majority opinion, which held:

The Confrontation Clause does not guarantee criminal defendants an *absolute* right to a face-to-face meeting with the witnesses against them at trial. The Clause's central purpose, to ensure the reliability of the evidence against a defendant by subjecting it to rigorous testing in an adversary proceeding before the trier of fact, is served by the combined effects of the elements of confrontation: physical presence, oath, cross-examination, and observation of demeanor by the trier of fact. Although face-to-face confrontation forms the core of the Clause's values, it is not an indispensable element of the confrontation right. If it were, the Clause would abrogate virtually every hearsay exception, a result long rejected as unintended and too extreme. Accordingly, the Clause must be interpreted in a manner sensitive to its purpose and to the necessities of trial and the adversary process. Nonetheless, the right to confront accusatory witnesses may be satisfied absent a physical, face-to-face confrontation at trial only where denial of such confrontation is necessary to further an important public policy and only where the testimony's reliability is otherwise assured. (p. 673)

In the *Craig* case, the testimony's reliability was assured by maintaining the essential elements of physical presence of the child in the courthouse, administration of the oath to the child witness, cross-examination of the child by defense counsel, and observation of demeanor of the child witness by the trier of fact. Specifically, the child, prosecutor, and defense counsel withdrew to another room where the child was examined and cross-examined. The judge, jury, and defendant remained in the courtroom where the testimony was displayed on a monitor. Although the child could not see the defendant, the defendant—Sandra Craig—could see the child and remained in electronic communication with her attorney. Objections could be made and ruled on as if the witness were in the courtroom.

This case has two important elements. First, using the procedures outlined above, the defendant "retained the essence of the right to confrontation" (p. 666). Second, based on expert testimony, the court found that the alleged victim (and other allegedly abused children who were witnesses) would suffer serious emotional distress if they were required to testify in the courtroom, distress so severe that each would be unable to communicate. Thus, unlike the situation in *Coy*, in *Craig* there was an individualized finding that the particular witnesses needed special protection. These two elements are essential to withstanding judicial scrutiny in child witness cases that involve nonstandard procedures.

Use of previously recorded videotaped testimony: The Supreme Court has yet to rule on a case that involves admitting into evidence a child's testimony videotaped prior to the trial, and this procedure has not been widely tested by the states. The Texas Legislature enacted article 38.071(2) of the Texas Code of Criminal Procedure, which provides for *ex parte* videotaping of the statement of a child victim and for the admissibility of such a videotaped statement in open court, provided that the child is available to testify. Under this statute, the prosecution need not call the child at any time during its case in chief in order for the *ex parte* statement of the child to be admissible. It is required, however, that the child be made available to the accused to call and cross-examine if he or she so chooses. Apparently, the Texas statute is based upon the idea that as long as the declarant of a hearsay statement is available to be called by the accused and examined at trial, the right to confrontation is satisfied (Graham, 1985).

Landwirth (1987) notes that, as with the use of simultaneous broadcasting, when a child's formal deposition via videotape is to be introduced at trial in lieu of a court appearance, special protections for the accused likely will be required. Unlike the Texas statute, Landwirth (1987) recommends that the court should be provided with convincing evidence that the child is "unavailable," that is, the court should be persuaded that the child's appearance at trial likely would cause further psychological harm. Furthermore, the defense attorney should be present and allowed to cross-examine the child at the taping session.

The hearsay rule and its exceptions. As noted above, courts typically refuse to admit into evidence statements referred to as *hearsay.* Rothenberg (1981) defines this legal concept as "[s]omething not heard or witnessed personally but which is based upon what was heard or witnessed by another" (p. 149). Such statements are excluded because they are considered, under most circumstances, to be less trustworthy than are statements made by a witness under oath, in court, in the presence of the accused. There are exceptions to the hearsay rule. According to Myers (1987, 1985-1986), such exceptions include the following:

(a) Present sense impressions—that is, statements describing or explaining an event made while the person was perceiving the event, or immediately thereafter (see Fed. R. Evid., 803.1);

(b) Excited utterances—that is, statements "relating to a startling event or condition made while the declarant was under the stress of excitement caused by the event or condition" (Fed.R.Evid. 803.2);

(c) Statements regarding the declarant's state of mind at the time of an event;

(d) Statements made for purposes of medical diagnosis or treatment;

(e) Statements made by young children alleging sexual abuse;

(f) Residual statements—that is, statements that do not fit under the categories listed above but that bear "circumstantial guarantees of trustworthiness" equivalent to those supporting the other exceptions. In other words, using this exception to the hearsay rule, courts must determine the likely trustworthiness of the statement: Was it made under oath? How much time elapsed between the incident and the statement? Was the declarant motivated to speak truthfully (or deceitfully)? Did the declarant have firsthand knowledge of the event in question? A combination of these factors is weighed by the court using a "totality of the circumstances" test.

In cases of child sexual assault, evidence to corroborate the child's allegations often is not available. So, when the child cannot or will not take the witness stand, prosecutors typically attempt to introduce into evidence the child's hearsay statements. Myers (1985-1986) notes:

> Because children are usually the only witnesses to abuse and because there is frequently a dearth of physical evidence, the state has a strong incentive to use the child's hearsay statements. The need is especially strong when the child recants, cannot remember, or is unavailable to testify. However, even when the child is available, the ability to put an adult on the stand to repeat what the child said at or near the time of the alleged abuse lends powerful support to the child's testimony. (p. 207)

Thus, hearsay evidence often assumes a central role in litigation involving children.

Currently, the courts are inclined to invoke exceptions to the hearsay rule when children are victims. But such exceptions must not be introduced capriciously, a position upheld by the U.S.

Supreme Court. In *Idaho v. Wright* (1990), the Court noted that the Confrontation Clause of the Constitution "bars the admission of some evidence that would otherwise be admissible under an exception to the hearsay rule" (p. 3146). Moreover, the Court outlined certain criteria for admission of hearsay evidence. First, the prosecution must either produce the declarant or demonstrate the unavailability of the declarant whose statement it wishes to use against the defendant. Second, if the witness is shown to be unavailable, then his statement is admissible only if it bears adequate "indicia of reliability" by virtue of its inherent trustworthiness, not by reference to other evidence at trial. In other words, the court must consider the totality of the circumstances surrounding the statement. Justice O'Connor, writing for the majority, noted:

> A statement made under duress, for example, may happen to be a true statement, but the circumstances under which it is made may provide no basis for supposing that the declarant is particularly likely to be telling the truth—indeed, the circumstances may even be such that the declarant is particularly *un*likely to be telling the truth. In such a case, cross-examination at trial would be highly useful to probe the declarant's state-of-mind when he made the statements; the presence of evidence tending to corroborate the truth of the statement would be no substitute for cross-examination of the declarant at trial. (p. 3150)

The Court concluded:

> [I]f the declarant's truthfulness is so clear from the surrounding circumstances that the test of cross-examination would be of marginal utility, then the hearsay rule does not bar admission of the statement at trial. (p. 3149)

We believe this trend is appropriate, and concur with Myers (1987), who comments:

> While the law maintains an equilibrium that is consistent with fundamental fairness, the balance tips toward receipt of out-of-court statements by children, a result which accords with the wise observation of Blackstone that children "often give the clearest and truest testimony." (p. 381, footnote omitted)

Use of an interpreter. Because children are especially prone to idiosyncracies of speech and because they often communicate by gesture rather than word, it may be particularly difficult for the trier of fact to understand their courtroom testimony (see chapter 4). Moreover, some children find the courtroom experience so embarrassing or intimidating that they refuse to speak above a whisper. Because of these circumstances, the presiding judge may appropriately rule that an interpreter should be appointed.

Appointment of an interpreter for a child witness should not be a capricious decision, however. In this regard, Wigmore (Cleary, 1984) writes:

> [I]t is clear that testimony must not be allowed to fail if some process of interpretation is available. The conditions under which it is to be resorted to are the simple dictates of cautious common sense. . . . Interpretation is proper to be resorted to *whenever a necessity exists,* but not till then. . . . (p. 277, footnote omitted)

As was noted in a New Jersey case, *In re* R.R. *(N.J.* 1979), "Any interpreter selected should also ordinarily be an individual who has no interest in the outcome of the case. (p. 86)" Thus, it is most appropriate for parents to be excluded from this role. In some cases, however, the parent is the only person who can translate accurately the child's utterances and gestures. In such cases, the court has shown leniency. For example, in 1979 the New Jersey Supreme Court reviewed the case of a four-year-old victim of sexual abuse. The trial court found the boy competent to testify and noted that he was able to express himself clearly most of the time. Occasionally, however, he used idiosyncratic gestures and speech patterns that only his mother could interpret. Consequently, the trial court appointed the mother to translate the relevant portions of her child's testimony. The New Jersey Supreme Court found the practice appropriate in this case, but cautioned:

> [S]uch an interested person should not be utilized unless and until the trial judge is satisfied that no disinterested person is available who can adequately translate the primary witness's testimony. . . . Even if this requirement is satisfied, however, the trial judge must still interrogate the "interested" interpreter in order to gauge the extent of his bias, and to admonish him that he must translate exactly what the primary witness has said. (*In re* R. R., 1979, p. 86).

Whether the interpreter is an interested or a disinterested party, Myers (1987) recommends that translation should proceed in an immediate and verbatim fashion as the child testifies. He clarifies this point as follows:

[S]uch "continuous" translation is preferred to "subsequent" translation which takes place after the child testifies, because "subsequent" translation involves the risk that the parent will forget the words spoken by the child or will inject biased or incorrect information. The parent should not suggest what the child "really means," nor should the parent reformulate questions put by the court or counsel. As an interpreter, the parent is a conduit for information, nothing more. (p. 93)

Although merely a "conduit," the interpreter may be crucial to the legal proceedings. Therefore, opposing counsel should have the opportunity to call the interpreter as a witness and to cross-examine for bias or error in the process of translation (Myers, 1987).

Great care must be taken whenever the court considers altering room arrangements or trial practice to accommodate child witnesses. Myers (1987) suggests that several factors should be evaluated in this regard:

Will the proposed alteration prejudice the party against whom the child testifies? Will the jury be confused? More important, will the modification focus unwarranted attention on the child's testimony, cause the jury to credit the testimony more than it should, or engender improper sympathy for the child? Does the child really need special accommodation? To what extent, if at all, does the modification inhibit cross-examination or face-to-face confrontation? Does the modification consume too much trial time? Could the child's needs be accommodated through more traditional means such as recesses? (p. 424)

SUMMARY

The criminal justice system was designed for adults. This system expects victims to undergo multiple interviews and court appearances, expects testimony to be detailed and articulate, and often confuses even the most sophisticated witnesses under cross-examination.

In child witness cases, courts often are caught on the horns of a dilemma: On the one hand, they must ensure that justice is served by using every legal and ethical means available to discover the truth of the matter, to guard against false accusations, and to protect the defendant's constitutional rights. On the other hand, it is incumbent upon the court system to protect victims—especially children—from further traumatization, badgering, and harassment. Like other witnesses who take the stand, child witnesses may expect to undergo both direct and cross-examination. The purpose of direct examination is to get the witness's story into the official record of the court, sometimes an arduous and delicate task with young children. Generally speaking, direct examination of the child witness should proceed in a supportive but factual manner. Legal precedent suggests that leading questions should be restricted; instead, the child should be encouraged to describe the alleged incidents in his or her own words. Similarly, use of demonstrative evidence may be beneficial in many cases, and even critical in some, but care should be taken that illustrative aids have been obtained without tainting the evidence.

The right to cross-examine witnesses is an essential component of the Sixth Amendment right to confront accusatory witnesses. Defendants, therefore, have a constitutionally protected right to confront even the youngest of accusers. Cross-examination has two purposes: (a) to elicit testimony favorable to the cross-examiner's theory of the case, and (b) to undermine direct testimony by challenging the witness's credibility and/or statements under direct questioning.

Innovative procedures for obtaining testimony from children and for making the courtroom experience less threatening to children currently are being tested—and challenged—in court. Courts generally have been sympathetic to courtroom and procedural changes that make the experience of testifying less traumatic for children, so long as defendants' constitutional rights are not unduly compromised in the process. Recent decisions by the Supreme Court suggest that the essence of the right to confrontation must be maintained, including physical presence of the child, administration of the oath, cross-examination by defense counsel, and observation of the child's demeanor by the trier of fact. Moreover, the Court has stated clearly that there must be an individualized finding of need when alteration of standard procedures is requested.

NOTES

1. "Children and the courts" by P. King, A. McDaniel, R. Sandza, and S. Doherty, 1984, *Newsweek*, p. 32.

2. The U.S. Supreme Court began addressing these issues in its 1988 and 1990 terms (see *Coy v. Iowa* [1988] and *Maryland v. Craig* [1990], described later in this chapter).

3. For deeper analysis of these issues, see *Fragile voices: Child witnesses in the American legal system* by L. McGough, in press, New Haven, CT: Yale University Press.

4. Interestingly, this opinion has been criticized for being literary rather than scholarly in the legal sense. As one commentator notes, "*Coy* has been subjected to excoriating criticism for its failure to analyze legal sources and its literalism, with only passing reference to the impact of confrontation upon *reliability*. Citing the Bible, Shakespeare and especially President Eisenhower to a lawyer is the act of a desperate analyst." (L. McGough, personal communication, 1990).

5. For a valuable, detailed description of the examination of children as witnesses in court, see \sec 3.22-3.28 of chapter 3 and chapter 4 in *Child witness law and practice* by J.E.B. Myers, 1987, New York: John Wiley.

6. For more information about CASA write to: NCASAA, 2722 Eastlake Ave. E., Suite 220, Seattle, WA 98102.

6

Resolving the Dilemmas: The Marriage of Social Science and the Law

Differing Roles in the Justice System

The Issues Revisited

Issue #1: Competence. How should the courts and society view the capabilities of children as witnesses?

Areas of agreement
Unresolved questions

How much trauma must the courtroom experience engender in child witnesses before reliability of their testimony is compromised?
How much should child witnesses be led on direct examination?
Degree of suggestion • Centrality of the information to be remembered
Strength of memory

Should evidence obtained using anatomical dolls be admissible?
Can child witnesses handle the sophisticated techniques commonly used during cross-examination?
Status of the questioner • Form of the questions posed
Interviewer's knowledge of the alleged crime

The effects of stress and intimidation
Paths to resolution

Issue #2: Credibility. When should the courts and society believe the testimony of children who have been judged competent to give evidence?

Areas of agreement
Unresolved questions

How can we determine the accuracy of the testimony provided by child witnesses?

Paths to resolution

Should expert witnesses be employed to inform the court?
Who may serve as an expert witness?
What is the purpose of expert testimony?

What are the applicable rules for admissibility of "scientific" evidence offered by an expert?

Paths to resolution

Issue #3: Children's rights. What rights should child witnesses have to protection from harm?

Areas of agreement
Unresolved questions

Should limits be placed on the cross-examination of child witnesses? Should videotaped testimony be allowed when a specific child has not been shown to be likely to experience trauma from testifying in court?

Paths to resolution

Issue #4: Defendants' rights. What rights should defendants have in cases involving child witnesses?

Areas of agreement
Unresolved questions
Paths to resolution

Summary

[I]t is generally acknowledged by practitioners in both fields—law and psychology—that they remain unfamiliar and uncomfortable when they move into the other's domain. . . . The question we face is: Can we optimize the divergence, i.e., move from one domain to the other to maximize knowledge and skill? And can we do this with some mutual respect for the complexities and the limitations of each field? . . .

It is reasonable to assume that the movement from one arena to the other will be fraught with some measure of difficulty and discomfort. It is also reasonable to assume that eventual decision-making in the interest of the public good would profit from the complementary contributions of both the law and behavioral science.

(Hall, 1989, pp. 451-452)

In chapter 1 we raised four fundamental issues associated with children testifying in court: (a) How should the courts and society view the capabilities of children as witnesses? (b) When should the courts and society believe the testimony of children who have been judged competent to give evidence? (c) What rights should child witnesses have to protection from harm? (d) What rights should defendants have in cases involving child witnesses?

In subsequent chapters we addressed these issues in a number of ways. Specifically, we looked at the question of competence by tracing the history of child witnesses from a legal perspective (chapter 2). We also considered credibility by describing the subjective reactions of lay persons and professionals to children as witnesses (chapter 2). We then described empirical findings from psychological studies regarding the abilities and shortcomings of developing children (chapters 3 and 4)— evidence that should be relevant to determination of both legal competence and credibility. Next, we discussed the constitutional issues that must be addressed—on behalf of both defendants and children—when minors testify (chapter 5).

In this chapter we revisit those issues and dilemmas in light of the evidence presented in subsequent chapters. The chapters have reviewed social science findings, as well as relevant legal definitions, laws, and court cases. Sometimes social science findings and legal decisions are in conflict. Thus, to provide a framework for later discussion of areas of agreement and disagreement related to each issue, we begin by discussing the differing roles of law and social science within the legal system.

DIFFERING ROLES
IN THE JUSTICE SYSTEM

Hall (1989) reminds us that law and the social sciences have different purposes within the justice system, purposes that sometimes put them at loggerheads with one another (see Box 6.1). She suggests that several reasons underlie this divergence:

> The sense of being on alien ground, using differing conceptual frameworks and separate languages, creates a reluctance on both sides to break down "trade" barriers, to brave the initial threat of being lost in a strange territory, and to discover optimal ways to function collaboratively within the court system. By processes of personal career selection, by traditions of training and professional identity, and by the unique values recognized within each profession, the "house of psychology" and the "house of law" appear to be built according to substantially divergent models. (p. 451)

The law demands concise and absolute (yes-or-no) answers to disputed questions. The legal focus is on rule and order and on adjudication of disputed issues by reliance on legal precedent. In addition, the law is concerned with protection of constitutional rights and doing justice in a system that is by its very nature adversarial.

The social sciences, on the other hand, rarely provide definitive answers to disputed questions. A common conclusion is that "more research needs to be done." At best, social scientists speak of "probabilities." In conducting empirical studies—instead of relying on precedents —behavioral scientists review all relevant hypotheses and data. While some irrelevant alternatives inevitably fall by the wayside, it is not uncommon for social scientists to invoke more than one theory to explain the behavior of a given person in

---

Box 6.1

Law and the Social Sciences:
Differing Roles in the Justice System

Law
  To focus on law, order, and the protection of constitutional rights
  To represent specific individuals and organizations within the legal
    system
  To resolve disputes by relying upon legal precedents
  To decide legal questions in an absolute (yes-no) fashion

Social Sciences
  To focus on upholding scientific and clinical standards
  To understand the behavior of individuals and groups involved with
    the legal system
  To resolve disputes by organizing, integrating, and interpreting
    data from empirical studies
  To inform the triers of fact so that they may make appropriate
    decisions

---

a particular situation. In other words, social scientists prefer to
consider *why* an individual behaves in a certain way rather than
judge the correctness or legality of the behavior. Therefore, social
scientists do not resolve disputes by applying absolutist precedents, but rather by organizing and evaluating the empirical
evidence supporting and refuting each side of the disagreement.

Weiss (1987) notes another area of divergence:

> Traditional litigation focuses on individuals. Lawyers and judges deal
> with specific people and organizations possessing particular charac-
> teristics. Social scientists come to conclusions about groups or classes
> ("employed mothers," "developmentally disabled children"). Courts
> may be skeptical about applying social science conclusions about
> categories of people to the specific individuals before them. (p. 66)

At first blush, it may appear that the disparate purposes of these
two professions—law and social science—render them impossible

bedfellows. Such is not the case. Indeed, we contend that the unique perspectives and methods provided by each one afford the legal system a means for ensuring that justice is better served.

Although the courts' use of social scientific findings is increasing and social scientists' understanding of the law is improving (Hafemeister & Melton, 1987), there still is a long way to go. As Hafemeister and Melton (1987) note:

> Courts appear unsure of whether and how to use social science to examine the policy questions that they have been asked to decide in recent decades. As a result, with the exception of a few judges who "specialize" in cases involving scientific expertise, reliance on social science is still largely a "liberal" practice of judges who have an expansive view of the judiciary's role in shaping legal doctrine and protecting disenfranchised groups. (p. 55)

What, specifically, is to be gained from social science involvement in the legal system? We believe that triers of fact and legal policy makers must make informed decisions, not ones based upon opinion or emotion—or even upon legal precedent alone. We live in an age of technological advances and rapid changes that were beyond the grasp of our ancestors. As scientific knowledge accumulates, it should be disseminated and used in the service of the public good. Within the legal system, sharing of social scientific findings can serve an important informative function.

This function is not without its risks, of course. Weithorn (1987) offers the following cautions:

> In judging whether research findings are "ready" for dissemination in a legal forum, there are no hard and fast rules. The researcher must honestly evaluate the strength of a body of data and its applicability for the particular proposed use. How strong are the findings with a range of methods? How much disagreement exists in the field? How appropriate is generalization from the laboratory to the specific legal context in which the findings will be applied? Scientists must keep in mind that even if they are confident as to the validity of their findings, a particular application may be inappropriate because it requires them to speculate too far beyond those variables actually studied (or permits others to do so). An evaluation of the strength and relevance of the research findings, and the possible benefits to society from disseminating them, must be balanced against an analysis of the possible harm resulting from such dissemination. (pp. 260-61)

With these caveats in mind, we return to the issues raised in chapter 1.

THE ISSUES REVISITED

In this section we address each of the issues separately. For each issue we summarize the areas of agreement and disagreement between social scientists and jurists, and offer paths to resolution of the remaining dilemmas.

Issue #1: Competence. How should the courts and society view the capabilities of children as legal witnesses?

Areas of Agreement

Research findings from the behavioral sciences confirm the ascending legal view that children generally possess the requisite characteristics for providing competent testimony. Remember that, in order to be deemed legally competent to provide evidence, potential witnesses of any age must possess the following characteristics: the capacity to observe, sufficient intelligence and adequate memory to store information, the ability to communicate, an awareness of the difference between truth and falsehood, and an appreciation of the obligation to speak truthfully. Recent statutes, as well as case law at both the federal and state levels, show that the courts now favor the view that a child of any age may testify if two conditions are met: (a) it can be demonstrated that the child possesses the requisite characteristics, and (b) the court is persuaded that the child has personal knowledge of the issue being litigated. As chapters 3 and 4 detail, ample empirical evidence supports the competence of most children as witnesses. To the extent that children are asked to testify about activities with which they are quite familiar, we can expect that their memories are at least as good, and on occasion better, than those of adults. If they are asked questions in a simple and straightforward manner, we can expect that children will be able to understand what is being asked of them and to communicate truthfully what they know.

Experts also agree, however, that the competence of a particular child as a witness depends upon a variety of factors. Age is one such factor, with younger children being considered a priori less competent than older children or adults. Indeed, younger children are more likely than older children or adults to leave out information from their reports to authorities. Of course, there are individual differences in accuracy for children and adults, with some youngsters outshining adult witnesses.

Experts further agree that age interacts in complex ways with other important factors. Centrality of the information to be remembered and reported, motivations to be truthful or dishonest, and characteristics of the questioner and of the courtroom situation all influence a given child's competence as a legal witness.

In our opinion, the area of competence most affected by these factors is the child's ability to communicate. If, for example, an allegedly abused child has been threatened that he or she will be harmed if the truth is disclosed, if the child perceives the presence of the defendant in the courtroom as a visible reminder of this threat, and if the child attributes power and authority to the defendant's attorney who conducts cross-examination, it is a small leap of faith to assume that the witness will be reluctant to disclose details of the abuse. Should this reluctance render the child incompetent as a witness? Social scientists and jurists generally think not. Experts disagree, however, about exactly how such a situation should be resolved (see next section).

Unresolved Questions

We believe that four critical questions concerning the competence of children as witnesses remain to be answered: (a) How much trauma must the courtroom experience engender in child witnesses before reliability of their testimony is compromised? (b) How much should child witnesses be led on direct examination? (c) Should evidence obtained using anatomical dolls be admissible? (d) Can child witnesses handle the sophisticated techniques commonly used during cross-examination?

How much trauma must the courtroom experience engender in child witnesses before reliability of their testimony is compromised? One central function of the court proceedings is to seek the truth of the matter in dispute. If witnesses are not competent, this fundamental purpose is abrogated. Currently, however, we have no litmus test of competence; each witness must be evaluated separately, using more or less subjective means.

The judge can ask relatively direct questions designed to test a given witness's intelligence, memory abilities, understanding of truth, appreciation of the obligation to speak truthfully, and capacity to observe the event in question. But questions regarding the ability to communicate are not so straightforward, especially where children are concerned. Remember that children do not understand much about the court, its personnel, and its procedures (see chapter 4). Therefore, asking them to imagine how they might feel about testifying in court in the presence of the defendant—and, more important, how this feeling might affect their ability to communicate at trial—probably is a fruitless endeavor.

How, then, should courts assess the impact of potential traumatization of the child witness in determining competence in the ability to communicate? This is an important question, for if the child "clams up" in court, he or she clearly is not a competent witness. In this situation, the criterion of ability to communicate is not met, and the witness is *de facto* incompetent.

It is common for social scientists, particularly those trained as clinicians, to favor the liberal use of procedures designed to elicit testimony from reluctant child witnesses—for example, use of screens, videotaped testimony, exceptions to the hearsay rule, leading questions, and such demonstrative evidence as anatomical dolls (Wehrspann, Steinhauer, & Klajner-Diamond, 1987). Clinicians tend to argue that such procedures should be permissible because they are more humane, not simply because they may serve to increase the competence of the witness.

Those trained in the law, on the other hand, are more likely to focus on the competence issue (although humaneness certainly is not ignored). Brooks and Milchman (1990) summarize the argument:

> [W]hen the alleged victim is young, traumatized and cannot communicate directly, the decision to avoid therapeutic techniques may be, in effect, a decision not to investigate the case. When therapeutic techniques are the only ones to which a child can respond, avoiding them may mean abandoning the child and forgoing justice. (p. 9)

U.S. Supreme Court Justice Sandra Day O'Connor alluded to this line of reasoning during the oral arguments presented in *Maryland v. Craig* (1990), the videotaped testimony case described in chapter 5:

O'Connor: Assume that you had a specific finding of trauma,
                           such that the child could not give testimony in the
                           courtroom. What then?

Counsel for
the Defendant: Then the truth-seeking function of the trial would be
                           ruined.

O'Connor: What if a psychiatrist finds that the child's testimony
                           would be more reliable if given outside the court-
                           room? Isn't the truth-seeking function of the court
                           enhanced in that case? (Oral Arguments, 1990,
                           p. 3688)

The issue raised here can be summarized in two relevant questions: Should special procedures be permissible *only* when the
child's ability to communicate is crippled? Or, should such procedures be invoked when the child is capable of communicating at
some level, but the trial judge determines that use of the procedure
may be more likely to produce reliable testimony, that is, testimony
that leads to the truth?

Legal experts are divided on this issue. The Supreme Court
decision in *Craig* suggests that courts should take a conservative
stand. If the child is completely incapacitated by the prospect of
testifying in court—that is, if the emotional distress suffered is so
serious that the child "cannot reasonably communicate" at trial—
then according to the *Craig* decision, a special procedure (in this
case, use of videotaped testimony) is permissible. Thus, the decision in *Craig* speaks directly to the issue of competence and only
indirectly to the question of traumatization of the witness. In
discussing the impact of this decision, McGough (in press) notes:

> The constitutional equation is not that trauma to the child per se
> justifies a special procedure but that trauma must have some pro-
> jected effect upon the child's ability to give reliable testimony. (Chap-
> ter 9)

Before the *Craig* decision was announced, some jurisdictions
used this line of reasoning to enact statutes that permitted more
liberal standards for using alternative procedures in child witness
cases. For example, a Florida statute (F.S. 92.53 [1985]) allows
introduction of the child's videotaped testimony if it is demonstrated that the child "would suffer *at least moderate* emotional or
mental harm" if required to testify in person. According to this

view, attorneys need not show that the alternative procedure would produce the *only* testimony possible from the child witness, the standard required in *Craig.*

Thus, while social scientists tend to favor the expansion of alternatives for obtaining testimony from child witnesses, legal opinion on this issue is divided. One legal scholar suggests, for example, that such procedures are "but one of a number of disturbing signals that courts are inclined to bend the usual rules of evidence in cases involving child sexual abuse, often beyond their breaking points" (McGough, in press, Chapter 9).

On this point, the waters are muddy. Currently, it is unclear how much trauma must be engendered in a child witness before reliability of the testimony is compromised and competence of the witness consequently is called into question.

Our position is that if the child meets the other criteria for competence and if he or she is able to communicate effectively about the incidents in question in some appropriate setting (e.g., judge's chambers, neutral office, on videotape), the truth-seeking function of the court is enhanced by using alternative procedures to obtain the child's testimony. We believe that the degree to which the child can communicate effectively in the presence of the accused should *not* speak to the child's competence as a witness, but rather should relate to the child's credibility. The child should be judged competent to give evidence, and the jury should decide what weight to give to the child's testimony.

How much should child witnesses be led on direct examination?
A second unresolved issue centers on the practice of asking leading questions to elicit testimony from children. Legal precedent clearly allows for the use of this technique, and mental health practitioners often advocate this approach. For example, Kee MacFarlane, chief interviewer for Children's Institute International during the McMartin Preschool investigation, previously had noted that most preschoolers will not disclose abuse unless a few leading questions are posed (Damon, Todd, & MacFarlane, 1987).

But psychological studies of the use of leading questions on children's memory have led to conflicting results. Some suggest that children's memories are more malleable than those of adults (see for example Ceci, Ross, & Toglia, 1987), while others show that children's memories are surprisingly resistant to suggestion (see for example Goodman, Hirschman, Hepps, & Rudy, in press;

Saywitz, Goodman, Nicholas, & Moan, 1989; Zaragoza, 1987; Zaragoza, in press). This fledgling line of research indicates that several factors must be considered whenever we attempt to deduce the effects of leading questions on children's memories. These factors include (a) degree of suggestion, (b) centrality of the information to be remembered, and (c) strength of memory.

Degree of suggestion: While children, like adults, are susceptible to the effects of suggestibility under certain circumstances, it is unusual for children to fabricate completely a series of events, assuming they have been given no motivation to lie (Goodman & Helgeson, 1985; Goodman & Reed, 1986; Marin et al., 1979). For example, research evidence suggests that children rarely fantasize or lie about the central incidents of a sexual assault (Goodman & Helgeson, 1985; Undeutsch, 1982). Goodman and Helgeson (1985) note that "the few cases in which fabrication has been documented involved a host of undesirable interviewing practices . . . e.g., parental influence, suggestive questioning, highly excessive and repetitive interviews, lengthy courtroom testimony, and questioning about peripheral detail" (p. 208).[1] The message is that, while young children rarely fabricate incidents on their own, they may succumb to suggestive questioning and coaching by adults with preconceived notions of what happened.

Not surprisingly, strong suggestions are more likely to elicit false agreement from a child than are mild suggestions. In this regard, Goodman and Helgeson (1985) note:

> [M]ild suggestion, such as "Did Uncle Henry touch your penis?" would be less likely to lead to an inaccurate report than a strong suggestion, such as "I bet Uncle Henry touched your penis, isn't that right?" or "Let's pretend that Uncle Henry touched your penis. How would he have done it?" (p. 189)

While leading questions are dangerous, there are times when mild suggestion may be beneficial. MacFarlane, as well as others in the mental health field, have noted that leading questions sometimes are necessary in sexual assault cases in order to break a frightened or embarrassed child's silence (MacFarlane, 1985; Wehrspann et al., 1987). Moreover, if a mild suggestion is offered but the child responds with a spontaneous report that differs from the suggestion, the interviewer can have somewhat greater confidence that the report is accurate (Goodman & Helgeson, 1985; Wehrspann et al., 1987).

Centrality of the information to be remembered: Children tend to remember details about actions particularly well and tend not to be suggestible when questioned about such details (Goodman et al., in press). On the other hand, suggestions regarding peripheral information are more likely to be adopted by both children and adults than are suggestions concerning central details (Goodman & Helgeson, 1985). Not surprisingly, the more attention one pays to central information, such as a culprit's face, the less time one can focus on peripheral detail.

Strength of memory: According to Penfield (1969), the brain does not contain a complete record of past experience. Similarly, Loftus and Loftus (1980) discuss the commonly held notion that memory is not stable. On this point experts agree.

But cognitive psychologists disagree about *why* memory may be malleable. Some contend that when a person is exposed to misleading information, memory impairment occurs by one of two means: (a) The misleading information actually may *replace* the original memory (Loftus & Loftus, 1980), or (b) the misinformation may render the original memory difficult or impossible to retrieve (Bekerian & Bowers, 1983; Christiaansen & Ochalek, 1983). If substitution occurs (the former hypothesis), theorists suggest that the original memory will be lost forever, irrevocably altered by the misleading suggestion. According to the latter view, however, the original memory is potentially retrievable. While the misleading information may mask the original memory—thereby blocking the person's access to it— if presented with the right cues, the person will be able to unearth the original memory, brushing aside the misleading information that temporarily obscured it (Zaragoza, in press).

Whichever view is correct, the fact remains that children, like adults, tend to be more suggestible if memory is weak (Goodman & Reed, 1986). Under this circumstance, either substitution of memories or the masking of memories is more likely to occur. In either case, testimony about the memory is more likely to be inaccurate.

Strong memories are resistant to change, however, even for children. Indeed, recent research suggests that when children are exposed to highly stressful, personally significant events, their memories are especially strong; that is, recall is better and suggestibility is reduced (Goodman et al., in press; Ochsner & Zaragoza, 1988).

Our view is that leading questions—especially strongly leading questions—should be avoided at all stages of interviewing. It is better to take the time necessary to establish rapport with the child (see chapter 7) than to risk compromising the outcome of a criminal case.

Should evidence obtained using anatomical dolls be admissible? Courts in the United States generally have found that anatomical dolls may be used as demonstrative evidence during the trial if they are sufficiently lifelike: The dolls' anatomy (specifically the genitalia) should be so realistic that neither the child witness nor the jury will be confused when using the dolls to point out particular anatomical parts (see for example *Cleaveland v. State*, 1986). Some states even have enacted statutes authorizing the use of anatomical dolls to facilitate the testimony of young children (see for example Ala. Code Ann. § 15-25-5 [1985]).

For a variety of reasons (discussed in chapter 5), use of the dolls *before* trial is not so commonly heralded. Difficulties include (a) wide variations in those dolls referred to as "anatomically correct," (b) the absence of standardized instructions for use of anatomical dolls, (c) lack of adequate training in the use of the dolls,[2] and (d) the risk that evidence provided via use of the dolls may be tainted. In this regard, one legal scholar offers these comments:

> The literature inspires little confidence regarding the validity of *any* proposition concerning the meaning of children's play with anatomically correct dolls. As usual, the clinical tail has been wagging the empirical dog. . . . The literature indicates that the conclusions drawn by mental health professionals from dolls-assisted interviews are nothing but clinical judgments dressed up in doll's clothing. . . . There is literally neither theoretical nor any empirical basis for drawing *any* conclusion about what a given child's play with the dolls means. . . . Mental health professionals who testify have made and, if the testimony is admissible, are likely to continue to make extravagant and baseless claims about the significance of children's play with the dolls. And because the dolls purport to be a scientific demonstration that establishes an "aura of infallibility," the implicit message of doll-play testimony is likely to be much more influential with fact finders than any other uncorroborated clinical conclusion by an expert. . . . In short, balancing the probative value of doll testimony against its likely prejudicial impact leads to the conclusion that it should not be admissible. (Levy, 1989, pp. 400, 402, 407)

Although Levy's argument is persuasive, his view is not shared by all. Consider these comments by Hall (1989):

> Reconstructive cues such as puppets, family dolls, drawing materials, and doll-house equipment may be useful memory aids for young children. The supportive nature of nonverbal aids, and especially the open-ended, nonsuggestive nature of most play materials, makes the information gathered in such sessions especially valuable. (p. 461)

After reviewing empirical studies and court cases regarding anatomical dolls, McGough (in press) drew these conclusions:

> Unlike preferred testimony that purports to divine when a child is telling the truth, reports of a child's behavior with any materials, including anatomically detailed dolls, does not seem unfairly prejudicial. Properly viewed as but one of a battery of evaluative techniques, anatomically detailed doll-play can provide helpful data to a skilled diagnostician or therapist and ultimately to the court or jury. Admittedly, there is some attendant risk of misinterpretation; however, sometimes doll play can stimulate a child to relate verbally details of an encounter which would otherwise remain unspoken. In a recent federal case, a four-year-old girl remembered during play that unlike the doll, her father's penis had been erect and had sprayed her face with "white mud." Perhaps the greatest utility of these dolls is as a more limited mechanism providing for reenactment of some witnessed encounter, thus helping a child to remember suppressed or forgotten details. (Chapter 9)

We agree with McGough's more reasoned approach to the problem of doll use. Certainly, the courts should be made aware of the fact that use of the dolls is not universally condoned and should be informed of the attendant risks in interpretation of dolls play. To routinely exclude dolls testimony as tainted goes too far. If properly educated about the benefits and risks of clinical dolls play, jurors should be able to consider the evidence presented, giving such evidence the weight they deem appropriate.

Can child witnesses handle the sophisticated techniques commonly used during cross-examination? As chapter 5 explained, cross-examination is a constitutional right protected by the Sixth Amendment to the U.S. Constitution. In *Chambers v. Mississippi* (1973), the Supreme Court reiterated the importance of this right:

The right of cross-examination is more than a desirable rule of trial procedure. It is implicit in the constitutional right of confrontation, and helps assure the "accuracy of the truth-determining process." . . . It is, indeed, "an essential and fundamental requirement for the kind of fair trial which is this country's constitutional goal." (cited in Myers, 1987, p. 192)

We contend, however, that the trial may be considered fair and the truth-determining process accurate only if witnesses can comprehend the meanings of questions put to them under oath. Many adults are stymied by the often convoluted questions and assertions of attorneys during cross-examination, and the confusion of such witnesses undoubtedly leads to abrogation of justice in some cases. For this reason, a judge may intervene during hostile cross-examination. The justice system affords other kinds of protection as well. For example, certain kinds of questioning are curtailed by law (e.g., rape shield laws). Thus, courts are cognizant that hostile cross-examination of adult witnesses may be risky business. We contend that the risk is much greater during cross-examination of child witnesses. Misunderstanding is more likely to occur with children, because their ability to decipher the spoken word is less well developed (see chapter 4).

As noted in chapter 5, attorneys have cultivated a number of cross-examination techniques specifically designed to baffle child witnesses. While the cleverness of these methods cannot be denied, their truth-serving function certainly must be called into question. Psychological studies of the effects of questioning provide ample justification for this opinion. These investigations have focused on several areas: status of the questioner, form of the questions posed, interviewer's knowledge of the alleged crime, and the effects of stress and intimidation.

Status of the questioner. Children are more likely to be suggestible if the questioner is perceived as having high status (Cohen & Harnick, 1980). When children are involved as witnesses in court cases, the questioner (police, attorney, or judge) likely will be perceived as possessing this quality. Depending upon the child's age and stage of moral development, responses to this perception may vary.

Indeed, for young children, truth-telling is highly contextual (Ceci, DeSimone, Putnick, Toglia, & Lee, 1990). Kindergartners, for example, may want to obey the authority figure even if it means sacrificing accuracy for obedience. Six- and seven-year-olds may want to be fair with the interviewer and thus have a tendency to say what the interviewer seems to want to hear. Similarly, older children (eight to eleven) may want to be perceived as "nice" and may act on this need by saying what the questioner seems to want to hear.

The McMartin Preschool case provides an apt example. Raymond Buckey's attorney, Bradley Brunon, viewed videotapes of a therapist's interview in which he thought a seven-year-old boy's agreeable nature had been manipulated. Describing this set of events, Girdner (1985) notes:

> [Brunon] then laughed the child through contradictions and retractions until his testimony was almost worthless to the prosecutors.

> "The first witness was a very gregarious and open, friendly boy," says Brunon. "I thought if I approached him in the same manner, it would reveal that information given to CII was given to please those who were friendly towards him." (p. 59)

As this example illustrates, if the truth-seeking function of the court is to be served, it is important that the questioner not act in an overbearing or solicitous manner. While it is helpful to impress upon the child the seriousness of the occasion, it is counterproductive either to overplay the role of authority figure or to act like the witness's "pal."

Form of the questions posed. The form of a leading question may determine how suggestive the query is to a child. Linguistic effects on memory and suggestibility depend upon whether the words used are (a) affirmative or negative, (b) definite or indefinite, and (c) describe actual or fictitious information. Dale, Loftus, and Rathbun (1978) studied the suggestibility of four- and five-year-old children, using 16 distinct question formats. The question formats combined the variables of (a) affirmation/negation (e.g., "Did you see. . . ?" versus "Didn't you see. . . ?"); (b) presence/absence (questions concerned events that either were part of the films shown or were fabrications by the researchers); (c) article/quantifier variability (e.g., *a* versus *the,* or *some* versus *any*). The researchers drew the following conclusion:

> If the question asked about an entity which was indeed present in the film, the form of the question did not matter. With probability 73-90%, the children responded *yes.* . . .

If, however, the question asked about an entity which was *not* present in the film, the form of the question significantly affected the probability of a *yes* response. In particular, questions of the form "Did you see *the* . . . ," "Did you see *any*. . . ," and "Didn't you see some. . ." were more likely to be answered *yes* than other question types. (pp. 274-275)

These results have obvious implications for the courtroom. The way a question is asked may determine whether it elicits accurate or inaccurate information. This is especially true if the witness's memory is weak or the question refers to misleading information. Other studies of linguistic effects on suggestibility indicate that adults, too, are influenced by the questioner's selection of specific words and syntactical constructions (see generally Loftus).

Interviewer's knowledge of the alleged crime. While the form of the question certainly is an important factor, its effects may be mitigated under some circumstances. Smith and Ellsworth (1987) found that misleading questions decrease the witness's accuracy when the questioner is assumed to be knowledgeable about the crime but have no effect on accuracy when the questioner is assumed to be naive. The critical variable is the respondent's *assumption* about the interviewer's knowledge, not the questioner's actual understanding of the facts.

In Smith and Ellsworth's (1987) study, subjects viewed a videotaped clip of a bank robbery and then were interrogated by a confederate of the experimenters. Subjects were questioned by an individual who was either knowledgeable or naive about the witnessed crime. In addition, half the subjects were asked misleading questions, while the other half were asked unbiased questions. The authors conclude:

> Our results indicate that the power of a misleading question to distort a listener's memory is not simply a matter of semantics or sentence construction, but involves the listener's perception of the social context.

> As in previous research, misleading questions generated incorrect answers when the witness could assume that the interrogator already knew a great deal about the crime. In a situation like this, unless the witness has a very clear memory that contradicts the facts presupposed by the knowledgeable questioner, he or she is not likely to doubt the accuracy of those facts, and will later remember them as part of the event. But when the witness knows that the interrogator

is ignorant of the facts, misleading questions have no effect. In a situation like this, the witness is the primary authority on the crime, and is unlikely to accept false presuppositions in the first place or to recall them later. Subjects who were asked misleading questions by an interrogator they knew to be naive were as accurate as subjects who were not asked misleading questions at all. (p. 299)

The problem, of course, is that witnesses do not assume that the cross-examining attorney is naive about the circumstances of the alleged crime. Indeed, the opposite is true: The attorney is presumed to be particularly knowledgeable. Thus, if a misleading question is asked, either inadvertently or intentionally, the accuracy of the witness's report is likely to suffer. The problem is compounded when children take the stand, because youngsters are especially likely to believe that adults are omniscient (see chapter 4).

The effects of stress and intimidation. Psychological research has shown that stress and intimidation can decrease a person's willingness and ability to retrieve information from memory (see e.g., Goodman & Helgeson, 1985). This phenomenon occurs with some frequency in the classroom when students suffer from test anxiety and are not able to summon information they have studied well. Similar anxiety may inhibit some victimized children from telling their stories accurately under stressful circumstances, for example, when the defendant is in the courtroom. In a study of age differences in eyewitness testimony, Goodman and Reed (1986) found that the performance of three-year-olds was inferior in almost every way to that of six-year-olds and adults. They cited evidence suggesting that the three-year-olds seemed to be more threatened by the research experience than were older subjects, and conjectured that this increased anxiety led to declines in performance.

But others have found that children's memories are not impaired by stress. For example, Goodman et al. (in press) conducted four studies to assess three- to seven-year-old children's memories for stressful events (venipuncture and inoculation) over time. Goodman and colleagues found that children's recollections of such events faded over time in much the same manner as would be expected for innocuous events. More importantly, in these studies, stress never was associated with a reliable negative effect on memory. Rather, when emotional impact was very high—that is, when children became "nearly hysterical with fear"—stress was associated with enhanced memory. The authors note that this finding is consistent with recent evidence that the release of adrenalin accompanying stressful situations aids consolidation of memory (Gold, 1987; McGaugh, 1989).

Ochsner and Zaragoza (1988) also report higher recall and reduced suggestibility in more highly stressed children. Similar results were obtained by Warren-Leubecker, Bradley, and Hinton (1988). These researchers tested the memories of children for a tragic event, the explosion of the space shuttle *Challenger*. Warren-Leubecker et al. (1988) found that children who rated themselves as more emotional about the space shuttle disaster recalled more about the event than did less emotional children, even two years after the tragedy.

On the other hand, Peters (1990) found that stress did have a negative effect on children's reports of their memories. Peters staged a robbery observed by children. In postevent interviews, half of the children were questioned in the presence of the thief, while the remaining half were interrogated in the absence of the perpetrator. He found that eyewitness accuracy of the child witnesses was compromised severely when the thief was present. In fact, when questioned immediately after the incident, more than five times as many children in the thief-absent condition than in the thief-present condition disclosed what they had witnessed.

This experiment combined both stress and intimidation—what Peters refers to as "confrontational stress." Certainly, this form of stress is qualitatively different from the stress induced in the studies of Goodman et al. (1990), Ochsner & Zaragoza (1988), and Warren-Leubecker et al. (1988). Moreover, we cannot conclude that because children in the thief-present condition tended not to give complete reports, their memories were impaired. Their willingness to communicate clearly was compromised, but we cannot know the state of their memories.

Bussey (1990) also found that when a child expects negative sanctions for disclosing information, truth-telling is compromised. Specifically, she found a developmental trend. Three-year-olds tended not to disclose after they had been threatened, while five-year-olds were least likely to disclose if they had been both threatened *and* offered a reward for maintaining secrecy.

These studies collectively suggest that stress generally does not have a negative effect on the memories of young children. Intimidation, however, results in reluctance to disclose. Because children generally are more easily bullied than adults, it is especially important to eliminate intimidation of child witnesses. In this way, suggestibility is likely to be reduced, and the truth-seeking function of the court is likely to be enhanced.

Paths to Resolution

We have documented the fact that, as a general rule, children possess most of the characteristics necessary to serve as competent witnesses: observational capacity, intelligence, memory, ability to differentiate fact from fantasy, and appreciation of the obligation to speak the truth. One area of competence remains troublesome, however—the ability to communicate. Several factors impinge upon this ability: the status of the questioner, the form of the question posed, the interviewer's knowledge of the alleged crime, and the effects of stress and intimidation. In our considered opinion, courts must deal constructively with these factors if the truth-seeking function of the legal system is to be served.

Toward this end, we offer the following policy recommendations:

1. *Allow the use of alternative procedures to enhance communication of child witnesses.* As noted above, if the child witness feels frightened or threatened, it is unlikely that relevant testimony will come to light.If such testimony is not disclosed, discovery of the truth is compromised and justice is not served. The Supreme Court advanced this view in its majority opinion in *Maryland v. Craig* (1990), noting:

> Indeed, where face-to-face confrontation causes significant emotional distress in a child witness, there is evidence that such confrontation would in fact disserve the Confrontation Clause's truth-seeking goal. (p. 686)

We agree and accordingly advocate increased use of live-broadcast videotaped testimony from children. The *Craig* decision certainly suggests that the judiciary will be sympathetic to this approach. We believe, however, that the *Craig* standard is vague. Recall that, in the case of *Craig,* alternative procedures were deemed appropriate because the distress likely to be suffered by the victim witness was so severe that the witness "could not reasonably communicate." *Craig* does not directly address the situation in which the victim can communicate at some level, but because of distress the testimony is incomplete or inaccurate (see Justice O'Connor's line of reasoning during oral arguments in *Craig,* quoted above).

We believe that every reasonable opportunity should be afforded to children who are alleged victims so that they may feel free to communicate what they know. Certainly, we must be aware of the possibility that protecting children from trauma also may make it easier for them to lie. Recent evidence from psychological studies indicates that even under circumstances that encourage open communication, there is little risk of children falsely reporting intimate touching, but a high risk that children who have genuinely experienced such touching will not reveal it (Ceci et al., 1990; Saywitz et al., 1989).

The dissenters in *Craig* (Justices Scalia, Brennan, Marshall, and Stevens) argued that "[F]or good or bad, the Sixth Amendment requires confrontation, and we are not at liberty to ignore it" (Justice Scalia, writing for the minority, p. 694). Although this is a compelling statement, we are persuaded by the majority view:

> The Confrontation Clause does not guarantee criminal defendants an *absolute* right to a face-to-face meeting with the witnesses against them at trial. The Clause's central purpose, to ensure the reliability of the evidence against a defendant by subjecting it to rigorous testing in an adversary proceeding before the trier of fact, is served by the combined effects of the elements of confrontation: physical presence, oath, cross-examination, and observation of demeanor by the trier of fact. Although face-to-face confrontation forms the core of the Clause's values, it is not an indispensable element of the confrontation right. If it were, the Clause would abrogate virtually every hearsay exception, a result long rejected as unintended and too extreme. Accordingly, the Clause must be interpreted in a manner sensitive to its purpose and to the necessities of trial and the adversary process. Nonetheless, the right to confront accusatory witnesses may be satisfied absent a physical, face-to-face confrontation at trial only where denial of such confrontation is necessary to further an important public policy and only where the testimony's reliability is otherwise assured. (p. 673, citations omitted)

The results of social science research support this view.

2. *Reduce or eliminate the use of leading questions.* Legal precedent argues for restricted use of leading questions, particularly during direct examination. In point of fact, however, courts fre-

quently permit the use of leading questions during the examination of children who experience difficulty testifying because of embarrassment, fear, or reluctance (Myers, 1987).

As discussed above, confusion and memory intrusions commonly result from the use of leading questions for both children and adults. Although the original memory may not be lost when a witness is subjected to leading questions (Zaragoza, in press), there are other compelling reasons to restrict the procedure, especially with children:

> [T]here are a number of other ways [in addition to memory impairment] that children might be suggestible. For example, in some cases suggested information may merely supplement and embellish information already in memory, or fill gaps in memory, without actually impairing a child's ability to remember originally-stored details. In addition, some types of suggestibility are entirely unrelated to memory, such as the tendency to conform or comply with the suggestions provided by an adult authority figure. Children may conform to suggestion because they are anxious to please an authority figure, feel pressure to conform to an adult's suggestions, or simply trust the information provided by an adult authority figure more than their own memory (Zaragoza, in press).

For these reasons, we believe that the use of leading questions during cross-examination of children should be curtailed. Other professionals—for example, the Association of Trial Lawyers in America—are likely to offer strong resistance to this suggestion. Some may even argue that the defendant has a constitutional right to ask leading questions during cross-examination of witnesses. But, as we have argued above, while such questioning techniques may be germane to seeking the truth when adults are witnesses, the same conclusion cannot be drawn when children testify.

Several factors are likely to subvert the truth-seeking function of the trial when children are led on cross-examination. First, children are likely to imbue the cross-examining attorney with high status and, therefore, are more likely to agree with assertions presented by this powerful person. Second, children are likely to be confused by the form of the leading questions posed. Third, children tend to assume that the interviewer is knowledgeable about the alleged crime, and further assume that the powerful adult would not be likely to mislead them, especially in front of the judge. Thus, to use leading questions on cross-examination of children is, in our estimation, akin to a subtle form of bullying. This practice does not serve the truth-seeking function of the trial and should, we believe, be eliminated.

3. *Use simple language.* Attorneys are renowned for using convoluted sentence constructions and "two-bit" words. But the use of "legalese" is confusing to many adult witnesses and incomprehensible to most children. Indeed, it is akin to speaking a foreign language. No court would dream of allowing an English-speaking child to be questioned in Chinese. Similarly, justice cannot be served if child witnesses are questioned using sophisticated sentence structure and reasoning. We recommend that attorneys who question children at any time during the course of resolving a legal case follow the guidelines described in chapter 4 ("Avoiding Communication Errors"). Use simple words and sentences illustrated by examples. Phrase sentences in the active voice. Eliminate double negatives and tag questions (those that ask for confirmation, e.g., "It's a nice day, *isn't it?*"). Avoid the use of abstractions and evaluative questions. Translate and define legal terms. Explain the premises underlying each question. Check separately the veracity of each point in the testimony.

Child witnesses cannot be considered competent if they cannot communicate what they know. By following the paths to resolution we have recommended, the courts should increase the ability of young witnesses to communicate effectively, thereby allowing them to serve as competent witnesses.

Issue #2: Credibility. When should the courts and society believe the testimony of children who have been judged competent to give evidence?

Areas of agreement

Both social scientists and legal professionals recognize that children tend not to be held in high regard as observers and witnesses. In fact, even children tend not to perceive themselves as influential when giving testimony (Hulse-Trotter & Warren, 1990). Not surprisingly, their credibility is enhanced if they are perceived as honest and capable of remembering significant details, characteristics that also add to the believability of adult witnesses. The results of scientific studies confirm the prevalent legal view that the demeanor and speaking style of the child witness affect jurors' impressions (see chapter 2). Thus, the factors that influence the credibility of children as witnesses are not in dispute.

Unresolved Questions

In the area of credibility, two significant questions remain troublesome, however: How can we determine the accuracy of the testimony provided by child witnesses? Should expert witnesses be employed to inform the court about the credibility of children's testimony?

How can we determine the accuracy of the testimony provided by child witnesses? Our system of justice rests on the twin assumptions that accurate witnesses are credible and that credible witnesses are accurate. Experience, however, proves otherwise. We know, for example, that confident witnesses tend to appear believable to jurors even when their testimony is in error (Deffenbacher, 1980; Smith, Kassin, & Ellsworth, 1989). In other words, credibility is not the same thing as accuracy, although the two undoubtedly are related.

Witness credibility is a complex issue when adults testify; it is much more complicated in the case of children. Saywitz (1988) summarizes the situation, stating, "Children's credibility is complex—a three-way interaction between what the listener (the court) and speaker (child witness) bring to the context (offering testimony in a courtroom)" (p. 39). Listeners bring preconceived notions about children as good witnesses; the child-speaker brings different levels of memory, communication, cognition, and suggestibility. Courtroom contexts vary, depending upon jurisdiction, type of case, presiding judge, and characteristics and tactics of the opposing attorneys.

Moreover, Saywitz (1988) suggests that cases involving child witnesses vary in at least four dimensions that are critical to evaluating credibility: the developmental, individual, clinical, and situational dimensions. First, as described in chapter 3, children of different ages or stages of development differ from one another (the developmental dimension). Second, children of the same age or stage of development differ (the individual dimension). Third, different children cope in varying ways with the stresses associated with experiencing and testifying about an incident, and they react in different ways when they are traumatized (the clinical dimension; see chapter 5). Fourth, an array of contextual factors varies with each incident (the situational dimension). These factors include, for example, the child's degree of familiarity with the alleged perpetrator, the number of criminal acts involved, and the duration of exposure. Thus, jurors who are called upon to evaluate the credibility of a given child's testimony must juggle the importance of these four factors to the case at hand.

Neither the courts nor anyone else has developed any surefire means for rating the believability of witnesses. Even so-called "lie-detector" tests (polygraphs) are fallible. The Anglo-American legal system has been designed to handle this deficiency. Our system of justice is based upon the premise that a jury of the defendant's peers should weigh the evidence before them and determine the credibility of each witness. As noted above, however, credibility and accuracy are not synonymous, yet the truth-seeking function of the legal system demands that the *accuracy* of testimony be ascertained. Remember that one of the purposes of cross-examination is to uncover inconsistencies in testimony that might reveal inaccuracy. Also recall that the jurors in a given case must consider the weight to be given any admissible testimony. Presumably, if either the testimony is inaccurate or the witness is deemed less than credible, the jurors will disregard the evidence.

Disentangling accuracy and credibility is no easy task when children testify. Psychological studies (described earlier in this chapter) show that a number of factors influence the accuracy of children's accounts in court. A model that predicts children's accuracy must take into account several factors: age of child, type of event experienced (simple or complex), degree and type of interrogation before trial, type of questions asked at trial, and responses desired (factual or interpretive). These are complex factors. How, then, can jurors—who are not experts in child development and witnessing behavior—be expected to evaluate the accuracy of a particular child's account?

Path to Resolution

Recently, clinicians, researchers, and legal scholars alike have suggested some promising approaches to this dilemma (Raskin, Boychuk, McGough, & Stellar, 1990; Raskin & Yuille, 1989; Wehrspann et al., 1987). For example, Raskin et al. (1990) suggest that the justice system must shift its focus away from *witness* credibility and toward *statement* credibility. The work of Raskin and colleagues centers on the use of a technique called "statement validity assessment" (SVA) (see Raskin & Stellar, in press; Raskin & Yuille, 1989; Yuille, 1988). Using this technique, children's allegations of sexual abuse are assessed, with statement analysis based on the premise that descriptions of events that actually were experienced differ in content, quality, and expression from those that are invented (Raskin & Yuille, 1989). The interview is conducted by a professional trained in SVA. Only the child and interviewer are present during questioning, and the session is videotaped. Questioning moves from the general to the specific. At the close of the interview, the child's statement is analyzed, first by assessing the overall quality of the statement, and then by proceeding to progressively more specific details and characteristics of the statement (see Stellar, Raskin, Yuille, & Esplin, in press). Each account is assigned a score ranging from zero to 38.

Boychuk and Raskin (reported by Raskin et al., 1990) field tested the technique in 40 cases of alleged sexual abuse. The cases were divided into two groups: confirmed and doubtful reports. Allegations were considered confirmed if the perpetrator confessed or produced a deceptive polygraph profile, an eyewitness corroborated the child's account, or evidence of vaginal or anal trauma existed. Reports were considered doubtful if the accused persistently denied the charges and gave a truthful polygraph result, no medical evidence existed, the child recanted, investigators found insufficient grounds to pursue criminal charges, or the court found for the defendant. The results showed that the SVA reliably discriminated between doubtful and confirmed accounts. SVA scores of zero to 10 were associated with doubtful evidence, whereas children's accounts in confirmed cases scored in the 16-34 range. Currently, Raskin and colleagues are conducting additional studies assessing the value of the SVA.

Others also have reported success using such procedures. For example, Undeutsch (1982) reported that, using statement analysis, the allegations of approximately 90 percent of the 1500 children in his sample were demonstrated to be valid. Moreover, convictions were obtained for perpetrators in 95 percent of these cases.

Courts in the United States may be reluctant to admit the results of procedures designed to assess statement validity, however, because expert opinion regarding the truthfulness of a child's testimony invades the province of the jury, whose task it is to determine the credibility of witnesses (McCord, 1986). This approach has been widely used in Germany since 1954, when in a landmark decision, the Federal Republic of Germany mandated that experts *must* be employed to assess the truthfulness of children's testimony if that is the major evidence and is not corroborated by other evidence (Raskin & Yuille, 1989). We believe that the time has come for the United States to follow suit and urge social scientists to agree upon the relevant criteria for assessment of veracity.

Wehrspann et al. (1987) suggest one set of criteria that may be used to assess the truthfulness of a child's account of sexual abuse:

1. Spontaneity of the account
2. Repetitions of the account over time
3. Repetitions that are internally consistent
4. Repetitions that are externally consistent
5. Occurrence of embedded responses (that is, verbal or behavior responses suggesting accuracy of the child's account that are triggered by a chance occurrence in everyday life)
6. Amount and quality of details
7. Story told from the child's viewpoint
8. Emotional state consistent with disclosure
9. Evidence of accommodation (that is, evidence that the child's responses to parents' or others' attempts have intimidated him or her into suppressing details of abuse or retracting what already has been said)
10. Consistency in the face of challenge
11. Sexually specific symptoms

We believe the approaches advocated by Raskin and colleagues, Undeutsch, and Wehrspann et al. hold great promise. We encourage social scientists to continue research in this area and urge the courts to consider the value of such evidence.

Should expert witnesses be employed to inform the court about the credibility of children's testimony? As the previous section suggests, some argue that expert witnesses might be employed by the court to address the issue of the credibility of children as witnesses (McCord, 1986). An expert might, for example, comment on the abilities and shortcomings of children in general, factors that relate to credibility. Alternatively, an expert might comment on the capabilities of a specific child witness, either enhancing or detracting from the child's credibility as a witness. Finally, an expert might comment on the behaviors of the child witness and how they relate (or fail to relate) to an evidentiary issue (e.g., whether the child has suffered abuse). Professionals representing both law and social science disagree about the usefulness of behavioral scientists as experts. Two commentators, referring to the testimony of mental health professionals, state bluntly, "[T]he involvement of experts wastes many hours of already too scarce court time and costs taxpayers millions of dollars" (Faust & Ziskin, 1988, p. 35). Some assert that experimental psychology should only speak in the courtroom when it can do so in a nonprobabilistic manner (McCloskey & Egeth, 1984). Others argue to the contrary:

> Now since our science rests on a rather large body of probabilistic statements, what is wrong with carefully presenting the relevant statements to triers of fact? After all, judges and jurors must constantly deal with probabilistic data from real life and are required to employ probabilistic criteria such as "preponderance of evidence" and "reasonable doubt." (Deffenbacher, 1984, p. 1067)

Although the academic debate on this topic may be interesting, more important practical considerations exist. Each time an attorney proposes to introduce expert testimony into evidence, the trial judge must rule on its admissibility. To understand how such decisions are made and how they apply in cases involving children as witnesses, we need to answer several questions: Who may serve as an expert? What is the purpose of expert testimony? What are the applicable rules for admissibility of "scientific" evidence offered by an expert?

Who may serve as an expert witness? By definition, an expert witness is any person with special knowledge in a particular sphere, such as an engineer, a scientist, or a physician (Rothenberg, 1981). Typically, in order to be considered an expert, an individual must have completed specialized training and established recognized credentials in the area of expertise. In addition, some suggest that an expert should be reasonably certain about the pertinent issues in a given case, not merely about the field in general (Faust & Ziskin, 1988). In fact, in order to be considered relevant, evidence provided by an expert "must make the existence of some fact in issue more or less likely" (McCormick, 1982, pp. 880-881). Most important, an expert witness "should be able to help the judge or jury reach a more valid conclusion than would be possible without the expert's testimony" (Faust & Ziskin, 1988, p. 31). In other words, the expert's testimony should help the trier of fact in deciding a disputed issue. These two factors—relevance to the case at hand and assistance to the trier of fact—provide general constraints concerning the admissibility of expert testimony. Applying these criteria to a particular case (for example, one involving children as witnesses), the presiding judge must decide whether to admit or exclude the testimony of each expert. McCormick (1982) explains:

> [T]he trial court must make judgments on matters not readily quantified and often not subject to empirical testing. The court must identify and evaluate the probative value of the evidence, consider how it might impair rather than help the factfinder, and decide whether truthfinding is better served by exclusion or admission. The rules give the court a range of discretion in determining whether the requisites for admissibility of expert testimony have been met and whether the evidence is likely to help the factfinder. (p. 881)

Courts generally recognize the expertise of certain individuals— for example, physicians, ballistics specialists, and engineers—and typically are willing to admit their testimony at trial. So long as proper foundation exists and the expert states an opinion, diagnosis, or conclusion "with reasonable [professional] certainty," it is likely to be admitted as evidence for the judge or jury to consider.

Other professionals do not share this widespread acceptance in the courtroom, however. Remember that the expert must pass a two-pronged test: relevance *and* helpfulness. While scientists often pass the relevancy test, the testimony they provide may not be considered "helpful" to the judge or jury. This situation applies particularly to social scientists, whose conclusions tend to be based upon probabilities. As Hall (1989) argues, however, the role of the social scientist as expert is not to provide certainty but rather to enhance knowledge:

> The crucial question, then, is not whether the psychologist as expert brings a totality of scientific "truth" or Olympian "wisdom" to the task, but whether what he or she can bring enriches the lay knowledge of the trier of fact—whether the probative value of the testimony

outweighs its possible prejudicial effect. The role of the psychologist is that of information processing, not decision making (p. 454).

What is the purpose of expert testimony? An expert must not usurp the role of the judge or jury in deciding a verdict. The evidence provided by the expert should have probative value; that is, it should make the existence of some fact in the case more or less likely (e.g., that an eyewitness had adequate opportunity to view a perpetrator). It is crucial, however, that the scientific evidence provided is not dispositive of the case; in other words, the expert's views should not render the verdict a foregone conclusion. In such a case, the testimony is considered prejudicial. For example, if the guilt of the defendant hinges to some degree on identification by an eyewitness, it may be probative for an expert to testify to the factors that influence accurate eyewitness identification (e.g., lighting conditions, duration of exposure, lineup procedures used). It would be dispositive, and therefore inappropriate, for the expert to conclude that because the conditions were favorable (or unfavorable) at the time of the incident, the eyewitness must be correct (or mistaken).

Hall (1989) cogently summarizes the role of the psychologist as expert witness:

> The psychologist in the courtroom is not an extension of the police investigator nor the scientific voice of the child protection service. The role demands autonomy, independence from the original fact-finding task force, and freedom to pursue the sole injunction to be an accurate and explicit scientific observer of human behavior and to provide a data-based opinion that serves to assist the trier of fact. This is true regardless of whether the psychologist is court-appointed or is hired by one of the parties. No matter how the psychologist enters the case, he or she is bound by the ethical principles of the profession and the contract to provide an "expert," i.e., a scientific, opinion. This includes maintaining "high standards of scholarship by presenting information objectively, fully, and accurately," being "alert to personal, social, organizational, financial, or political situations and pressures that might lead to misuse of their influence," and avoiding "any action that will violate or diminish the legal and civil rights of clients or of others who may be affected by their actions."

> The assumption is that if the information is fair and accurate, it will, whether the expert be court- or party-appointed, serve the needs of the fact finder and, therefore, will aid the public. (pp. 452-453)

What are the applicable rules for admissibility of "scientific" evidence offered by an expert? Determining when scientific evidence is probative as opposed to prejudicial is no easy matter, although such evidence is offered in a significant number of trials.[3] Each time such evidence is offered, the trial judge must rule on its admissibility by selecting an appropriate test or standard for evaluation. Under Rule 702 of the Federal Rules of Evidence, now used in more than half the states, the court has discretion to admit expert testimony if it will assist the jury. Rule 702 also comments on scientific testimony specifically:

> If scientific, technical, or other specialized knowledge will assist the trier of fact to understand the evidence or to determine a fact in issue, a witness qualified as an expert by knowledge, skill, experience, training, or education, may testify thereto in the form of an opinion or otherwise. (Fed. R. Evid. 702)

Admission or exclusion of expert testimony must not be capricious; rather, the court must employ a standard of admissibility:

> The admissibility standard functions as the device through which the values of the legal system are imposed on scientific knowledge and determines the rapidity and readiness with which scientific information becomes evidence. Thus, the standard has vital evidentiary ramifications. (McCormick, 1982, p. 879)

Most courts use one of two generally accepted tests of admissibility for scientific evidence: the *Frye* test and the relevancy approach. The former is considered to be the more conservative; the latter, the more liberal (Giannelli, 1980). The testimony of any social scientist who provides evidence concerning purportedly scientific procedures—such as the methods used in determining whether a child has been sexually abused—may be subjected to one of these tests.

The *Frye* standard was articulated in *Frye v. United States* (1923). In *Frye,* the United States Court of Appeals for the D.C. Circuit ruled that the trial judge's exclusion of a purportedly scientific procedure was appropriate. Frye, the defendant in a murder case, had sought to demonstrate his innocence by introducing into evidence favorable results of a "systolic blood pressure deception test" he had taken. In upholding the trial judge's exclusion of the blood pressure evidence (a forerunner of the polygraph), the appellate court commented:

Just when a scientific principle or discovery crosses the line between the experimental and demonstrable stages is difficult to define. Somewhere in this twilight zone the evidential force of the principle must be recognized, and while courts will go a long way in admitting expert testimony deduced from a well-recognized scientific principle or discovery, the thing from which the deduction is made must be sufficiently established to have gained *general acceptance* in the particular field in which it belongs. (p. 1014)

The court further held that the technique in question had "not yet gained such standing and scientific recognition among physiological and psychological authorities" (p. 1014).

The *Frye* "general acceptance" test has dominated the admissibility of scientific evidence for nearly 70 years, although the D.C. Court provided no explanation for adoption of this standard. This is a curious omission, considering the stringent guidelines implied by *Frye:*

In effect, *Frye* envisions an evolutionary process leading to the admissibility of scientific evidence. A novel technique must pass through an "experimental" stage in which it is scrutinized by the scientific community. Only after the technique has been tested successfully in this stage and has passed into the "demonstrable" stage will it receive judicial recognition. What is unique about the *Frye* opinion is the standard it establishes for distinguishing between the experimental and demonstrable stages. . . . [I]t is not enough that a qualified expert, or even several experts, believes that a particular technique has entered the demonstrable stage; *Frye* imposes a special burden—the technique must be *generally accepted by the relevant scientific community.* (Giannelli, 1980, p. 1205)

Since its adoption, courts adhering to the general acceptance standard have offered supporting rationales omitted from the D.C. Court opinion. Four main arguments have been offered in behalf of *Frye:* (a) the test guarantees that "a minimal reserve of experts exists who can critically examine the validity of a scientific determination in a particular case" (*United States v. Addison,* 1974, p. 744); (b) the general acceptance standard "may well promote a degree of uniformity of decision" (*People v. Kelly,* 1976, p. 31); (c) the test eliminates the need for time-consuming hearings on the validity of innovative techniques (*Reed v. State,* 1978); and (d) it "establishes a *method* for ensuring the reliability of scientific evidence" (Giannelli, 1980, p. 1207).

Although the *Frye* standard is used widely it is not without its critics. Giannelli (1980) notes several bones of contention:

> In particular, courts must decide *who* must find the procedure acceptable, they must define exactly *what* must be accepted, and they must determine what methods will be used to establish general acceptance. (p. 1208)

Because many scientific techniques do not fall exclusively within the domain of one academic discipline or professional field, deciding who must find the procedure acceptable may prove troublesome. Even if this problem is overcome, the percentage of those in the field who must accept the technique never has been clearly delineated. In this regard, one legal commentator notes, "The resulting standard, something greater than acceptance by the expert himself but less than acceptance by all experts in the field, is obviously somewhat lacking in definiteness" (Strong, 1970, cited in Giannelli, 1980, p. 1211). Moreover, it is unclear whether the *Frye* standard requires general acceptance of the scientific technique only or of both the underlying principle and the technique applying it. In addition, the standard has been criticized for excluding reliable evidence and for admitting unreliable evidence. After all, "general acceptance" by experts is not synonymous with reliability; if it were, early explorers *would* have fallen off the edge of the earth when they set sail for the horizon!

The problems associated with the general acceptance standard have led to inconsistencies in its application. Thus, Giannelli (1980) suggests:

> . . . the critical issue is whether other approaches can better achieve the *Frye* objective of "prevent[ing] . . . the introduction into evidence of specious and unfounded scientific principles or conclusions based upon such principles." If such alternative approaches exist, then the conservatism implicit in the *Frye* test is not an "advantage," but rather an unjustified obstacle to the truth-determining process. (p. 1224, footnotes omitted)

One commonly accepted alternative to the *Frye* standard is the "relevancy approach." According to this approach, the admissibility of scientific evidence depends upon a three-step process: First, the probative value of the evidence is determined; that is, the judge must determine whether the expert testimony will tend to make the existence of any fact that is relevant to determining a verdict more probable or less probable than it would be without the expert testimony. Second, relevant dangers of the proposed testimony are identified. (Is it likely, for example, that the evidence will mislead the jury?) Third, the probative value of the evidence must be balanced against the identified dangers (Giannelli, 1980).

McCormick (1982) cautions that courts should take several factors into account when applying the relevancy approach. He enumerates them as follows:

> (1) the potential error rate in using the technique, (2) the existence and maintenance of standards governing its use, (3) presence of safeguards in the characteristics of the technique, (4) analogy to other scientific techniques whose results are admissible, (5) the extent to which the technique has been accepted by scientists in the field involved, (6) the nature and breadth of the inference adduced, (7) the clarity and simplicity with which the technique can be described and its results explained, (8) the extent to which the basic data are verifiable by the court and jury, (9) the availability of other experts to test and evaluate the technique, (10) the probative significance of the evidence in the circumstances of the case, and (11) the care with which the technique was employed in the case. (pp. 912-913, footnotes omitted)

Under the relevancy approach, some evidence will be excluded by the trial judge, but most will pass the threshold requirements for admissibility (Giannelli, 1980). Indeed, this is the preference of the courts adhering to the relevancy approach. In *United States v. Baller* (1975), for example, the Court commented:

> Unless an exaggerated popular opinion of the accuracy of a particular technique makes its use prejudicial or likely to mislead the jury, it is better to admit relevant scientific evidence in the same manner as other expert testimony and allow its weight to be attacked by cross-examination and refutation. (p. 466)

Thus, although the relevancy approach hinges to some degree on admissibility, in actuality the focus is on the *weight* to be attributed to the evidence by judge or jury. Imwinkelried (1981) suggests:

If a technique's interpretive standards have been experimentally verified as being reliable, the expert's interpretation is entitled to great weight. . . . [But] when the witness cannot point to hard proof of the reliability of his or her interpretive standard, the trier of fact should ascribe little weight to the expert's interpretation. (pp. 282-283, 285)

As Giannelli (1980) notes, one of the assumptions underlying the use of this standard is that jurors are capable of evaluating scientific evidence. He cites the opinion of the Court in *United States v. Ridling* (1972):

[I]t is important to understand how different juries are today than they were when the restrictive rules of evidence were first developed. On the whole they read widely. Largely because of television they know generally what is going on in the world. Their educational background is extensive. They think. They reason. They are really very good at sorting out good evidence from bad, of separating the credible witness from the incredible, and of disregarding experts who attempt to inject their opinions into areas of which they have little knowledge. (pp. 1239-1240)

Unfortunately, the *Ridling* Court is sadly mistaken. Empirical studies show that jurors cannot discriminate between accurate and inaccurate eyewitnesses (Lindsay, Wells, & Rumpel, 1981; Wells, Lindsay, & Ferguson, 1979; Wells, Lindsay, & Tousignant, 1980). Thus, one of the major assumptions of the relevancy approach is unfounded.

Even with procedural safeguards—e.g., adequate notice and discovery of the evidence that the opposing party intends to introduce at trial, full disclosure, and preservation of evidence —the relevancy approach may fail to protect adequately against the misuse of unreliable scientific evidence. Thus, its major shortcoming (failure to protect against admission of unreliable evidence) is the opposite of the most significant weakness of the *Frye* test (failure to admit reliable scientific evidence).

Some scholars have attempted to find a middle ground between the excessive strictness of the *Frye* test and the unwarranted leniency of the relevancy approach. For example, Giannelli (1980) has suggested that the burden of proving reliability of scientific evidence should fall on the proponent of the evidence and that the judge should determine as a preliminary question of fact whether the burden of proof has been satisfied. Moreover, he recommends that the proponent of the evidence should be required to establish its validity at the strictest level required by law, "beyond a reasonable doubt" (pp. 1247-1248).

Giannelli (1980) contends that his proposal accepts the premise of *Frye* but rejects its strict standard (general acceptance). This seems to us a specious argument. As mentioned above, nowhere do the courts define "general acceptance" in statistical terms. Thus, "general acceptance" could constitute the view of a significant minority of scholars, or it could require virtually 100 percent conformity. Because "beyond a reasonable doubt" generally is assumed by judges to be certainty of 90 percent or greater (Kagehiro, 1990; McCauliff, 1982; Simon, 1969; *United States v. Fatico,* 1978), it is quite possible that Giannelli's approach is even *more* stringent than that set forth in *Frye.*

McCormick (1982) summarizes other alternatives. For example, some have suggested abandoning the *Frye* standard in favor of establishing an expert tribunal to evaluate and pass judgment on the validity and reliability of new scientific developments. Proponents argue that such a tribunal could survey scientific opinion regarding the evidence in question. They contend that because decisions would be made by neutral, qualified parties not engaged in an adversarial process, the search for truth would proceed more smoothly (McCormick, 1982). Critics have argued that use of a scientific tribunal could be excessively costly and time-consuming and that there is no guarantee that conclusive results would be achieved.

On this point, McCormick (1982) concludes:

It might be preferable to maintain the present dichotomy between the roles of science and law. This does not mean scientists and lawyers should not cooperate in official and informal ways to assist in the assimilation of valid and reliable scientific developments into the legal system. (p. 907)

As illustration, McCormick (1982) cites the joint publication of an official statement of the American Bar Association and the American Medical Association on the use of blood testing in establishing paternity. The report identified, analyzed, and discussed more than 60 test systems and recommended that 7 of these were appropriate for routine use in cases of disputed paternity. Mc-Cormick notes:

The value of the report is twofold. First, it is an authoritative analysis of existing knowledge in the field, and second, it is equally authoritative as an endorsement of the reliability of the legal adaptation of this knowledge. This joint effort of lawyers and scientists is an excellent example of bringing scientific advancements to the courtroom in a systematic and deliberate way. If similar efforts were undertaken in other areas of controversy, it is possible that questions about validity and reliability could be answered more expeditiously and accurately. (p. 908)

We wholeheartedly concur that social scientists and jurists should maintain their distinctive roles. Social scientists should be employed to inform the court but should not usurp the fact-finding role of the jury.

Indeed, recent studies show that expert testimony may help jurors examine the evidence before them (Cutler, Dexter, & Penrod, 1989; Goodman & Loftus, 1988). For example, in a comparison of three studies of the influence on jurors of expert testimony regarding eyewitnesses, Hosch (1980) concludes:

[E]xpert psychological testimony regarding eyewitness identification benefits the courts by causing jurors to increase their consideration of the evidence in a case. It is not startling that jurors consider eyewitness identification evidence more carefully when an expert testifies that accurate identification is a complex phenomenon. The unexpected finding that jurors also increase their examination of the other relevant evidence suggests that expert testimony can have a profound and nonintuitive impact on the process of jury deliberations. Justice can best be served to the degree that jurors make the most considered, rational decision possible. Expert testimony appears to serve this end. (p. 301)

We agree.

Paths to Resolution

We believe that the courts and society should believe the testimony of children who have been judged competent to give evidence when the accuracy of their reports can be determined. Therefore, expert testimony that considers the means for assessing the accuracy of children's reports is warranted. Scientific evidence on this issue should be admitted and submitted to standard tests of its weight. We, therefore, (a) encourage expert witnesses to discuss the factors that impinge upon the accuracy of a child's allegations (see above), and (b) refrain from commenting on the accuracy of a specific child's report. In this regard, Goodman and Loftus (1988) comment:

> An expert who reports accepted scientific findings about the average behavior of hundreds of subjects over hundreds of tests does not provide testimony that can be characterized as "too speculative." It is crucial, however, that the expert not violate statistical principle or invade the province of the jury by applying statistical findings to one member of the group. Decisions about the applicability of the research findings to the defendant must be made by the jury, which, as the state of Washington has long recognized, may always accept or reject all or part of the expert's opinion. (p. 120, citation omitted)

We also believe that the justice system should consider use of court-appointed expert witnesses. Their purpose would be to inform the triers of fact in a nonpartisan, nonadversarial fashion. A similar approach has been advocated recently by the American Psychology-Law Society. APLS is encouraging the preparation and dissemination of *amicus curiae* briefs to inform the court on such psycholegal issues as the traumatization of child witnesses (APA, nd., Amicus Curiae 7-13). We believe that court-appointed experts could use such briefs effectively, coupled with the results of recent scientific studies, in giving nonpartisan evidence at trial.

Finally, we believe that experts should inform the court whether they are testifying in a nonadversarial fashion (as research scientists) or in an adversarial role (as clinician-advocates for their clients). Such disclosure serves to inform the triers of fact of the potential vested interest of the expert and the potential bias of the testimony.

Issue #3: Children's rights. What rights should child witnesses have to protection from harm?

Areas of Agreement

Social scientists and legal experts agree on two important points: (a) courtroom appearances generally are traumatic for children, and (b) children have no special, constitutionally protected rights within the legal system.

As chapter 5 details, testifying in court generally is stressful for children, as well as for adults, although it is not necessarily incapacitating. In fact, in some cases, the experience may be simultaneously traumatic and therapeutic.

Also, clinicians, researchers, and jurists alike have recognized the importance of protecting children from unnecessary harm. For example, statutes in each of the 50 states make the abuse of children illegal (Fraser, 1981). And, as the *Craig* opinion notes, "[T]hat a significant majority of States has enacted statutes to protect child witnesses from the trauma of giving testimony in child abuse cases attests to the widespread belief in the importance of such a public policy" (p. 683). Likewise, in its decision in *Globe Newspaper Co. v. Superior Court* (1982), the Supreme Court held that a state's interest in the physical and psychological well-being of a victim of tender years was sufficiently weighty to justify depriving the press and public of their constitutional right to attend criminal trials (where the trial court makes a case-specific finding that closure of the trial is necessary to protect the welfare of the minor witness). More recently, in *Maryland v. Craig* (1990), the Court concluded that a state's interest in the well-being of a child abuse victim may be sufficiently important to outweigh, "at least in some cases, a defendant's right to face his or her accusers in court" (p. 683).

There are other encouraging developments as well. In 1977 the federal government formally recognized the special concerns of child witnesses by funding two programs specifically devoted to children as victim-witnesses: Children's National Hospital and Medical Center in Washington, DC, and the Sexual Assault Center at Harborview Medical Center in Seattle, WA (Berliner, 1985). Berliner (1985) notes:

> The goal of the programs at these institutions was to develop social, medical and legal responses to child victims which recognized and accommodated the children's special needs and encouraged their successful participation in the criminal justice process. The programs were identified as national models and were awarded exemplary status in 1981. (p. 169)

More recently, the federal government's Office of Juvenile Justice and Delinquency Prevention (OJJDP) funded research development projects in four jurisdictions: Polk County (Des Moines),

IA; Ramsey County (St. Paul), MN; Erie County (Buffalo), NY; and San Diego County, CA. These programs are designed to improve the way the judicial system treats child victims. Through this project, OJJDP hopes to provide carefully tested approaches that can be used to change prosecution policies and practices so that they become more supportive of child victims and witnesses.[4]

Despite these encouraging trends, however, the fact remains that children have no *constitutionally* protected rights to be shielded from harm. It is ludicrous to assume that the justice system would not want to protect children as long as the defendant's due process rights are not abrogated. But as the recent decisions in *Coy* and *Craig* suggest, it is difficult indeed to draw the line of demarcation between protection of young witnesses and protection of the rights of defendants. As one legal commentator notes, "[I]t would be a horrifying concept if the search for truth was compromised by any desire to protect children" (L. McGough, personal communication, 1990).

Unresolved Questions

The central question that remains unanswered, then, is this: What alternative procedures designed to protect child witnesses from traumatization at trial are acceptable? In answering this question, two corollaries must be considered: Should limits be placed on the cross-examination of child witnesses? Should video-taped testimony be allowed when a specific child has *not* been shown to be likely to experience trauma from testifying in court?

Should limits be placed on the cross-examination of child witnesses? As discussed earlier, cross-examination is a right of constitutional magnitude, designed to protect the defendant from false allegation. Therefore, procedures to limit cross-examination must be considered especially carefully (see, for example, *Maryland v. Craig,* 1990).

Refusing to limit cross-examination of child witnesses also may subvert justice. When the child is confused or intimidated by opposing counsel, his or her testimony on critical points may *appear* unreliable. Thus, protection of the defendant's constitutional right to cross-examination may in fact hinder the truth-seeking function of the court. Therefore, it is our considered opinion that limits should be placed on the cross-examination of witnesses of tender years. Certainly bullying and intimidation should be

curtailed, but the more subtle ways of confusing young witnesses
described above also should be avoided.

*Should videotaped testimony be allowed when a specific child has
not been shown to be likely to experience trauma from testifying in
court?* Coy and Craig offer important guidelines with regard to
confrontation:

1. "The Confrontation Clause guarantees the defendant a face-to-face
   meeting with witnesses appearing before the trier of fact" (*Coy v.
   Iowa*, 1988, p. 280, citing *Kentucky v. Stincer*, 1987).
2. "We have never held, however, that the Confrontation Clause guarantees criminal defendants the *absolute* right to a face-to-face
   meeting with witnesses against them at trial" (*Maryland v. Craig*,
   1990, p. 677).
3. "A State's interest in the physical and psychological well-being of
   child abuse victims may be sufficiently important to outweigh, at
   least in some cases, a defendant's right to face his or her accusers
   in court" (*Maryland v. Craig*, 1990, p. 683).
4. "The requisite necessity finding must be case specific. The trial
   court must hear evidence and determine whether the procedure's
   use is necessary to protect the particular child witness's welfare;
   find that the child would be traumatized, not by the courtroom
   generally, but by the defendant's presence; and find that the emotional distress suffered by the child in the defendant's presence is
   more than de minimis" (*Maryland v. Craig*, 1990, p. 674).

The unanswered question, however, is: What constitutes requisite showing? Clearly, *Craig* establishes that the trauma likely to
be experienced must relate directly to the presence of the defendant and must be more than minimal. But how much more than
minimal? The *Craig* opinion concluded that:

> where necessary to protect a child witness from trauma that would
> be caused by testifying in the physical presence of the defendant *at
> least where such trauma would impair the child's ability to commu-
> nicate,* the Confrontation Clause does not prohibit use of a procedure
> that, despite the absence of face-to-face confrontation, ensures the
> reliability of the evidence by subjecting it to rigorous adversarial
> testing and thereby preserves the essence of effective confrontation.
> (p. 686)

The boundaries for the admissibility of videotaped testimony are set: on the one hand, "more than mere nervousness or excitement or some reluctance to testify," and on the other hand, inability to communicate (*Craig,* 1990, p. 685). But the middle ground remains to be tested.

Paths to Resolution

Allowing the use of alternative procedures to enhance communication (see Issue #1 above) has the twin result of reducing traumatization. Therefore, we believe that, whenever possible, procedures should be implemented to reduce the likely stress of a child witness so long as they do not directly assault the defendant's right to confrontation. Specifically, we advocate the following approaches:

1. *Allow children to testify via live-broadcast videotape.* This technique reduces the distress likely to be experienced by children who must face alleged perpetrators while protecting the defendants' constitutional rights (see chapter 5 and Issue #1 above).

2. *Limit the techniques used during cross-examination of child witnesses.* Require cross-examining attorneys to use simple, clear language and to eliminate attempts to confuse or cajole child witnesses. Such techniques are as unfair as are deliberate attempts to bully witnesses; they subvert the truth-seeking function of the court. Due process *cannot* be served if child witnesses are traumatized and are not afforded the opportunity to give complete and accurate testimony.

3. *Prepare all child witnesses for the experience of providing testimony.* This recommendation should go without saying, as it has no constitutional implications.

Issue #4: Defendants' rights. What rights should defendants have in cases involving child witnesses?

Areas of Agreement

Our justice system assumes the innocence of the defendant and has developed a number of constitutional rules to ensure protection of defendants' rights. There is no dispute that, in most circumstances, we should uphold the defendant's rights to public trial and to confront accusatory witnesses. Jurists and social scientists agree, however, that the defendant's right to a public trial may be abridged when the state has an overriding public concern (see chapter 5).

Unresolved Questions

The central question that remains unanswered is this: What are the parameters of confrontation? The recent Supreme Court decisions in the *Coy* and *Craig* cases begin to carve out the special exceptions in this area. But, as noted above, there still is room for interpretation. Surely common sense dictates that the defendant does not have the right to traumatize accusatory witnesses. Although children are not constitutionally protected from harm, the state does have an overriding interest in shielding them from hurt. It is equally clear that the defendant has a right to confront accusatory witnesses and that this right must be vigorously protected. We argue, however, that the right is misapplied when zealous cross-examination leads to confusion and distress of child witnesses. The allegations of young witnesses *should* be put to the test of rigorous questioning, but not questioning that seeks to confuse the witness or to twist his or her words. Such techniques are questionable with adult witnesses, and travesties of justice when applied to child witnesses.

Finally, the courts are not unanimous in their opinions concerning whether the defendant has the right to see the child witness *in vivo*. *Coy* argues for face-to-face confrontation, while the more recent decision in *Craig* suggests that in individual cases meeting the requirements outlined by the Court (e.g., sufficient indicators of trauma, inability to communicate), the defendant's right pales.

Paths to Resolution

We believe that the Court is correct in requiring case-by-case showing of individual need. Some children are quite capable of and willing to testify in court without the use of special, alternative procedures. Those children who can face the defendant in open court should do so. But we believe that the courts must clarify the gray area with regard to "requisite showing": How much likely trauma must be demonstrated before alternative procedures are invoked? We believe that adhering to the standard defined in the Maryland Statute (Md. Cts. & Jud. Proc. Code Ann. § 9-102(a)(1)(ii) [1989]) in *Maryland v. Craig*—that the child witness must "suffer serious emotional distress such that the child cannot reasonably communicate"—is too stringent. In our considered opinion, if the distress likely to be experienced by the child witness restricts his or her ability to "tell the truth, the whole truth, and nothing but the truth," special exceptions should be acceptable.

SUMMARY

In this chapter we revisited the four psycholegal issues raised in chapter 1, in light of the scientific evidence presented in previous chapters. Although the disparate purposes of law and the social sciences sometimes make them difficult companions, we argue that justice may be served better in the case of child witnesses if evidence from the two fields is considered.

Ample experimental evidence supports the competence of most children as witnesses. However, the competence of a particular child witness depends upon a variety of factors: age, centrality of the information to be remembered and reported, motivations to be truthful or dishonest, and characteristics of the questioner and of the courtroom situation.

Four critical questions regarding the competence of children as witnesses remain unresolved: (a) How much trauma must the courtroom experience engender in child witnesses before reliability of the testimony is compromised? (b) How much should child witnesses be led on direct examination? (c) Should evidence obtained using anatomical dolls be admissible? (d) Can child witnesses handle the sophisticated techniques commonly used during cross-examination?

On the first issue, our position is that if the child meets the other criteria for competence and if he or she is able to communicate effectively about the incidents in question in some appropriate setting (e.g., judge's chambers, neutral office, on videotape), the truth-seeking function of the court is enhanced by using alternative procedures to obtain the child's testimony. On the second issue professionals disagree about how much a child witness should be led on direct examination. On this point, several factors must be considered: (a) degree of suggestion, (b) centrality of information to be remembered, and (c) strength of memory. The stronger the suggestion, the more peripheral the details to be recalled; the weaker the original memory, the more likely it is that leading questions will result in inaccurate testimony. Our view is that leading questions should be avoided at all stages of interviewing children—from the initial interview through cross-examination.

On the third issue, the use of so-called anatomical dolls is not universally condoned by the courts when child witnesses provide testimony. Courts should be made aware of this fact and should be informed of the attendant risks in interpretation of dolls play. We believe that if jurors are properly educated about the benefits and risks of clinical dolls play, they should be able to consider the evidence presented, giving such evidence the weight they deem appropriate.

On the fourth issue, attorneys have developed a number of cross-examination techniques specifically designed to baffle child witnesses. We argue that such methods are inherently unfair and subvert the truth-seeking function of the court.

With regard to the competence of child witnesses, we offer the following policy recommendations: (a) Allow the use of alternative procedures to enhance communication of child witnesses, (b) reduce or eliminate the use of leading questions when interviewing children, and (c) use simple language when questioning witnesses of tender years.

In the area of credibility, both social scientists and legal professionals recognize that children tend not to be held in high regard as observers and witnesses. Two central questions must be addressed: (a) How can we determine the accuracy of the testimony provided by child witnesses? (b) Should expert witnesses be employed to inform the court about the credibility of children's testimony?

Recently, clinicians, researchers, and legal scholars alike have suggested some promising approaches to the dilemma of assessing the accuracy of a child's report. One technique, statement validity analysis (SVA), has been used widely in Germany and offers encouraging possibilities. Some researchers offer sets of criteria to consider when assessing the truthfulness of a child's account of sexual abuse, and these also seem promising. We urge the courts to consider the value of such evidence.

Professionals representing both law and social science disagree about the usefulness of behavioral scientists as experts. By definition, an expert witness is any person with special knowledge in a particular sphere. The testimony of an expert should help the trier of fact in deciding a disputed issue. But an expert must not usurp the role of the judge or jury in deciding a verdict. The problem is that determining when scientific evidence is probative as opposed to prejudicial is no easy matter.

Most courts use one of two generally accepted tests of admissibility for scientific evidence: the *Frye* test (more conservative) and the relevancy approach (more liberal). The former requires that evidence to be presented by an expert must have gained "general acceptance" in the field. According to the latter, admissibility of scientific evidence depends upon a three-step process: (a) determine the probative value of the evidence, (b) identify the relevant dangers of the proposed testimony, and (c) balance the probative value of the testimony against the identified dangers. Some have attempted to find a middle ground between the excessive strictness of the *Frye* test and the unwarranted leniency of the relevancy approach, but such efforts have met with mixed results.

We argue that social scientists and jurists should maintain their distinctive roles. We agree that social scientists should be employed to inform the court but must not usurp the fact-finding role of the jury. We believe that expert testimony regarding children's testimony can be a valuable piece of information for jurors to consider. We encourage expert witnesses to discuss the factors that impinge upon the accuracy of a child's allegations but to refrain from commenting on the accuracy of a specific child's report. We also believe that the justice system should consider use of court-appointed expert witnesses to inform the triers of fact in a nonpartisan, nonadversarial fashion.

It is agreed that courtroom appearances generally are traumatic for children. Recently, clinicians, researchers, and jurists alike have recognized the importance of protecting children from unnecessary harm when they give evidence. However, the fact remains that child witnesses have no constitutionally protected rights to be shielded from harm. Thus, what alternative procedures designed to protect child witnesses from traumatization at trial should be considered acceptable?

We argue that limits should be placed on the cross-examination of children at trial. When the child is confused or intimidated by opposing counsel, the testimony on critical points may appear unreliable. Protection of the defendant's constitutional rights to cross-examination may in fact hinder the truth-seeking function of the court.

Moreover, allowing the use of alternative procedures to enhance communication also results in reducing traumatization. Whenever possible, we believe such procedures should be implemented. Specifically, we advocate use of the following approaches: (a) Allow children at risk for traumatization to testify via live-broadcast videotape, (b) limit the techniques used during cross-examination of child witnesses, and (c) prepare all child witnesses for the experience of providing testimony.

There is no dispute between jurists and social scientists that in most circumstances we should uphold the defendant's rights to public trial and to confront accusatory witnesses. But what are the limits of confrontation? We believe that the courts are correct in requiring case-by-case showing of individual need to use procedures that infringe upon the defendant's rights. But the courts must determine just how much trauma a specific child must experience before invoking special procedures. In our opinion, if the distress restricts the child witness's ability to "tell the truth, the whole truth, and nothing but the truth," special exceptions should be acceptable.

NOTES

1. Note that all of these undesirable practices occurred in the investigation of the McMartin Preschool case.

2. A 1985 survey in North Carolina found that less than half of the child protective workers using anatomical dolls for interviews had *any* training (cited in Levy, 1989).

3. A survey of judges and attorneys conducted in 1980 by the National Center for State Courts found that 44 percent of those responding had encountered scientific evidence in at least 30 percent of their cases (cited in Imwinkelried, 1981).

4. This project now is drawing to a close. Results of at least a preliminary nature should be published relatively soon.

7

In the Aftermath of *McMartin:* Society's Rights to Accurate Testimony

The Issue of Accuracy Revisited: Whose Responsibility Is It?

What Psychologists, Psychiatrists, and Social Workers Need To Do

Clinicians
Preparing for involvement in court proceedings
Knowing the relevant laws
Reviewing the standards for and the pitfalls of serving as an expert witness
Interviewing the child • Preparing the child for the courtroom experience

Expert witnesses

Researchers

What Interviewers Need To Do
Preparing for the interview
Conducting the interview(s)
Assessing the credibility of the child's statement

What Officers of the Court Need To Do

Investigators • *Judges* • *Attorneys* • *Jurors*

Policy Recommendations

Conclusions

Summary

A criminal justice system which does not accommodate a whole class of victims, especially those who are the most vulnerable, helpless, and deserving of protection, does not serve society well. It is intolerable that the opportunity for justice so unevenly depends on the state where the child is victimized. The basic procedural changes should be immediately extended to all jurisdictions.

(L. Berliner, social worker, Sexual Assault Center, University of Washington, 1985, p. 179)

While I have no desire to see sexual abusers turned loose to prey on innocent children, I similarly have no desire to live under a system that will guarantee the conviction of all persons against whom such allegations are made. The recent rash of legislative proposals in this area of the law leads me to the conclusion that this is indeed the direction in which we are presently headed. I personally find it very difficult to explain to an individual against whom an unfounded allegation of sexual abuse has been made, that he or she must be convicted, forever labeled a child molester, and sentenced to prison, so we can thereby assure ourselves that the truly guilty will also share that fate.

(Roy N. Howson, public defender and former prosecutor, King County, Washington, 1985, p. 6)

THE ISSUE OF ACCURACY REVISITED: WHOSE RESPONSIBILITY IS IT?

Box 7.1 reviews several recent books on the topic of child abuse in the United States. While these volumes approach their subject from differing perspectives, on one point the message is unanimous: Children are victimized by crime in staggering numbers. Estimates of sexual abuse alone suggest that from 3 to 38 percent of children experience this trauma (Whitcomb et al., 1985). For example, in two counties in Maine, populated by 100,000 individuals, a sexual assault hotline receives 20 to 25 calls per month just from 12- to 18-year-olds (V. Ritchie, Washington and Hancock

Counties, personal communication, 1990). During the 1980s, child protection agencies across the country received allegations of child maltreatment (of various forms) affecting an estimated 1.5-4 million children annually (Gothard, 1990; Whitcomb et al., 1985). The FBI's Uniform Crime Reports, which publishes crime statistics contributed by nearly 16,000 law enforcement agencies covering 97 percent of the American population, notes that nearly 5 percent of the victims of murder are children under the age of 15. While these facts are sobering indeed, they surely reflect only the tip of the iceberg. Whitcomb et al. (1985) summarize the situation as follows:

> The Bureau of Justice Statistics estimates that only one-third of all crimes, and 47 percent of violent crimes, are reported to police. Moreover, young victims are only half as likely as the total population to report crimes to police. (p. 2)

Even when crimes against children are reported, only a portion of the cases result in charges being filed. A still smaller number result in cases being tried in court. In other words, large numbers of perpetrators remain at large, victimizing and revictimizing children.

Society pays for this set of circumstances in a variety of ways. Children who have been victimized suffer mental health consequences. Some engage in delinquent activity, for which we all pay the price. Others suffer a private torment, often resulting in poor academic performance, problems in developing and maintaining healthy social relationships, stunting of personal potential, and/or serious emotional problems. Clearly, such victims pay a heavy toll, but society also loses, in an albeit less direct manner. We pay for remedial programs and special counselors in school, increased health care costs, and loss of productivity in the workplace. When children are victimized, we all suffer the consequences.

Some might argue that the cure is simple: Bring more cases to trial. This response is too simplistic. Merely bringing a case to trial does not ensure that the cost is less devastating. If the evidence presented at trial is weak, poorly gathered or organized, or confusing, justice may not result. The McMartin Preschool case illustrates this point. Two trials, spanning more than three years and costing the taxpayers nearly $15 million, failed to produce a single

Box 7.1

A Selected Bibliography of Recent Books on Child Abuse

Recently, a number of books have appeared that seek to inform the general reading public about child abuse. Five of these are described below.

Hechler, D. (1988). *The battle and the backlash: The child sexual abuse war.* Lexington, MA: Lexington. (Paperback, $9.95).

This is an objective book, written by an investigative reporter. Several case studies are described in great detail, cases not widely publicized in the media. Also, more publicized cases are covered in depth, such as the Jordan, Minnesota case (10 pages) and the McMartin Preschool case (20 pages). The author seeks to deal with issues that span a number of cases, including the denial and minimization of child sexual abuse, the difficulty in prosecuting abusers, the legitimate rights of defendants, the proper role of expert witnesses, and the role of the media. An appendix contains excerpts from interviews with five individuals of divergent opinions on these issues; one of them is a defense attorney who represented a McMartin Preschool teacher who was a defendant for a period of time.

Dziech, B. W., & Schudson, Judge C. B. (1989). *On trial: America's courts and their treatment of sexually abused children.* Boston: Beacon. (Hardcover, $24.95).

Written by a professor of language arts (who is an experienced trade-book author) and a Wisconsin circuit court judge, this book is pro-children. The emphasis is on the failure of the courts to recognize children's abilities and needs, along with the urgency of reforms to facilitate justice for those children who are victims. Chapters are devoted to a history of treatment of children by the courts and on the knowledge we have from developmental psychology about children's language and comprehension skills. A chapter is given to a case so disguised that all we know about its location is that it was in the Northeast. The Jordan (Minnesota), McMartin Preschool, and Country Walk cases also are described.

Much of value may be found in this book, with many nuggets of interesting information. Unfortunately, errors also are present. For example, *voir doir* is substituted for *voir dire* (p. 128) and the authors incorrectly describe Kohlberg's Stage 1 as "conventional morality"

(p. 55). Controversial positions sometimes are offered as givens, as in this statement: "Despite his indisputable contribution to the modern age, Freud either misunderstood or intentionally rejected evidence about sexual abuse of female children" (p. 6). There is much overlap with Hechler's book. An appendix contains a state-by-state listing of resources for victims.

Crewdson, J. (1988). *By silence betrayed: Sexual abuse of children in America.* New York: Harper & Row. (Paperback, $8.95).

Written by a former reporter and editor for the *Chicago Tribune,* who spent a year researching the topic, this book has goals and an orientation similar to those by Dziech and Schudson and by Hechler. It has somewhat more coverage of abusers and pedophiles (separate chapters on each) than do the other two, however. There is chapter-length coverage of the Jordan and McMartin Preschool cases. It is empathetic to Jeffrey Masson (who claimed that Freud abandoned the seduction theory) but open-minded on the issue. Many cases are described briefly.

Although each of these five books is quite well written, this one is especially readable.

Hollingsworth, J. (1986). *Unspeakable acts.* New York: Congdon and Weed. (Hardcover, $18.95; now available in paperback).

Coverage of the Country Walk Babysitting Service child sexual abuse case in Florida, one of the first to receive nationwide publicity. The account of the case, chronologically organized, is long (592 pages) but readable. There is extensive coverage of the trial. An index would have made the book more useful. It is recommended as an example of a detailed account of one case from its beginning to its end.

Johnson, J. (1990). *What Lisa knew: The truth and lies of the Steinberg case.* New York: G. P. Putnam. (Hardcover, $22.95).

This book is of less relevance to the topic of children as eye-witnesses and of more relevance to the topic of physical abuse of children by their parents. Lisa Steinberg was a first-grader at the time she was illegally adopted by Joel Steinberg and Hedda Nussbaum. In January 1989, in a highly publicized trial, Joel Steinberg was found guilty of first-degree manslaughter in the death of Lisa Steinberg. The book is useful because of its concern with the general theme of physical and sexual abuse of children. Coverage of the trial is interpretive and provocative.

conviction. In the process, jurors devoted more than two years of their lives to the case, three individuals associated with the case died under suspicious circumstances, the key defendants spent several years in jail despite their presumed innocence, the lives of those accused were ruined emotionally and financially, and the children who claimed victimization felt crushed by a system that had failed, in their eyes, to produce justice. Clearly, neither lack of prosecution nor overzealous prosecution is acceptable. In either case, the price paid by all members of society is too great. What is the answer? Of course, there is no simple solution. We believe that one important piece of the solution is to achieve accuracy of reporting. Each member of the system must endeavor to seek the truth in a given case, eschewing preconceived notions of outcome and fanatic advocacy. Accuracy must be the responsibility of every player in the system. Accordingly, we offer the following suggestions for members of the legal, law enforcement, and helping professions.

WHAT PSYCHOLOGISTS, PSYCHIATRISTS, AND SOCIAL WORKERS NEED TO DO

Mental health professionals may serve different functions in legal cases involving child witnesses. They may be clinicians who assess the capabilities of children or who are engaged to help heal traumatized children, experts called to testify about children generally or regarding specific issues in a particular case, or researchers who study children as legal witnesses.

Clinicians

Clinicians may work with child witnesses in a variety of professional capacities. A psychologist or psychiatrist may be retained specifically to assess the competence of a particular child to give testimony in court. Alternatively, a mental health professional may be involved in an ongoing therapeutic relationship with a child. During the course of therapy, the child may reveal information that ultimately will lead to a criminal trial in which the child may be called as a witness. In either case, the clinician must take several steps in working with the child who may be called to testify.

Preparing for Involvement in Court Proceedings

Knowing the relevant laws. Whether the professional person, the client, or both will testify in pretrial hearings or at the trial, the clinician must become familiar with relevant statutes for the state in which he or she is practicing. As Melton and Wilcox (1989) note, "[p]sychologists must be knowledgeable about diverse areas of law if they are to provide much assistance in the law's response to the needs of children and families" (p. 1215). The same may be said for psychiatrists and social workers. Mental health professionals need to understand the relevant laws of their state and how local authorities tend to interpret these statutes. They should be knowledgeable about laws in the following areas:

1. *Children's competence to testify.* All states have developed guidelines concerning children's competence to testify; clinicians must be aware of these. It is important to know whether the state relies upon a given age in determining competence of the child to testify or whether it follows the Federal Rules of Evidence approach.

2. *Use of alternative procedures designed to reduce traumatization of child witnesses.* Some jurisdictions have passed legislation regarding the use of alternative procedures designed to reduce the traumatization of child witnesses (such as videotaped testimony in lieu of a courtroom appearance; see chapter 6). Becoming conversant with these laws reduces the possibility of inadvertently tainting evidence—evidence that then could be excluded from the trial. Without such evidence the outcome of the case might be doomed, illustrating the fact that ignorance of the law in this area could have devastating consequences.

3. *Defendants' constitutional rights.* As Melton and Wilcox (1989) caution, ". . . in the desire to 'do something' to help families in crisis or children who may have been victimized, psychologists must be careful to avoid inadvertent intrusions on civil rights" (p. 1216). It is essential to know the rights extended to the defendant and how these rights have been interpreted in case law (see for example, *Coy v. Iowa* [1988], *Idaho v. Wright* [1990], *Kentucky v. Stincer* [1987], *Maryland v. Craig* [1990]; see also chapter 5 of this volume).

4. *Admissibility of hearsay evidence.* Mental health professionals should become familiar with the circumstances under which hearsay evidence is allowed in child witness cases. Recall (from chapter 5) that the hearsay rule excludes statements made outside the

courtroom because such evidence is considered to be less trustworthy than live, in-court testimony. Under certain circumstances, however,—especially in cases involving children as witnesses— exceptions to the hearsay rule are permitted and even encouraged. Professional persons should become familiar with the commonly accepted exceptions to the hearsay rule and how they are applied in a given jurisdiction. They must know the "indicia of reliability" of the hearsay evidence required in their area and how "particularized trustworthiness" of the testimony must be demonstrated.

Reviewing the standards for and the pitfalls of serving as an expert witness. Clinicians may or may not be called to give expert testimony in cases involving child witnesses. Certainly, it is better to be prepared for the eventuality of being asked to give evidence. Even if clinicians do not take the stand, it is prudent for them to become knowledgeable about evidentiary issues, for such information may prevent inadvertent tainting of the evidence provided by the young client. Box 7.2 suggests several valuable resources for learning the ins and outs of giving expert testimony. We recommend that mental health professionals become familiar with such resources.

Interviewing the Child

See p. 236, "What Interviewers Need to Do."

Preparing the Child for the Courtroom Experience

It is the attorney's job to prepare the child for testifying in court or via videotape. The attorney should explain the roles of the various players in the system, as well as the legal maneuverings that are likely to occur (see below). Still, it helps most children to have multiple explanations, assuming the descriptions offered are not contradictory. Thus, clinicians may find themselves in a particularly good position to provide helpful information and support to children who will testify.

Cora Lynn Goldsborough, a Virginia psychologist with 35 years experience in child-clinical practice, offers these comments:

> Many therapists say they feel that if there is a relationship between therapist and the child, then testifying in court will interfere with the relationship. I feel just the opposite. I find that oftentimes the therapeutic relationship is strengthened in that the child feels that you are willing to go into court and stand up for them.

Box 7.2

Serving as an Expert Witness: Valuable Resources

Alberts, F., & Blau, T. (1988). *The cue book: The courtroom companion.* Tampa, FL: Psychological Seminars.

American Bar Association. (1989). *ABA criminal justice mental health standards* (Part III: Pretrial evaluations and expert testimony). Washington, DC: Author.

Appelbaum, P. S. (1987). In the wake of *Ake:* The ethics of expert testimony in an advocate's world. *Bulletin of the American Academy of Psychiatry and Law, 15,* 15-25.

Blau, T. H. (1984). *The psychologist as expert witness.* New York: John Wiley.

Expert witness: Psychology and beyond. (1989, August). (Cassette Recording No. 89-090). Washington, DC: American Psychological Association.

McGough, L. (In press). Expert testimony: Assessing a child's credibility and interpreting behaviors. In L. McGough, *Fragile voices: Child witnesses in the American legal system* (Chapter 9). New Haven, CT: Yale University Press.

Nichols, J. F. (1980, July). The marital/family therapist as an expert witness: Some thoughts and suggestions. *Journal of Marital and Family Therapy,* 293-299.

I tell the child I'm going to testify, and I ask the child if there are any things we have been talking about that they don't want me to bring up; or if there are any things they do want me to talk about. I tell them I'm going to go to tell the judge what you're like, what you're thinking about, and feeling. And I explain a little bit about what goes on: . . . the judge listens to all kinds of people and makes a decision. This is why I am there, to make the judge understand about you. ("Telling it," March 1989, pp. 1, 3)

Sometimes it is permissible for the professional person to accompany the child to court when he or she testifies. In other cases, this practice is neither possible nor permissible. For example, if subpoenaed to serve as an expert witness in the case, the individual may be excluded from the courtroom while the child testifies. If the professional cannot accompany the client and no friend or relative of the child is available to do so, it may be possible to arrange for a court-appointed "special advocate" to assist the young witness.[1]

It is imperative that children receive as much support as possible when they testify in court. As chapter 5 discusses, giving evidence at trial is a demanding experience even for the most sophisticated of witnesses; for children, the process tends to be both stressful and baffling.

Expert Witnesses

In the event that the mental health worker volunteers to serve as an expert witness or is called to do so by the court or by one of the parties in the dispute, we suggest that he or she read the materials recommended in Box 7.2 and follow these guidelines:

1. *Understand the role of the expert witness.* Your role as an expert witness is to inform the court of the relevant issues and to make the existence of some fact in question more or less likely. Although you may be called by one party in the dispute, your role is not to serve as a zealous advocate for that side. The *American Bar Association Criminal Justice Mental Health Standards* (1989) speak clearly on this issue:

> Mental health or mental retardation professionals, like other expert witnesses, serve as impartial sources of information for and assistance to triers of fact. Therefore, their expert opinions should rest on impartial, objective evaluations and reflect clinical findings derived impartially and objectively. Evaluations, clinical findings, and mental health or mental retardation expert opinions should not be affected or modified according to the partisan needs of the attorneys who elicit them at trial. . . . [T]he professional role of expert witness occupies a middle ground between an adversary witness and a wholly impartial and disinterested source of data. (Standard 3.14, p. 150)

MacDonald (1969, cited in Nichols, 1980) similarly states:

> The medical witness should never take sides in a case, but should endeavor to be fair, impartial, and free from prejudice. He should regard himself as an independent witness for the court and should not act as an auxiliary advocate for the prosecution or defense. (p. 293)

Indeed, attorneys who fail to explain this role or to adequately prepare expert witnesses may face charges of ineffective assistance of counsel and may be subject to professional discipline (*ABA Criminal Justice Mental Health Standards,* p. 150).

2. *Understand the concepts of "confidentiality" and "privilege" and how they are addressed in a court of law.* "Confidentiality" refers to the information protected under applicable law by the professional-client relationship. Information that is "privileged" is protected from being divulged. Be aware that there are two categories of privilege, "qualified" and "absolute." A qualified privilege can be waived by the client, whereas an absolute privilege is maintained and not waived (Nichols, 1980). Prevailing state law distinguishes one from the other, but surprisingly few professionals understand the parameters of confidentiality and privilege.

3. *Know the circumstances for providing testimony.* If expertise is volunteered, it is sufficient to be cognizant of the confidentiality requirements. If the professional is issued a subpoena, however, he or she must be able to interpret its meaning. There are two forms of such an "invitation": a *subpoena* and a *subpoena duces tecum.* Nichols (1980) clarifies the difference:

> A "subpoena" is an instrument drawn by the attorney and issued by the court clerk requiring the therapist to appear at a certain time, date and place for the purpose of possibly giving sworn testimony regarding the patient or the patient's family. A "subpoena duces tecum" is a subpoena which also requires the possible production of records in the possession or under the control of the therapist. (p. 293)

4. *Consult with all relevant parties.* Expert witnesses should obtain from the client (or the client's legal guardian) a signed authorization form for the release of information. They should request a pretrial conference with the attorney who issued the subpoena to determine what will be expected in court. In addition, they should advise the client of the results of this conference and, if necessary, consult their own attorneys.

5. *Prepare for the trial.* Experts should prepare two files, one that includes unaltered original documents (for which there are signed release forms) and one that includes clean copies of the original documents that can be left with the court. The original documents never should be changed; if changes or clarifications are required, supplemental records should be included.

Each professional person also must determine a fee for serving as an expert witness. The amount may be a lump sum or may be based upon an hourly wage, but never should it be contingent upon the outcome of the case. Attaching a fee to the verdict labels the expert clearly as an advocate, not as an impartial educator.

    6. *Maintain professional demeanor in the courtroom.* Nichols (1980) offers a helpful list of witness stand "dos and don'ts":

1. Always tell the truth. One slight falsehood destroys the credibility of the therapist's testimony.
2. Listen to the question that is asked and answer only the question that is asked. Any other answer may be objected to as being "non-responsive."
3. If on cross-examination a therapist's answer requires further explanation in order to put the answer into proper context, ask to explain the answer. If the request is denied, the patient's attorney will make a note to ask the therapist to explain the answer on re-direct examination.
4. Do not be an advocate. The therapist is called to the witness stand to give impartial objective testimony and not to be the advocate for the patient. Advocacy is for the attorney.
5. Wait until the complete question is asked before attempting to answer. "Eager beavers" generally turn into advocates.
6. Do not "false start" in answering. A "false start" is when the therapist attempts to answer the question without really knowing what the answer is going to be ahead of time and, upon further consideration starts over again in an attempt to answer the question. If the question asked is not clear, have it repeated so that it is understood before attempting to answer. If the therapist does not ask that the question be repeated, it will be assumed that the question was understood.
7. On cross-examination, do not look at the patient's attorney before answering. The patient's attorney cannot answer the question for you.
8. Dress neatly and professionally.
9. Be polite and non-defensive.
10. Be prepared to testify as to the cost of time taken to come to court, the amount of any outstanding bills, and the fairness and reasonableness of the bills and time taken for testimony.
11. Upon being released from the witness stand, the therapist should thank the judge for allowing him to be put on the witness stand. . . . This will leave a favorable impression on the judge and the therapist may be called back to the witness stand later on in the case.
12. Do not stay in the court and listen to the rest of the testimony after being released from the witness stand unless asked to stay by the court or attorneys. This shows partiality. (p. 296)

Researchers

Although the topic of children as legal witnesses has received periodic attention in the professional literature for decades, only recently has it received such sustained interest. In 1984 the *Journal of Social Issues* published a volume devoted entirely to the topic of "The Child Witness." Numerous articles in several journals, including *Law and Human Behavior* and *Behavioral Sciences and the Law,* have addressed the topic. In addition, books on children as legal witnesses are beginning to appear with some regularity. (See for example, Ceci, Ross, & Toglia, 1989 [*Perspectives on children's testimony*]; Ceci et al., 1987 [*Children's eyewitness memory*]; McGough, in press [*Fragile voices: Child witnesses in the American legal system*]; Myers, 1987 [*Child witness law and practice*].) Professional meetings also have centered on this issue. (See for example, Ceci, 1989, Cornell Conference on the Suggestibility of Children's Recollections, June 1989[2], papers and symposia presented at the American Psychology-Law Society meeting, April, 1990[3]) Clearly, the topic of children as legal witnesses has come of age.

This volume (and others) attest to the fact that great strides have been made in understanding the abilities and shortcomings of children as witnesses in court. But gaps in our knowledge remain. We believe it would be profitable for psycholegal researchers to focus on the following areas of inquiry and empirical questions:

Competence

1. What factors influence the child's ability to communicate at trial? Presence or absence of the defendant? Number of court officials and/or spectators in attendance? Visibility of a videocamera? Presence or absence of support persons (e.g., relatives, therapist, court-appointed advocate)? Special adaptations in the appearance of the courtroom?
2. How do these factors interact with age or other characteristics of the child in determining ability to communicate at trial?

Credibility

1. What factors influence truth-telling in children? Offers of reward and/or threats by the defendant? By a non-offending parent? By an attorney or other officer of the court?
2. Are these factors age-dependent?

3. Is it possible to assess successfully the validity of statements made by children (or other witnesses, for that matter)? What factors reliably point to validity of the statement?

4. Is there "general acceptance" among the scientific community (as is required by the *Frye* test) of what constitutes a credible statement by a child witness?

Traumatization

1. Under which specific circumstances do child witnesses feel traumatized? During the preliminary interviews and hearings? During the deposition? During videotaping? At trial?

2. Specifically, how does traumatization (at different levels) affect the child's ability to communicate and to provide accurate testimony?

3. What specific procedures help children weather the courtroom experience and thereby communicate effectively and accurately?

Answers to these questions would help us to determine whether additional reforms of the system are required to serve the truth-seeking function of the court.

WHAT INTERVIEWERS NEED TO DO

In the course of a legal proceeding, police officers, mental health professionals, attorneys, and others may question children. The tasks of the interviewer are likely to include the following: to enlist the cooperation of the child, to assess the situation by gathering facts and data, to assess the competence of the child in providing information in a legal setting, to determine the accuracy of the child's account, to formulate a plan of action, to provide emotional support, and to evaluate any immediate danger to the child. In other words, the interviewer must wear several hats simultaneously. While it is vital that the trust and cooperation of the child be gained so that he or she feels comfortable sharing difficult or embarrassing information, it is equally imperative not to lead the child through inappropriate questioning or to empathize with the child to the point of losing objectivity. Box 7.3 suggests several sources of information on conducting successful interviews of children who will serve as legal witnesses.

One helpful approach is proposed by Brooks and Milchman (1990), who offer the "clinician-as-researcher" model. The authors suggest that, when conducting interviews, clinicians (and others)

Box 7.3

Conducting Interviews: Helpful Resources

Jones, D. P. H., & McQuiston, M. G. (1988). *Interviewing the sexually abused child.* London: Gaskell.

Myers, J. E. B. (1988). Examining the young witness: Paint the child into your corner. *Family Advocate, 10,* 42-47.

Myers, J. E. B. (1987). *Child witness law and practice* (Chapter 2: Interviewing the child witness— preparation for testimony). New York: John Wiley.

Perry, N. W., & Teply, L. L. (1984-1985). Interviewing, counseling, and in-court examination of children: Practical approaches for attorneys. *Creighton Law Review, 18,* 1369-1426.

Rich, J. (1968). *Interviewing children and adolescents.* London: Macmillan.

Spaulding, W. (1987). *Interviewing child victims of sexual exploitation.* Louisville, KY: National Center for Missing and Exploited Children.

Whitcomb, D., Shapiro, E. R., & Stellwagen, L. D. (1985). *When the victim is a child: Issues for judges and prosecutors* (Appendix) (Contract #J-LEAA-011-81). Washington, DC: National Institute of Justice.

must collect data without having formed conclusions (e.g., that the child was abused). Instead, the child's observed and reported behaviors must be considered in light of the following:

1. empirical standards of normalcy for the behavior of children of the same age, developmental level, gender, and cultural group.
2. reported behaviors of the same child before the alleged incident occurred.
3. alternative explanations for the behaviors (observed or reported).

Considering all of these factors improves the likelihood that the clinician-as-researcher will reach a valid conclusion.

Preparing for the Interview

Ideally, several tasks should be completed before the interview is held (Jones & McQuiston, 1988):

1. *Obtain necessary preliminary information.* Certainly, this includes the child's name, age, gender, and family situation. It must be determined who has custody or legal guardianship of the child. It also is helpful to obtain basic information about the family (how it is structured, what the rules are, etc.) and details of the child's everyday life (who cares for the child, what the daily routines are, who the child's teacher is, what the child's hobbies are, etc.).

2. *Obtain prior records and histories.* If an allegation has been made, it is advisable to know all the relevant details and to obtain access to prior records and histories (although interviewers must be particularly careful not to let such information cloud their objectivity while conducting the session).

3. *Obtain consent from the relevant authority to conduct the interview.* In some cases, an evaluation is ordered by the court and no further consent is required; at other times, consent must be obtained from the parent(s). In this regard, Jones and McQuiston (1988) caution, "There should not be a delay between the request for consent to the interview and the evaluation itself. If there is, inordinate parental pressure may be placed on the child to keep him or her silent" (p. 19).

Consider the case of three young children (ages three, four, and six) who had provided their therapist with independent and consistent reports of repeated sexual assault by their stepfather. Charges were filed with the county attorney. Subsequently, the therapist was asked to provide details of the children's accounts for a bill of discovery, the legal document filed for the purpose of compelling a defendant to answer the charges against him. The therapist was reluctant to do so, fearing that the children might be harmed or threatened if their stepfather was informed of the details of their allegations. But without her report, no further legal steps could be taken. Reluctantly, she complied with the request of defense counsel. At the next therapeutic visit— which followed the youngsters' regular visitation with "Daddy Don"—the children, who had been "warm, open, and expressive" on previous occasions, acted "withdrawn and fearful" and adamantly refused to discuss topics relating to physical intimacy. (V. Bones, personal communication, 1990). It is likely that during the delay the defendant threatened or coerced the children, causing the changes in their behavior.

Conducting the Interview(s)

In some instances only one interview is required to glean the applicable information. More commonly, however, several interviews are required, particularly in the case of children who have been threatened with harm should they disclose the details of criminal activity.

Several authors describe the complexity of issues associated with conducting interviews of children and provide helpful suggestions regarding how such interviews should be completed. A sample of resources is provided in Box 7.3, and we recommend that you consult them.

Several steps must be taken by interviewers who question children who may serve as legal witnesses.

1. *Select an appropriate setting for the interview.* Spaulding (1987) notes:

Selection of the interview site is a critical decision in the interview process. Both the interview site and the pre-interview setting can significantly affect the responsiveness of the child. (p. 13)

While a number of sites may be comfortable for the child and conducive to communication, we recommend that the interview occur in a professional office with videotaping capabilities. It may require more time to establish rapport with a child/victim in such a formal setting, but it is important that the child understand from the outset that the situation is serious. Moreover, the importance of making a permanent record of the interview should not be underestimated.

Ideally, the room should be large enough to allow some movement and to avoid the feeling that personal space is being intruded upon, but not so large that videotaping is hampered. It may be helpful to have drawing materials and simple toys available to help the child communicate.

2. *Eliminate distractions and interruptions.* It is essential that the interview room be private so that interruptions and distractions are avoided. It is difficult enough for a child to disclose the embarrassing details of a sexual encounter or physical assault after rapport and trust have been established; to ask the child to disclose when there are interruptions is inappropriate.

3. *Decide whether to allow support persons in the interview room.*
This is a controversial point. Whitcomb et al. (1985) suggest, "If
the child wishes a parent or other person present, it should be
allowed. A frightened or insecure child will not give a complete
statement" (p. 123). Other professionals disagree. Consider the
comments of Jones and McQuiston (1988):

> There may be unforeseen problems if a parent is present. The parent
> may appear to be supportive and non-abusive, but at the start of the
> interview this is unknown. We have seen so-called non-abusive par-
> ents become experts at non-verbally reminding the child to keep the
> secret while saying "tell the truth." Therefore, while the interviewer
> is in the stage of not fully understanding either child or family, it is
> best to see the child alone, if at all possible. If the parent must be
> present, then he must sit to one side, and be instructed not to help,
> nor to express his feelings or fears. (p. 20)

We agree with Jones and McQuiston that an interested party
should not be present in the room. Certainly it may be possible for
a parent to view the interview through a one-way mirror (if the
interview room provides such a feature) or alternatively to view
videotapes of the interview(s). In addition, we recommend that the
child know the whereabouts of the caregiver at all times during the
interview. The child may be shown where the parent will be waiting
and may even practice walking from the interview room to where
the parent is waiting. Finally, the child may be given permission
to leave the interview if necessary to check on the parent.

4. *Video/audiotape the interview.* We recommend thorough doc-
umentation of interview sessions. Videotapes that record running
time are the first choice, but for a variety of reasons videotaping
may not be practical. Moreover, no advantage is gained if the
recording is of poor quality. If high-quality videotaping is not
possible, record the interview on audiocassette. Keeping only written records of the interview is a poor, last alternative.

Recording of interviews is not universally praised, however, for
the procedure raises some interesting ethical dilemmas. For example, the interviewer must consider whether taping the session is
likely to "reduce spontaneity or even frighten the child" (Jones &
McQuiston, 1988). On the other hand, availability of a high-quality
videotape may obviate the need for the child to provide live testimony in court.

Any tapes made are potentially subject to laws of discovery; that is, they may need to be made available to counsel for the defendant. Therefore, they must be stored and not erased, in case legal action is taken at some later date. To protect confidentiality of the client, great care must be taken to store the tapes safely and securely.

5. *Establish rapport.* Nothing will more thoroughly subvert the truth-seeking function of the interview than failing to establish rapport with the child. Inexperienced interviewers are likely to fall prey to the desire to "get straight to the heart of the matter." In their zeal to uncover the facts, they may well close the channels of communication. It is essential to spend the time necessary to establish rapport, even if it requires more than one session to do so.

Investigators must recognize that in order to establish a good working relationship with the client, they must be aware that children as interviewees differ from their more mature counterparts. They tend to be put off by a cold greeting but also by one that is too friendly. Freeman and Weihofen (1972) note:

> Like anyone else, a child feels more at home in a situation that is familiar or at least expected. An unduly warm greeting may therefore be disconcerting. Advancing on him with outstretched hand and a toothy smile may take him aback. (p. 458)

Indeed, in the case of a child who has been sexually assaulted, such an enveloping greeting may be reminiscent of the perpetrator who criminally invaded the child's personal space.

An interview with a child may be opened in several ways, and no single approach is the "proper" one. We think it is appropriate for adults to introduce themselves and to explain their role, using words the child can understand. It also is helpful to tell the child what already is known about him or her and to explain that there are some things the interviewers don't know and that the child can help them learn. It is appropriate to ask if the child knows why the interview is being conducted and to assure him or her that the adults are there to try to help.

Even if the child is able to discuss the nature of the interview at the outset, it is best to retreat from the central issues for a while. Spend some time "chitchatting." Interviewers should find out about the child's interests, hobbies, and pets and be willing to talk about their interests as well. It is difficult for one person to divulge information if the other one refuses to reciprocate. It is best to avoid sensitive topics at this stage, even discussion of how the child is doing in school.

6. *Assess developmental level.* It is helpful to ask general questions that assess the child's intelligence, social and moral maturity, memory, ability to discern fact from lie (or fantasy), understanding of the obligation to tell the truth, and ability to communicate. For example, ascertain the following:

> Does child read, write, count, tell time; know colors or shapes; know the day or date; know birthdate; remember past events (breakfast, yesterday, last year); understand before and after; know about money; assume responsibilities (goes around neighborhood alone, stays at home alone, makes dinner, etc.). (Whitcomb et al., 1985, p. 124)

If there is uncertainty about the child's capacities, it is wise to arrange for an assessment by a professional trained in child development.

7. *Obtain a history of the alleged assault(s).* After rapport has been established and the participants feel comfortable with one another, it is time to ask about the alleged assault(s). It is important to ask for a free narrative first to avoid the possibility of—or even the appearance of—"planting suggestions." Jones and McQuiston (1988) suggest these opening questions:

> Is there anything you feel uncomfortable about—that you would like to talk about?
>
> [or]
>
> I have spoken with X, and it sounds as though a lot of things have been happening in your family. Can you tell me a little bit about that?
>
> [or]
>
> I know you have had to leave your family and are now in a foster home. Can you tell me how that happened?
>
> [or]
>
> You told me that you were here talking with me today because someone in your family did something that he shouldn't have [reiterate what the child said]—can you tell me a little bit more about that? (p. 26)

If the child is reluctant to talk, it is better to return to more neutral material. After a period of time, the interviewer may return to the sensitive issue. With some children several such verbal retreats may be necessary before disclosure is forthcoming. When discussing sensitive topics, Myers (1988) suggests the following strategies:

- Don't act shocked by what the child says.
- Let the child proceed at his or her own pace.
- Be prepared to move quickly away from sensitive topics. Let the child talk about safe subjects for a while, then gradually move back to sensitive areas.
- Reassure the child that it's okay to tell what happened.
- Encourage the child with nods and an occasional, "I see" or "Um-hummm."
- Reassure the child that he or she is not blameworthy. (p. 47)

Although Myers (1988) suggests that "[L]eading questions may be necessary to help the child discuss sensitive topics" (p. 47), we think it is imperative that leading questions be avoided at this stage of the process. Remember that the investigator's role in the interview is to determine *whether* abuse occurred, not to *prove* that it did.

Several methods may be used to facilitate disclosure, but keep in mind that any of these may be considered suspect in court. We urge professional persons to use such techniques sparingly and only when appropriate videotape records can be made to verify the procedures followed.

Jones and McQuiston (1988) suggest that "[i]f open-ended questions produce no answers, and the interviewer remains suspicious, then more enabling questions may be used" (p. 27). The authors offer these examples:

"Did anyone, even a grown-up who you are close to, ever touch the private parts of your body, like where your swimsuit goes?" (Direct question)

"I talk to a lot of children and sometimes to children who have been touched on private parts of their bodies. It can help to talk about things like that. Has anything like that ever happened to you?" (Permission-giving and ending with a direct question)

"Some kids are touched in private places on their body by people who are close to them, like someone in their family who they know very well. Has anything like that ever happened to you?" (Permission-giving and ending with a direct question)

Questions such as these avoid suggesting to the child a particular person as a possible abuser. On the other hand, if one were to ask, "Did Daddy touch you . . . ?", the result could be highly misleading. (pp. 27-28)

Other approaches that may facilitate disclosure include allowing the child to play with toys (especially dolls, puppets, and clay) and to draw pictures. In some cases, the interviewer may elect to let the child use anatomical dolls to illustrate alleged abuse, although evidence obtained using such dolls may not be admissible in court (see Levy, 1989). Raskin and Yuille (1989) state the case as follows:

Aids and props, such as anatomically detailed dolls, puppets, and drawings, should be viewed as tools of last resort. They should be considered only if the interviewer has failed to elicit adequate infor-mation by means of the standard interview methods. . . . Since the use of such aids and props may actually create more problems than they solve, a systematic and properly conducted interview appears to be the best available procedure. (p. 194)

We agree.

8. *Guard against suggestion and undue influence.* Generally, as we have repeatedly stressed, it is advisable to refrain from sugges-tive questioning of children. Whenever leading questions are used, the interviewer runs the risk of eliciting inaccurate statements. This risk may be especially pernicious when questioning cogni-tively sophisticated children who understand the subtler nuances of language and when interviewing very young children who have a tendency to acquiesce to suggestion. If leading questions must be used, it is well to ensure that only mild suggestion is offered. For example, use the "enabling" (mild suggestion) question form described by Jones and McQuiston (1988; see above):

"Did anyone, even a grown-up who you are close to, ever touch the private parts of your body, like where your swimsuit goes?"

rather than a strongly leading suggestion such as:

"Did Daddy touch the private parts of your body?

or

"Daddy touched your private parts, didn't he?" Did he do it like this?" (demonstrating with a doll)

Especially with children under age six or seven, it is helpful to ask questions primarily concerning the central aspects of the event, rather than the peripheral elements. It is more useful to ask a variety of questions about central details than to go on a "fishing expedition" for tangential information. Questioning on peripheral matters is likely to confuse (and perhaps intimidate) children.

To ensure accurate testimony, it may be beneficial to use the technique of "stacking and counterstacking" questions (Freeman & Weihofen, 1972). With this method, the interviewer first asks questions that call for a positive reply. This is followed by questions calling for a negative reply to achieve the same answer. Use of stacking and counterstacking enables the questioner to ascertain whether the child truly understands what is being asked.

If a child's memory is weak, it is best to ask only a few questions and to limit these to the central incident. Probing further, especially using leading questions, may result in inaccurate testimony (Loftus & Loftus, 1980).

When asking questions about events known to have happened, the form of the question is less vital than whether the questions refer to unsubstantiated information. When probing for details regarding unsubstantiated information, consider the linguistic form of the question. It is particularly important to avoid questions that include definite articles (e.g., *the*) or quantitative qualifiers (e.g., *any* and *some*). These linguistic forms plant the suggestion that the entity in question actually was present during the event. Instead, it is better to ask such simply phrased, nonleading questions as, "Did you see *a* car?" rather than "Didn't you see *the* car?" or "I'll bet you saw *some* cars, right?" Finally, in order to optimize the chances of obtaining accurate reports from children, intimidation and stress should be avoided. Every effort should be made to help the child feel comfortable. Such techniques as videotaping one interview (rather than subjecting the child to numerous interviews), allowing a supportive parent or advocate to remain nearby while the child is being interviewed, and conducting the interview through one highly trained, neutral questioner (rather than a variety of adversarial professionals) may help reduce the child's level of stress.

9. *Close the interview(s).* Closing the interview sessions requires nearly as much finesse as opening them. The child needs to be reassured that the session was important and that the child played a valuable role in helping concerned adults get at the truth. Interviewers should tell the child that they appreciate how he or she may have struggled to overcome the guilty or otherwise unpleasant feelings associated with divulging once-secret information.

The child also needs to be prepared for what will happen next. It is helpful to explain that there will be other interviews and to describe with whom these interviews will take place. If it is unlikely that the professional will see the child again, this fact should be explained honestly and directly, and the child thanked for his or her cooperation. It is vital not to make promises to the child that cannot be kept, or to extract promises from the child (e.g., that he or she will testify).

Finally, it is advisable to reassure the child that there are "safe" adults who can be trusted to help throughout the process. The interviewer should help the child identify who these advocates are and how to reach them. At this stage, as in all others, the child must be treated with honesty, care, and respect.

Assessing the Credibility of the Child's Statement

At the close of the interview, the validity of the child's report must be assessed, which sometimes is a gargantuan task. Although there is no general consensus about when to believe a child's allegations, several factors are mentioned by a variety of sources (see Box 7.4 for a list of relevant sources): consistency of the account, vocabulary appropriate to the child's developmental level, lack of motivation to fabricate the account, appropriate affect (e.g., fear, guilt), spontaneity, consistency with the laws of nature and with corroborative evidence (see, for example, Raskin & Yuille, 1989). One promising technique developed by Raskin and colleagues ("statement validity analysis") currently is being tested in the United States.[4]

Assessment of the validity of the child's statement is a vital step in the process of litigation. As Howson (1985) notes, in our enthusiasm to protect children from harm, we may have taken steps that encourage us *not* to assess validity of the claims made. He notes, for example, that in some jurisdictions (such as King County in the state of Washington), the police take an abbreviated initial report

Box 7.4

Assessing Validity of the Child's Statement:
Helpful Resources

Benedek, E. P., & Schetky, D. H. (1987a). Clinical experience: Problems in validating allegations of sexual abuse. Part 1: Factors affecting perception and recall of events. *Journal of the American Academy of Child and Adolescent Psychiatry, 26,* 912-915.

Benedek, E. P., & Schetky, D. H. (1987b). Clinical experience: Problems in validating allegations of sexual abuse. Part 2: Clinical evaluation. *Journal of the American Academy of Child and Adolescent Psychiatry, 26,* 916-921.

Jones, D. P. H., & McGraw, J. M. (1987). Reliable and fictitious accounts of sexual abuse to children. *Journal of Interpersonal Violence, 2,* 27-45.

Raskin, D. C., & Yuille, J. C. (1989). Problems in evaluating interviews of children in sexual abuse cases. In S. J. Ceci, D. F. Ross, & M. P. Toglia (Eds.), *Perspectives on children's testimony* (pp. 184-207). New York or Berlin: Springer Verlag.

---

and then transport the complainant to the hospital and/or sexual assault center, "but themselves do not attempt an in-depth interview with the complainant" (p. 10). He speculates:

> I suspect the same considerations that have caused the police to abandon the investigative interview have influenced prosecutors to limit their interview. It is simply not politic to ask questions which may cause other people to believe that the interviewer suspects a false allegation. (p. 10)

Howson (1985) correctly concludes that, under such circumstances, "the defendant-victim suffers all of the most serious consequences (with the exception of physical punishment) not as a result of conviction or sentencing but as a result of the *filing* of criminal charges" (p. 10), while the complainant's allegations avoid appropriate scrutiny.

WHAT OFFICERS OF THE COURT NEED TO DO

Investigators

Law enforcement officers typically are the first to formally interview the children who later may serve as witnesses in court. How they handle the initial questioning is of paramount importance in terms of obtaining accurate information, preserving untainted evidence for use in court proceedings, and reducing the stress experienced by the young complainants. For these reasons, it is vital that law enforcement officers who will be assigned the duty of interviewing children receive special training.

Specifically, they need to understand child development, including the normative ages at which certain developmental milestones are attained, and the typical issues faced by children of various ages. They also need to be aware of how children communicate, why they sometimes are reluctant to do so, and why they may even recant allegations. Police officers who work with child victims need to understand the dynamics of sexual exploitation of children as well as how the cycle of abuse is perpetuated in chronically abusive families. General training in child psychology and the sociology of the family should prove helpful.

Specialized training should be obtained as well. It is especially important that police officers in this line of duty learn how to conduct comprehensive but nonsuggestive interviews with child victims. One helpful model for interviewing children is offered by the National Center for Missing and Exploited Children, a model developed by police Lieutenant William Spaulding of the Criminal Intelligence Division of Police in Louisville, KY(1987). We cannot overemphasize the importance of training for police officers who interview children. Children often have idiosyncratic ways of communicating, and because they typically want to please authority figures (especially the police!), they may be especially susceptible to suggestive questioning by an officer. Specialized training is essential.

This point was illustrated by Dent (1982), who asked experienced police officers to question child witnesses following a staged incident. She notes, "the performance of the three experienced policemen indicates that certain important lessons are not invariably learned through experience" (p. 294). Indeed, all three elicited very inaccurate descriptive information by succumbing to the temptation of using suggestive, leading questioning. Consider the following dialogue, which demonstrates how even an experienced police officer can lead a child into compounding an initial error by requesting increasingly specific details. In this example the officer is questioning the child concerning the appearance of a woman suspect:

Officer:	Wearing a poncho and a cap—?
Child:	I think it was a cap.
Officer:	What sort of cap was it? Was it like a beret, or was it a peaked cap, or—?
Child:	No, it had sort of, it was flared with a little piece coming out (demonstrates with hands). It was flared with a sort of button thing in the middle.
Officer:	What—sort of—like that—was it a peak like that, that sort of thing?
Child:	Ye-es.
Officer:	Like a sort of orange segment thing, like that, do you mean?
Child:	Yes!
Officer:	Is that right?
Child:	Yes.
Officer:	That's the sort of cap I'm thinking you're meaning, with a little peak out there.
Child:	Yes, that's top view, yes.
Officer:	That sort of thing, is it?
Child:	Yes.
Officer:	Smashing. Um—what color?
Child:	Oh! Oh—I think this was um black or brown—
Officer:	Think it was dark, shall we say?
Child:	Yes—it was a dark color I think, and I didn't see her hair. (Dent, 1982, pp. 290-291)

In fact, the woman was not wearing anything on her head, nor was she wearing a poncho!

Extrapolating from her research findings, Dent (1982) provides a description of productive and counterproductive interviewing strategies commonly used by police officers:

> The most counter-productive interviewing occurred when the interviewer formed a strong preconceived impression about what happended [*sic*] in the incident, based on the minimal information given in the instructions. This resulted in the phrasing of particularly suggestive questions and a lack of receptiveness on the part of the interviewer to information relevant to the incident but which did not fit into the preconceived version of the incident. A similar situation occurred when interviewers accepted the first and perhaps the second

child's version of the incident, as a complete, accurate account, and as a result became unreceptive to alternative or extra information volunteered by subsequent children.

A similar counter-productive strategy consisted of heavily structuring the interview so that information not specifically requested was rejected, at least until its relevant slot occurred. . . .

Frequent, strong prompting of recall occurred, despite most interviewers' recognition of the dangers of suggestion, or "putting words into the child's mouth", and avowed attempts to guard against this. It is interesting that the worst offenders were mainly experienced interviewers, who were all theoretically aware of the dangers of suggestion.

The task of taking a statement had an adverse effect on some interviewers' performances. This took the form of continually interrupting the child's initial flow of recall in order to have time to write everything down. A more successful strategy was to obtain total recall first, then to go through the incident a second time in order to write the statement.

The most obvious productive interviewing strategy consisted of asking the children to recount the appropriate day's activities from some point to the lesson in which the incident occurred. (pp. 288-289)

Clearly, amount of field experience did not relate well to ability to interview children successfully. For this reason, we believe that specialized training of police officers who work with children should be mandatory. Additionally, we urge law enforcement agencies to consider using a team approach to investigation of cases involving children. For example, professionals trained in interviewing children could question young victim-witnesses while the police observe the session through a one-way mirror. Questions could be relayed to the interviewer via the "bug in the ear" technique.

Judges

Because of the central role they play in orchestrating trial proceedings, it is particularly important that judges be educated adequately regarding the special issues attendant on working with children as legal witnesses. Yates (1987) suggests that the most expeditious and positive changes of the legal system might be attained through education of the judiciary:

> Through the judge's discretionary powers, child witnesses may be seen in chambers, granted recesses, or be accompanied to the courtroom by a familiar supportive adult. The judge may caution attorneys who question children inappropriately and may speak directly to the child. The court may appoint a special attorney with a background in child development to examine the child. This attorney would use questions supplied by the other attorneys and would have the right to object to questions that might confuse or be unduly upsetting to the child. (p. 479)

A number of alternatives exist for continuing education of the judiciary. First, we recommend that, in order to obtain a good background in issues and techniques, judges read books and articles such as those recommended in Boxes 7.1-7.4.

Second, we applaud organized efforts to educate the judiciary on the issue of children as legal witnesses. For example, in February of 1990, the Nebraska District Judges Association and the Nebraska County Judges Association presented a joint education program entitled "Child Sexual Abuse in Criminal, Juvenile, and Divorce Cases" (Boys Town Conference, 1990). This session focused on three areas: (a) children as witnesses, (b) medical evidence of sexual abuse, and (c) child development issues. Presentations were offered by a cross-section of professional persons interested in psycholegal issues—judges, attorneys, psychologists, social workers, and physicians. We urge other jurisdictions to follow suit.

Third, we encourage judges to review recent Supreme Court decisions bearing on children as witnesses (see for example, *Coy v. Iowa* [1988], *Idaho v. Wright* [1990], *Maryland v. Craig* [1990]) and to encourage the use of alternative procedures designed to reduce traumatization of child witnesses without infringing upon the defendant's constitutional rights. For instance, we encourage the use of these procedures[5]:

1. *Permit live-broadcast videotaped testimony of child witnesses when the defendant can be represented by counsel during the taping.* Do not require the stringent standard that the child be "unable to communicate" in court before allowing the use of this procedure; if the truth is more likely to be uncovered because the child finds it easier to communicate in chambers, then allow the use of this alternative procedure.

2. *Use court-appointed (non-partisan) experts to inform the court.* Experts might testify on such matters as (a) how children perceive, encode, store, and retrieve memories; (b) how children understand language and communicate with others; (c) how children may be misled by suggestion; (d) how to guard against suggestion when interviewing children; and (e) why children's actions may appear fickle and their allegations may be recanted.

3. *Admit expert evidence regarding the validity of witnesses' statements.* When scientific means have been used to assess validity, allow testimony to explain the procedures used.

4. *Caution attorneys not to use leading questions or sophisticated language when examining and cross-examining child witnesses.*

5. *Instruct jurors about children's abilities and shortcomings as witnesses.* It is preferable to provide instruction *before* evidence is presented, with a reminder being given before deliberation begins.

With proper education of the judiciary, implementation of these procedures can be accomplished without infringing upon defendants' rights.

Attorneys

Prosecution and defense attorneys, like all others in the system who work with children, need education. They should become familiar with the resource materials and interviewing techniques described throughout this chapter.

In addition, attorneys need to prepare their child clients for the courtroom experience, as well as to prepare the system for working with a child witness. Here are some important steps to be taken:

1. *Explain to the child the charges against the defendant.* By the time a case reaches the trial stage, interested adults likely will have a good idea of the charges against the defendant. Children may not be so enlightened. Although they as victim-witnesses certainly have some understanding of what happened and of the fact that the events were "bad," they are likely to have little appreciation for the nuances of the law. Attorneys should explain the charges, using language the child can comprehend. They should avoid saying, for example, "Jimmy, the alleged perpetrator is charged with lewd and lascivious conduct and with the commission of sodomy, which is a first degree sexual assault punishable by ____ years of imprisonment according to the relevant statutes of our state." Jimmy won't have any idea what the lawyer is talking about! Instead, the attorney might explain the situation as follows:

"Jimmy, you told me that Uncle George touched you in private places on your body and that sometimes he put his pee-pee (as you call it) inside your bottom and that hurt you. Where we live, Jimmy, adults aren't allowed to do that to children. Our state has laws that say that grown-ups can't do that. So, whenever we find out that a grown-up man has done that to a boy, we try to find out as much as we can about what happened. Then we take all that information to a place called a courtroom, and we let someone who is very smart about these things—the judge—see if we have enough information to be very sure that Uncle George should be punished for putting his pee-pee in your bottom. Because this is a very difficult problem and because we don't want to punish Uncle George if he didn't do something wrong, the judge in our courtroom is going to have some helpers. These helpers are called "the jury," and they are people who will sit in a special part of the courtroom that I will show you. Our job is to help the judge and jury see that you are telling the truth, that Uncle George really did break the law when he put his pee-pee in your bottom."

2. *Describe the roles of the actors in the system.* Attorneys should use child-friendly descriptions of each person involved in the process (at least each person the child will encounter). Because very few good materials are commercially available for children, some organizations may want to write simple books that can be read to children by the attorney, parent, or special advocate.

3. *Tour the courtroom.* A field trip can go a long way in helping children understand their role in court. We urge attorneys to show any child witness where each of the actors will sit or stand during the trial. Let the child sit in the witness chair and in the seats reserved for the audience. Allow the child to walk around the room and to touch objects. Sometimes actually touching objects will elicit important questions that need to be answered. For example, a frightened child may ask, "If Uncle George sits here, who will keep him from jumping up and getting me?"

4. *Explain who will be present and what will happen at trial.* Attorneys should describe how direct and cross-examination will proceed and should engage the child in role-playing how these processes occur. To avoid the possibility of the child's testimony sounding coached, witness examination could be role-played using questions that do not relate to the trial at hand. If questioning will occur in chambers, the attorney might arrange for the child to see the judge's office and where the videotape machine will be.

5. *Prepare the child for the competency exam* (if applicable).
Myers (1987) offers these suggestions for preparing the child for
the competency examination:

- Ask the child to describe objects in the interview room. By this means
  the adult can assess the child's present capacity to observe.
- Ask the child's parent or caretaker whether the child possessed
  normal vision and observational capacity at the time the alleged
  incident(s) occurred. Such information is vital, because a child who
  lacked such ability at the time of the occurrence(s) may be deemed
  incompetent to testify at trial.
- Ask the child simple, factual questions that probe short-term memory
  and long-term memory unrelated to the alleged incident(s). In other
  words, play memory games that help ascertain whether the child
  possesses sufficient memory to be considered competent at trial.
- Ask simple questions to determine whether the child can differentiate
  between the truth and a falsehood (again, unrelated to the alleged
  incident). Then encourage the child to explain *why* something is true
  or false.
- Explain to the child the obligation to tell the truth in court. Ask the
  child to describe what happens to children who do not tell the truth
  (at home, in school, etc.). Further explain that giving false testimony
  ("telling a lie") may lead to punishment.
- Explain to the child the procedures followed during a competency
  examination. (pp. 42-44)

6. *Secure emotional supports for the child.* In addition to preparing the child witness, it is important for attorneys to inform the
child's parent, relative, or court-appointed special advocate of what
will happen at the trial and of how the child is likely to respond to
these challenging circumstances. If necessary, they may arrange
for the child to receive therapeutic intervention.

7. *Encourage the judge to allow videotaped live broadcast testimony of the child witness from chambers.* As discussed in chapters
5 and 6, this procedure is likely to reduce intimidation experienced
by the child and to result in better communication.

8. *Allow the child to take a favorite toy (or other source of comfort)
to the stand.* Some jurisdictions permit a child to sit on a trusted
parent's lap while giving testimony; others do not. Rarely would a
judge forbid a child to take a favorite toy to the witness chair.

9. *Encourage frequent recesses.* Children need breaks when giving testimony. Attorneys should ask the court's indulgence in

allowing frequent recesses when a child must give testimony over an extended period of time.

10. *Strenuously object to cross-examination that is incomprehensible, suggestive, or confusing to the child.* Legal professionals must insist that questions be phrased in ways that the child can understand. They should not allow the child to be "trapped" into agreeing with misleading suggestions on cross-examination.

Jurors

Jurors also need to be educated about children as legal witnesses. Judges and attorneys alike have the opportunity to provide a "crash course" in this subject. Jurors need to understand how children perceive, remember, and report events. They need to understand why leading questions occasionally may be necessary (on direct) for obtaining the truth from child witnesses. They also need to understand why leading questions (especially on cross-examination) may be particularly problematic for child witnesses. Finally, jurors need to understand why children often recant their statements after allegations have been made and how to assess the credibility of statements made by children. Without such education, jurors cannot render informed decisions in cases for which children serve as legal witnesses.

POLICY RECOMMENDATIONS

Our review of the scientific literature and the legal cases concerning children as witnesses in court leads us to conclude that the following policies should be encouraged:

1. All personnel working with cases involving child witnesses should receive general education regarding child development and family dynamics as well as specialized training in interviewing children.

2. Interviews of children should be conducted by trained personnel and should be videotaped (using a running time record). The number of interviews held and the number of people conducting such sessions should be limited. All unessential interviews and duplications of effort should be eliminated.

3. Specially trained workers should be assigned to child witnesses for the purpose of conducting interviews and represent-

ing their testimony to the court, a procedure often used in other countries (see Landwirth, 1987).

4. A multidisciplinary team involving the prosecutor, police, and social services resource personnel should be utilized in the investigation and prosecution of cases in which a child is alleged to be the victim of or witness to abuse (see ABA, 1985; Brooks & Milchman, 1990).

5. Courtrooms should be made child-friendly to the degree possible without infringing upon the rights of the defendant (see, for example, Parker, 1982).

6. Empirical studies of procedural reforms should be conducted to assess the impact of such changes on all participants involved in the process. One large-scale study of this sort currently is being conducted by the U.S. Department of Justice, Office of Juvenile Justice and Delinquency Prevention. The goals of the study are (a) to examine a wide range of techniques for investigating and prosecuting child sexual abuse cases, (b) to assess empirically the circumstances under which alternative techniques are used, and (c) to evaluate how well these innovations reduce victim trauma and increase successful prosecution of offenders. Multidisciplinary teams from each of four counties will address the research questions: (a) Erie County, NY: What are the effects on children of not having to swear out arrest complaints or testify at preliminary hearings? (b) San Diego County, CA: What effects result from child witnesses attending "court school" to prepare them for testifying at preliminary hearings? (c) Polk County, IA: How might services be improved for child victims of nonfamilial sexual abuse? (d) Ramsey County, MN: What are the effects of flagging cases requiring expedited disposition?[6]

Empirical efforts, such as the OJJDP project described in the previous paragraph, are a step in the right direction. We believe that more research studies of this sort are sorely needed.

7. State legislatures should enact appropriate legislation to permit modification of court procedures and evidentiary rules when children testify (see ABA, 1985). For example, they might extend the statute of limitations in cases involving the abuse of children, establish (or enhance) special assistance programs for victim-witnesses who are children, or define the circumstances under which alternative methods of giving evidence are permissible for child witnesses.

Procedural reforms are likely to be more influential—and thus to better serve justice—if all elements of the system are working in concert.

CONCLUSIONS

This volume has addressed four basic issues that must be considered whenever a child is asked to provide testimony in court: (a) How should the courts and society view the capabilities of children as witnesses? (b) When should the courts and society believe the testimony of children who have been judged competent to give evidence? (c) What rights should child witnesses have to protection from harm? (d) What rights should defendants have in cases involving child witnesses?

Recent court cases involving children as witnesses demonstrate the fact that jurisdictions within the United States have varying levels of sophistication in handling the issues we have raised. At times, child witness cases are litigated in a particularly adroit manner, as in the case of "Susie" (Jones & Krugman, 1986), described in chapter 1. At other times, the process is so convoluted that it may appropriately be labeled "bungled" (e.g., the McMartin Preschool case).

We believe that enough evidence currently exists to warrant some general conclusions with regard to children as witnesses in court. The scientific evidence and legal opinions described in this book lead us to the following conclusions regarding the four central questions we have investigated:

1. The vast majority of children, even as young as age four (and in some cases younger), meet the criteria for competence. In most cases they should be judged competent to offer testimony at trial.

2. The credibility of children as witnesses is a complex issue, one that requires education of all parties involved in a legal case—judges, attorneys, therapists, parents, children, special advocates, interviewers, and jurors. Those who attempt to determine credibility of the young witness must consider the diverse factors we have discussed in detail throughout this book.

3. Although children have no specific constitutional rights to protection from harm during court proceedings, legal precedent has established that the state has an overriding interest in shield-

ing children from trauma. Recent Supreme Court decisions indicate that the tide may be turning in favor of making the courts more child-oriented. This is a trend we wholeheartedly support.

4. The defendant's constitutional rights in a case involving a child victim-witness are adequately protected when (a) the trial is speedy, (b) the trial is as public as it can be without unduly harming any participant, and (c) the elements of confrontation (presence of defense counsel at the questioning of the child, ability to ask questions of the young witness, and opportunity to object to questions by opposing counsel) are preserved, even if face-to-face confrontation of the accuser is denied.

SUMMARY

Whose responsibility is it to see that the statements made in cases involving child witnesses are accurate? We believe that every member of the legal system must be accountable, for society is affected in many adverse ways when the truth of the matter is not uncovered. Each person who interacts with child witnesses must strive for accuracy. Moreover, each professional person involved should understand child development, and those who question children victim-witnesses should receive specialized training in the techniques appropriate to interviewing children.

Clinicians must take several steps in working with a child who may be called to testify in court. They should prepare for possible involvement in court proceedings by becoming familiar with the relevant laws and reviewing the standards for and the pitfalls of serving as an expert witness. They should follow acceptable interviewing practices and prepare the child for the courtroom experience.

Expert witnesses should understand the impartial nature of their role and should know how the issues of confidentiality and privilege are addressed in a court of law. Additionally, they should know the circumstances under which they are being called to testify, consult with all relevant parties, prepare for the trial, and maintain professional demeanor in the courtroom.

Although psycholegal researchers have made great progress in recent years, much work is still to be done. Research especially is needed in answering these questions: What factors influence the **child's ability to communicate at trial? What factors influence** truth-telling in children? Is it possible to assess successfully the validity of statements made by children? Under which specific circumstances do child witnesses feel traumatized? What specific procedures help children to weather the courtroom experience, and thereby to communicate effectively and accurately?

The tasks of the interviewer include the following: to enlist the cooperation of the child, to assess the situation by gathering facts and data, to assess the competence of the child to provide information in a legal setting, to determine the accuracy of the child's account, to formulate a plan of action, to provide emotional support, and to evaluate any immediate danger to the child. Interviewers need to obtain information in preparing for the interview and to resolve several issues in conducting questioning sessions with children. They also must assess the validity of statements provided by children.

Investigators need to be particularly careful not to form preconceived notions about alleged crimes when interviewing children. They need to become familiar with the productive and counterproductive techniques for obtaining information from children.

Because of the central role judges play during the course of legal proceedings, the judiciary especially needs to be well informed about the issues surrounding children as legal witnesses. We believe that judges should be encouraged to permit live-broadcast videotaped testimony of child witnesses, to use court-appointed experts to inform the triers of fact, to admit expert evidence regarding the validity of witnesses' statements, and to ensure that questions posed to child witnesses are comprehensible and neither leading nor confusing.

Attorneys need to prepare their child clients for the courtroom experience, as well as to prepare the system for working with a child witness. They should explain to the child the charges against the defendant, describe the roles of the actors in the system, allow the child to tour the courtroom, explain who will be present and what will happen at trial, prepare the child for the competency exam (if applicable), secure emotional supports for the child, and encourage the court to adopt procedures designed to safeguard the child from harm while testifying.

This chapter also offers policy recommendations and general conclusions regarding children as legal witnesses.

NOTES

1. For more information about court-appointed special advocates write to NCASAA, 2722 Eastlake Ave. E., Suite 220, Seattle, WA 98102.

2. For information on this conference, contact Stephen J. Ceci, Ph.D., Department of Human Development and Family Studies, Martha Van Rensselaer Hall, Cornell University, Ithaca, NY 14853-4401.

3. For information on this meeting, contact Cathleen Oslzly, Department of Psychology, 209 Burnett Hall, University of Nebraska, Lincoln, NE 68588-0308.

4. This technique has been used in Germany for approximately 30 years.

5. Many of these procedures are recommended by the American Bar Association (1985).

6. Results of this study should be available during the year 1991.

References

After the verdict, solace for none. (1990, February 5). *People Weekly, 33* (5), 70-80.

Ainsworth, M. D. S., Blehar, M. C., Waters, E., & Wall, S. (1978). *Patterns of attachment: A psychological study of the strange situation.* Hillsdale, NJ: Lawrence Erlbaum.

Alabama Code Ann. § 15-25-5 (1985).

Alberts, F., & Blau, T. (1988). *The cue book: The courtroom companion.* Tampa, FL: Psychological Seminars.

American Bar Association (1985). *ABA guidelines for the fair treatment of child witnesses in cases where child abuse is alleged.* Washington, DC: Author.

American Bar Association. (1989). *ABA criminal justice mental health standards.* Washington, DC: Author.

American Jurisprudence. (1960). Rochester, NY: Lawyers Co-Operative.

American Jurisprudence Trials. (1966). San Francisco: Bancroft Whitney.

American Psychiatric Association. (1980). *Diagnostic and statistical manual of mental disorders.* (3rd ed.). Washington, DC: Author.

American Psychological Association. (nd.). Amicus Curiae #7-13. Washington, DC: Author.

Anglin, J. M. (1977). *Word, object, and concept development.* New York: Norton.

Appelbaum, P. S. (1987). In the wake of *Ake:* The ethics of expert testimony in an advocate's world. *Bulletin of the American Academy of Psychiatry and Law, 15,* 15-25.

Atkinson, R. D., & Shiffrin, R. M. (1968). Human memory: A proposed system and its control processes. In K. W. Spence & J. T. Spence (Eds.), *The psychology of learning and motivation* (Vol. 2). New York: Academic Press.

Beach, B. H. (1983, January 31). Out of the mouth of babes. *Time,* p. 58.

Bekerian, D. A., & Bowers, J. M. (1983). Eyewitness testimony: Were we misled? *Journal of Experimental Psychology: Learning, Memory, and Cognition, 9,* 139-145.

Benedek, E. P., & Schetky, D. H. (1987a). Clinical experience: Problems in validating allegations of sexual abuse. Part 1:Factors affecting perception and recall of events. *Journal of the American Academy of Child and Adolescent Psychiatry, 26,* 912-915.

Benedek, E. P., & Schetky, D. H. (1987b). Clinical experience: Problems in validating allegations of sexual abuse. Part 2: Clinical evaluation. *Journal of the American Academy of Child and Adolescent Psychiatry, 26,* 916-921.

Berliner, L. (1985). The child witness: The progress and emerging limitations. *University of Miami Law Review, 40,* 167-179.

Berliner, L., & Barbieri, M. K. (1984). The testimony of the child victim of sexual assault. *Journal of Social Issues, 40,* 125-137.

Birmingham Ry., Light & Power v. Wise, 149 Ala. 492, 42 So. 821 (1906).

Blau, T. H. (1984). *The psychologist as expert witness.* New York: John Wiley.

Bloom, L., & Lahey, M. (1978). *Language development and language disorders.* New York: John Wiley.

Bole v. Bole, 76 Cal. App. 2d 344, 172 P.2d 936 (1946).

Bottoms, B. L., Goodman, G. S., Schwartz-Kenney, B., Sachsenmaier, T., & Thomas, S. (1990, March). *Keeping secrets: Implications for children's testimony.* Paper presented at the meeting of the Americal Psychology-Law Society, Williamsburg, VA.

Boys Town Conference (1990, February). *Child sexual abuse in criminal, juvenile, and divorce cases.* Boys Town, NE: Author.

Brant, R. S. T., & Tisza, V. B. (1977). The sexually misused child. *American Journal of Orthopsychiatry, 47,* 80-90.

Brigham, J. C., & Wolfskeil, M. P. (1983). Opinions of attorneys and law enforcement personnel on the accuracy of eyewitness identifications. *Law and Human Behavior, 7,* 337-349.

Brooks, C. M., & Milchman, M. S. (1990). Child sexual abuse allegations in the context of child custody litigation: A multi-disciplinary project to resolve conflicts between mental health professionals' testimony. *Lawyers for children.* Washington, DC: American Bar Association Center on Children and the Law.

Brown, A. L., Bransford, J. D., Ferrara, R. A., & Campione, J. C. (1983). Learning, remembering, and understanding. In J. H. Flavell & E. M. Markman (Eds.), *Handbook of child psychology* (4th ed.). *Vol. 3. Cognitive development* (pp. 77-166). New York: John Wiley.

Bruner, J. (1973). *Beyond the information given.* New York: Norton.

Bulkley, J. (1982). *Recommendations for improving legal intervention in intrafamily child sexual abuse cases.* Washington, DC: American Bar Association.

Bulkley, J. (1989). The impact of new child witness research on sexual abuse prosecutions. In S. J. Ceci, D. F. Ross, & M. P. Toglia (Eds.), *Perspectives on children's testimony* (pp. 208-229). New York or Berlin: Springer Verlag.

Burton, R. V. (1976). Honesty and dishonesty. In T. Lickona (Ed.), *Moral development and behavior* (pp. 173-197). New York: Holt, Rinehart, & Winston.

Bussey, K. (1990, March). Adult influences on children's eyewitness testimony. In S. Ceci (Chair), *Do children lie? Narrowing the uncertainties.* Biennial Meeting of the American Psychology-Law Society, Williamsburg, VA.

California Penal Code § 868 (West 1986).

California v. Green, 399 U.S. 149 (1970).

Callicott v. Callicott, 364 S.W.2d 455 (1963).

Carey, S. (1978). A case study: Face recognition. In E. Walker (Ed.), *Explorations in the biology of language* (pp. 175-201). Montgomery, VT: Bradford Books.

Carey, S., & Diamond, R. (1977). From piecemeal to configurational representation in faces. *Science, 195,* 312-315.

Ceci (1989, June). *Some overarching issues in the child suggestibility debate.* Paper presented at the Cornell Conference on the Suggestibility of Children's Recollections, Ithaca, NY.

Ceci, S. J., DeSimone, M., Putnick, M., Toglia, M., & Lee, J. M. (1990, March). Motives to lie. In S. Ceci (Chair), *Do children lie? Narrowing the uncertainties.* Biennial Meeting of the American Psychology-Law Society, Williamsburg, VA.

Ceci, S. J., Ross, D. F., & Toglia, M. P. (1987). Suggestibility of children's memory: Psycholegal implications. *Journal of Experimental Psychology: General, 116,* 38-49.

Ceci, S. J., Ross, D. F., & Toglia, M. P. (1989). *Perspectives on children's testimony*. New York or Berlin: Springer Verlag.

Ceci, S. J., Toglia, M. P., & Ross, D. F. (1987a). *Children's eyewitness memory*. New York or Berlin: Springer Verlag.

Ceci, S. J., Toglia, M. P., & Ross, D. F. (1987b, October). *The suggestibility of preschoolers' recollections: Historical perspectives on current problems*. Paper presented at the Third Emory Cognition Symposium, Atlanta, GA.

Chambers v. Mississippi, 410 U.S. 284 (1973).

Chance, J. E., & Goldstein, A. G. (1984). Face-recognition memory: Implications for children's eyewitness testimony. *Journal of Social Issues, 40,* 69-85.

Chase, S. (1938). *The tyranny of words*. New York: Harcourt Brace.

Chi, M.T.H., & Koeske, R. D. (1983). Network representation of a child's dinosaur knowledge. *Developmental Psychology, 19,* 29-39.

Christiaansen, R. E., & Ochalek, K. (1983). Editing misleading information from memory: Evidence for the coexistence of original and postevent information. *Memory and Cognition, 11,* 467-475.

Clark, E. V. (1983). Meanings and concepts. In J. H. Flavell & E. M. Markman (Eds.), *Handbook of Child Psychology* (4th ed., pp. 787-840). *Vol. 3: Cognitive development*. New York: John Wiley.

Clarke-Stewart, A., Thompson, W., & Lepore, S. (1989, April). Manipulating children's interpretations through interrogation. In G. S. Goodman (Chair), *Do children provide accurate eyewitness reports? Research and social policy implications*. Society for Research in Child Development Meetings, Kansas City, MO.

Cleary, E. W. (1984). *McCormick on evidence*. St. Paul, MN: West.

Cleaveland v. State, 490 N.E.2d 1140 (Ind.Ct.App. 1986).

Cohen, R. L., & Harnick, M. A. (1980). The susceptibility of child witnesses to suggestion. *Law and Human Behavior, 4,* 201-210.

Cohen, R. L., Perlmutter, M., & Myers, N. A. (1977). *Memory for location of multiple stimuli by 2- to 4-year olds*. Unpublished manuscript, University of Massachusetts.

Cole, C. B., & Loftus, E. F. (1987). The memory of children. In S. J. Ceci, M. P. Toglia, & D. F. Ross (Eds.), *Children's eyewitness memory* (pp. 178-208). New York or Berlin: Springer Verlag.

Collins, G. B., & Bond, E. C. (1953). Youth as a bar to testimonial competence. *Arkansas Law Review, 8,* 100-107.

Collins, W. A., Wellman, H., Keniston, A., & Westby, S. (1978). Age-related aspects of comprehension and inferences from a televised dramatic narrative. *Child Development, 49,* 389-399.

Commonwealth v. Anderson, 552 A.2d 1064 (Pa.Super. 1988).

Commonwealth v. Berry 355 Pa.Super. 243, 513 A.2d 415 (1986).

Constitution of the United States (Amendments I and VI).

Coy v. Iowa, 108 S.Ct. 1798, 487 U.S. 1012 (1988).

Crewdson, J. (1988). *By silence betrayed: Sexual abuse of children in America*. New York: Harper & Row.

Cutler, B. L., Dexter, H. R., & Penrod, S. D. (1989). Expert testimony and jury decision making: An empirical analysis. *Behavioral Sciences and the Law, 7,* 215-225.

Dale, P. S., Loftus, E. F., & Rathbun, L. (1978). The influence of the form of the question on the eyewitness testimony of preschool children. *Journal of Psycholinguistic Research, 7,* 269-277.

Damon, L., Todd, J., & MacFarlane, K. (1987). Treatment issues with sexually abused young children. *Child Welfare, 66,* 125-137.

Day, M. C. (1975). Developmental trends in visual scanning. In H. W. Reese (Ed.), *Advances in child development and behavior* (Vol. 10, pp. 154-193). New York: Academic Press.

Deffenbacher, K. (1980). Eyewitness accuracy and confidence: Can we infer anything about their relationship? *Law and Human Behavior, 4,* 243-260.

Deffenbacher, K. (1984, September). Experimental psychology actually can assist triers of fact. *American Psychologist,* pp. 1066-1067.

DeFrancis, V. (1969). *Protecting the child victim of sex crimes committed by adults.* Denver, CO: American Humane Association.

Dent, H. R. (1982). The effects of interviewing strategies on the results of interviews with child witnesses. In A. Trankell (Ed.), *Reconstructing the past: The role of psychologists in criminal trials* (pp. 279-297). Stockholm: Norstedt.

Dent, H. R., & Stephenson, G. M. (1979). An experimental study of the effectiveness of different techniques of questioning child witnesses. *British Journal of Social and Clinical Psychology, 18,* 41-51.

Doek, J. E. (1981). Sexual abuse of children: An examination of European criminal law. In P. B. Mrazek & C. H. Kempe (Eds.), *Sexually abused children and their families* (pp. 75-84). Elmsford, NY: Pergamon.

Duggan, L. M. III, Aubrey, M., Doherty, E., Isquith, P., Levine, M., & Scheiner, J. (1989). The credibility of children as witnesses in a simulated child sex abuse trial. In S. J. Ceci, D. F. Ross, & M. P. Toglia (Eds.), *Perspectives on children's testimony* (pp. 71-99). New York or Berlin: Springer Verlag.

Duncan, E. M., Whitney, P., & Kunen, S. (1982). Integration of visual and verbal information in children's memories. *Child Development, 53,* 1215-1223.

Dunning, D. (1989). Research on children's eyewitness testimony: Perspectives on its past and future. In S. J. Ceci, D. F. Ross, & M. P. Toglia (Eds.), *Perspectives on children's testimony* (pp. 230-248). New York or Berlin: Springer Verlag.

Dziech, B. W., & Schudson, C. B. (1989). *On trial: America's courts and their treatment of sexually abused children.* Boston: Beacon.

Egan, D., Pittner, M., & Goldstein, A. G. (1977). Eyewitness identification: Photographs vs. live models. *Law and Human Behavior, 1,* 199-206.

Elkind, D. (1977). Perceptual development in children. In I. Janis (Ed.), *Current trends in psychology* (pp. 121-129). Los Altos, CA: Kaufmann.

Erickson, M. T. (1987). *Behavior disorders of children and adolescents.* Englewood Cliffs, NJ: Prentice-Hall.

Erikson, E. (1963). *Childhood and society(* 2nd rev. ed.). New York: Norton.

Expert witness: Psychology and beyond. (1989, August). (Cassette Recording No. 89-090). Washington, DC: American Psychological Association.

Faller, K. C. (1984). Is the child victim of sexual abuse telling the truth? *Child Abuse and Neglect, 8,* 473-481.

Fantz, R. L. (1965). Visual perception from birth as shown by pattern selectivity. *Annals of the New York Academy of Science, 118,* 793-814.

Fantz, R. L. (1966). Pattern discrimination and selective attention as determinants of perceptual development from birth. In A. H. Kidd & J. E. Rivoire (Eds.),

Perceptual development in children (pp. 181-224). New York: International Universities Press.

Faust, D., & Ziskin, J. (1988). The expert witness in psychology and psychiatry. *Science, 24,* 31-35.

Federal Rules of Evidence 403.

Federal Rules of Evidence 601.

Federal Rules of Evidence 603.

Federal Rules of Evidence 611.

Federal Rules of Evidence 615.

Federal Rules of Evidence 702.

Federal Rules of Evidence 803.

Fisher, R. P., Amador, M., & Geiselman, R. E. (1989). Field test of the cognitive interview: Enhancing the recollection of actual victims and witnesses of crime. *Journal of Applied Psychology, 74,* 722-727.

Fisher, R. P., Geiselman, R. E., Raymond, D. S., Jurkevich, L. M., & Warhaftig, M. L. (1987). Enhancing enhanced eyewitness memory: Refining the cognitive interview. *Journal of Police Science and Administration, 15,* 291-297.

Fisher, R. P., & Quigley, K. L. (1989). *Improving epidemiological investigations with the Cognitive Interview: Tracing the source of food-borne outbreaks of disease.* Unpublished manuscript, Florida International University, Miami.

Flapan, D. (1968). *Children's understanding of social interaction.* New York: Teachers College Press.

Flavell, J. H. (1977). *Cognitive development.* Englewood Cliffs, NJ: Prentice-Hall.

Flavell, J. H. (1985). *Cognitive development* (2d ed.). Englewood Cliffs, NJ: Prentice-Hall.

Flin, R. H., Davies, G. M., & Stevenson, Y. (1987). Children as witnesses: Psycholegal aspects of the English and Scottish system. *Medicine and Law, 6,* 275-291.

Florida Statute 92.53 (1985).

Folkman, S., & Lazarus, R. S. (1985). If it changes it must be a process: Study of emotion and coping during three stages of a college examination. *Journal of Personality and Social Psychology, 48,* 150-170.

Fraser, B. G. (1981). Sexual child abuse: The legislation and the law in the United States. In P. B. Mrazek & C. H. Kempe (Eds.), *Sexually abused children and their families* (pp. 55-74). Elmsford, NY: Pergamon.

Freeman, H. A., & Weihofen, H. (1972). *Clinical law training: Interviewing and counseling.* St. Paul, MN: West.

Freeman, K. R., & Estrada-Mullaney, T. (1988). Using dolls to interview child victims: Legal concerns and interview procedures. *NIJ Reports,* No. 207, 2-6.

Frye v. United States, 293 F. 1013 (D.C. Cir. 1923).

Furth, H. G., & Milgram, N. A. (1973). Labeling and grouping effects in the recall of pictures by children. *Child Development, 44,* 511-518.

Furth, H. G., Ross, B. M., & Youniss, J. (1974). Operative understanding in reproductions of drawings. *Child Development, 43,* 63-70.

Galin, D., Johnstone, J., Nakell, L., & Herron, J. (1979). Development of the capacity for tactile information transfer between hemispheres in normal children. *Science, 204,* 1330-1332.

Gander, M., & Gardiner, H. (1981). *Child and adolescent development.* Boston: Little, Brown.

Geiselman, R. E., Fisher, R. P., Cohen, G., Holland, H., & Surtes, L. (1986). Eyewitness responses to leading and misleading questions under the cognitive interview. *Journal of Police Science and Administration, 14,* 31-39.

Geiselman, R. E., Fisher, R. P., Firstenberg, I., Hutton, L. A., Sullivan, S. J., Avetissian, I. V., & Prosk, A. L. (1984). Enhancement of eyewitness memory: An empirical evaluation of the cognitive interview. *Journal of Police Science and Administration, 12,* 74-80.

Geiselman, R. E., Fisher, R. P., MacKinnon, D. P., & Holland, H. L. (1985). Eyewitness memory enhancement in the police interview: Cognitive retrieval mnemonics versus hypnosis. *Journal of Applied Psychology, 70,* 401-412.

Gelles, R. J., & Cornell, C. P. (1985). *Intimate violence in families.* Beverly Hills, CA: Sage.

Georgia Code Ann. § 24-9-5 (1982).

Giannelli, P. C. (1980). The admissibility of novel scientific evidence: *Frye v. United States,* a half-century later. *Columbia Law Review, 80,* 1197-1250.

Gibbens, T. C. N., & Prince, J. (1963). *Child victims of sex crimes.* London: Institute for the Study and Treatment of Delinquency.

Gibson, E. J. (1969). *Principles of perceptual learning and development.* Boston: Little, Brown.

Gilligan, C. (1982). New maps of development: New visions of maturity. *American Journal of Orthopsychiatry, 52,* 199-212.

Girdner, B. (1985). Out of the mouths of babes. *California Lawyer, 5,* 57-61.

Globe Newspaper Co. v. Superior Court, 457 U.S. 596 (1982).

Gold, P. E. (1987). Sweet memories. *American Scientist, 75,* 151-155.

Gonzales v. State 748 S.W.2d 513 (Tex. App.—Beaumont 1988).

Goodman, G. S. (1984a). The child witness: An introduction. *Journal of Social Issues, 40,* 1-7.

Goodman, G. S. (Ed.) (1984b). Children's testimony in historical perspective. *Journal of Social Issues, 40,* 9-31.

Goodman, G. S. (1984c). The child witness [special issue]. *Journal of Social Issues, 40.*

Goodman, G. S., & Aman, C. (In press). Children's use of anatomically detailed dolls to recount an event. *Child Development.*

Goodman, G. S., Bottoms, B. L., Herscovici, B. B., & Shaver, P. (1989). Determinants of the child victim's perceived credibility. In S. J. Ceci, D. F. Ross, & M. P. Toglia (Eds.), *Perspectives on children's testimony* (pp. 1-22). New York or Berlin: Springer Verlag.

Goodman, G. S., Golding, J. M., & Haith, M. M. (1984). Jurors' reactions to child witnesses. *Journal of Social Issues, 40,* 139-156.

Goodman, G. S., Golding, J. M., Helgeson, V. S., Haith, M., & Michelli, J. (1987). When a child takes the stand: Jurors' perceptions of children's eyewitness testimony. *Law and Human Behavior, 11,* 27-40.

Goodman, G. S., & Hahn, A. (1987). Evaluating eyewitness testimony. In I. B. Weiner & A. K. Hess (Eds.), *Handbook of forensic psychology* (pp. 258-292). New York: John Wiley.

Goodman, G. S., & Helgeson, V. S. (1985). Child sexual assault: Children's memory and the law. *University of Miami Law Review, 40,* 181-208.

Goodman, G. S., Hirschman, J., Hepps, D., & Rudy, L. (In press). Children's memory for stressful events. *Merrill-Palmer Quarterly.*

Goodman, G. S., & Michelli, J. A. (1981, November). Would you believe a child witness? *Psychology Today,* pp. 83-84, 86, 90-92.

Goodman, G. S., & Reed, R. S. (1986). Age differences in eyewitness testimony. *Law and Human Behavior, 10,* 317-332.

Goodman, G. S., Taub, E. P., Jones, D. P. H., England, P., Port, L. K., Rudy, L., & Prado, L. (1990). *Emotional effects of criminal court testimony on child sexual assault victims.* Manuscript submitted for publication.

Goodman, J., & Loftus, E. (1988, March). The relevance of expert testimony on eyewitness memory. *Journal of Interpersonal Violence,* 115-121.

Gothard, S. (1990, February). *The battle and the backlash: Myths, realities and hidden agendas in sexual abuse of children.* Paper presented at the Nebraska District Judges Association and Nebraska County Judges Association Joint Education Program, Boys Town Campus, Omaha, NE.

Graham, M. H. (1985, August). Difficult times for the Constitution: Child testimony absent face-to-face confrontation. *The Champion,* pp. 18-21.

Graham, M. (1986). *Handbook of federal evidence.* (2nd ed.) St. Paul, MN: West.

Greenhouse, L. (1990, June 28). Child abuse trials can use television. *New York Times,* pp. A1, A12.

Grisso, T. (1981). *Juveniles' waiver of rights: Legal and psychological competence.* New York: Plenum.

Grossberg, S. J. (1985). A stepping stone to truth: Hypnosis and the preparation of the child witness. *Journal of Juvenile Law, 9,* 53-66.

Hafemeister, T. L., & Melton, G. B. (1987). The impact of social science research on the judiciary. In G. B. Melton (Ed.), *Reforming the law: Impact of child development research* (pp. 27-59). New York: Guilford.

Hale, G. A. (1979). Development of children's attention to stimulus components. In G. A. Hale & M. Lewis (Eds.), *Attention and cognitive development* (pp. 43-64). New York: Plenum.

Hall, M. D. (1989). The role of psychologists as experts in cases involving allegations of child sexual abuse. *Family Law Quarterly, 23,* 451-464.

Hall, E., Lamb, M., & Perlmutter, M. (1986). *Child psychology today.* New York: Random House.

Harris, J., & Liebert, R. (1984). *The child.* Englewood Cliffs, NJ: Prentice-Hall.

Harris, J., & Liebert, R. (1987). *The child.* (2nd ed.). Englewood Cliffs, NJ: Prentice-Hall.

Harrold v. Schluep, 264 S.2d 431 (Fla. App. 1972).

Hartshorne, H., & May, M. A. (1928). *Studies in deceit.* New York: Macmillan.

Haugaard, J. J. (1988). Judicial determination of children's competency to testify: Should it be abandoned? *Professional Psychology: Research and Practice, 19,* 102-107.

Hecaen, H., & Albert, M. L. (1978). *Human neuropsychology.* New York: Wiley-Interscience.

Hechler, D. (1988). *The battle and the backlash: The child sexual abuse war.* Lexington, MA: Lexington Books.

Heeney, T. L. (1985, August). Coping with "The abuse of child abuse prosecutions": The criminal defense lawyer's viewpoint. *The Champion,* pp. 12-17.

Herbert v. Superior Court, 117 Cal.App.3d 661, 172 Ca.Rptr. 850 (1981).

Hetherington, E. M., & Parke, R. D. (1986). *Child psychology: A contemporary viewpoint.* New York: McGraw-Hill.

Higgins-Trenk, A., & Gaithe, A. (1971). Elusiveness of formal operational thought in adolescents. *Proceedings, 79th Annual Convention, American Psychological Association.*

Higgs v. District Court, 713 P.2d 840 (Colo—Douglas County 1985).

Hollingsworth, J. (1986). *Unspeakable acts.* New York: Congdon and Weed.

Hopkins, E. (1988, January 11). Fathers on trial. *New York,* pp. 42-49.

Horowitz, M. J., Wilner, M., Kultreider, N., & Alvarez, W. (1980). Signs and symptoms of post-traumatic stress disorder. *Archives of General Psychiatry, 37,* 85-92.

Hosch, H. M. (1980). A comparison of three studies of the influence of expert testimony on jurors. *Law and Human Behavior, 4,* 297-302.

Howson, R. N. (1985, August). Child sexual abuse cases: Dangerous trends and possible solutions. *The Champion,* pp. 6-11, 45.

Hubel, D. H. (1979, September). The brain. *Scientific American, 241,* 44-53.

Hulse-Trotter, K., & Warren, A. R. (1990). *Do children believe in their own believability?* Poster presented at the American Psychology and Law Society Meetings, March 1990, Williamsburg, VA.

Idaho Code § 9-202 (Supp. 1986).

Idaho v. Wright, 110 S.Ct. 3139 (1990).

Imwinkelried, E. J. (1980). *Evidentiary foundations.* Charlottesville, VA: Michie.

Imwinkelried, E. J. (1981). A new era in the evolution of scientific evidence—A primer on evaluating the weight of scientific evidence. *William & Mary Law Review, 23,* 261-290.

Inhelder, B., & Piaget, J. (1958). *The growth of logical thinking from childhood to adolescence.* New York: Basic Books.

In re R.R. 79 N.J. 97, 398 A.2d 76 (1979).

James, W. (1890). *Principles of psychology.* New York: H. Holt.

Jewish Encyclopedia. (1916). New York: Funk & Wagnalls.

Johnson, J. (1990). *What Lisa knew: The truth and lies of the Steinberg case.* New York: G. P. Putnam.

Johnson, M. K., & Foley, M. A. (1984). Differentiating fact from fantasy: The reliability of children's memory. *Journal of Social Issues, 40,* 33-50.

Jones, D. P. H., & Krugman, R. D. (1986). Can a three-year-old child bear witness to her sexual assault and attempted murder? *Child Abuse & Neglect, 10,* 253-258.

Jones, D. P. H., & McGraw, J. M. (1987). Reliable and fictitious accounts of sexual abuse to children. *Journal of Interpersonal Violence, 2,* 27-45.

Jones, D. P. H., & McQuiston, M. G. (1988). *Interviewing the sexually abused child.* London: Gaskell.

Kagehiro, D. K. (1990). Defining the standard of proof in jury instructions. *Psychological Science, 1,* 194-200.

Kail, R. V., Jr., & Hagen, J. W. (1977). Introduction. In R. V. Kail, Jr., & J. W. Hagen (Eds.), *Perspectives on the development of memory and cognition* (pp. xi-xiii). Hillsdale, NJ: Lawrence Erlbaum.

Kalish, R. (1981). *Death, grief, and caring relationships.* Belmont, CA: Brooks/Cole.

Kastenbaum, R. (1967). The child's understanding of death: How does it develop? In E. Grollman (Ed.), *Explaining death to children.* (pp. 89-108). Boston: Beacon.

Katz , S., & Mazur, M. A. (1979). *Understanding the rape victim.* New York: John Wiley.

Kelly, R. J. (1984). *Gender and incest factors in reaction to adult-child sex.* Unpublished doctoral dissertation, State University of New York at Buffalo, Buffalo, NY.

Kentucky Rev. Stat. Ann. § 421.200 (Baldwin 1981).

Kentucky v. Stincer, 482 U.S. 730, 107 S.Ct. 2658 (1987).

King, P., McDaniel, A., Sandza, R., & Doherty, S. (1984, May 14). Children and the courts. *Newsweek,* p. 32.

Kirby v. United States, 174 U.S. 47, 19 S.Ct. 574 (1899).

Kobasigawa, A. (1974). Utilization of retrieval cues by children in recall. *Child Development, 45,* 127-134.

Kobasigawa, A. (1977). Retrieval strategies in the development of memory. In R. V. Kail, Jr., & J. W. Hagen (Eds.), *Perspectives on the development of memory and cognition* (pp. 177-201). Hillsdale, NJ: Lawrence Erlbaum.

Kohlberg, L. (1963). The development of children's orientations toward a moral order: I. Sequence in the development of moral thought. *Vita Humana, 6,* 11-33.

Kohlberg, L. (1976). Moral stages and moralization: The cognitive developmental approach. In T. Lickona (Ed.), *Moral development and behavior: Theory, research, and social issues* (pp. 31-53). New York: Holt, Rinehart & Winston.

Kosslyn, S. M. (1983). *Ghosts in the mind's machine.* New York: Norton.

Kübler-Ross, E. (1969). *On death and dying.* New York: Macmillan.

Landwirth, J. (1987). Children as witnesses in child sexual abuse trials. *Pediatrics, 80,* 585-589.

Lefrancois, G. R. (1989). *Of children.* (6th ed.). Belmont, CA: Wadsworth.

Leippe, M. R., Brigham, J. C., Cousins, C., & Romanczyk, A. (1989). The opinions and practices of criminal attorneys regarding child eyewitnesses: A survey. In S. J. Ceci, D. F. Ross, & M. P. Toglia (Eds.), *Perspectives on children's testimony* (pp. 110-130). New York or Berlin: Springer Verlag.

Leippe, M. R., & Romanczyk, A. (1987). Children on the witness stand: A communication/persuasion analysis of jurors' reactions to child witnesses. In S. J. Ceci, M. P. Toglia, & D. F. Ross (Eds.), *Children's eyewitness memory* (pp. 155-177). New York or Berlin: Springer Verlag.

Lenneberg, E. H. (1967). *Biological foundations of language.* New York: John Wiley.

Levy, R. J. (1989). Using "scientific" testimony to prove child sexual abuse. *Family Law Quarterly, 23,* 383-409.

Lickona, T. (1983). *Raising good children: Helping your child through stages of moral development.* New York: Bantam Books.

Linberg, M. (1980). The role of knowledge structures in the ontogeny of learning. *Journal of Experimental Child Psychology, 30,* 401-410.

Lindsay, R. C. L., Wells, G. L., & Rumpel, C. (1981). Can people detect eyewitness identification accuracy within and across situations? *Journal of Applied Psychology, 66,* 79-89.

Lipton, J. P. (1977). On the psychology of eyewitness testimony. *Journal of Applied Psychology, 62,* 90-95.

Loftus, E. F. (1979). *Eyewitness testimony.* Cambridge, MA: Harvard University Press.

Loftus, E. F., & Davies, G. M. (1984). Distortions in the memory of children. *Journal of Social Issues, 40,* 51-67.

Loftus, E. F., & Loftus, G. R. (1980). On the permanence of stored information in the human brain. *American Psychologist, 35,* 409-420.

Loftus, E. F., & Palmer, J. C. (1974). Reconstruction of automobile destruction: An example of the interaction between language and memory. *Journal of Verbal Learning and Verbal Behavior, 13,* 585-589.

Macaulay, S. (1987). Images of law in everyday life: The lessons of school, entertainment, and spectator sports. *Law and Society Review, 21,* 185-218.

Macfarlane, A. (1977). The psychology of childbirth. Cambridge, MA: Harvard University Press.

MacFarlane, K. (1985). Diagnostic evaluations and the use of videotapes in child sexual abuse cases. *U. Miami Law Review, 40,* 135.

MacFarlane, K., & Bulkley, J. (1982). Treating child sexual abuse: An overview of current program models. In J. Conte & D. Shore (Eds.), *Social work and child sexual abuse* (pp. 69-91). New York: Haworth.

Maclean, P. D. (1970). The triune brain, emotion, and scientific bias. In R. O. Schmitt (Ed.), *The neurosciences: Second study program.* New York: Rockefeller University Press.

Mahady-Smith, C. M. (1985, Spring). The young victim as witness for the prosecution: Another form of abuse? *Dickinson Law Review,* 721-749.

Mandler, J. M. (1983). Representation. In P. H. Mussen (Ed.), *Handbook of child psychology* (4th ed.). Vol. 3: J. H. Flavell & E. M. Markman (Eds.), *Cognitive development* (pp. 420-494). New York: John Wiley.

Marin, B. V., Holmes, D. L., Guth, M., & Kovac, P. (1979). The potential of children as eyewitnesses. *Law and Human Behavior, 3,* 295-306.

Marvin, R. S., Greenberg, M. T., & Mossler, D. G. (1976). The early development of conceptual perspective taking: Distinguishing among multiple perspectives. *Child Development, 47,* 511-514.

Maryland Statutes (Maryland Cts. and Jud. Proc. Code Ann. § 9-102 [1989]).

Maryland v. Craig, 110 S. Ct. 5157, 111 L.Ed.2d 666 (1990).

Massachusetts Gen. Laws Ann. Ch. 233, § 20 (West 1986).

McCauliff, C. M. A. (1982, November). Burdens of proof: Degrees of belief, quanta of evidence, or constitutional guarantees? *Vanderbilt Law Review,* 1293-1335.

McCloskey, M., & Egeth, H. E. (1984, September). Process and outcome considerations in juror evaluation of eyewitness testimony. *American Psychologist,* pp. 1065-1066.

McCord, D. (1986). Expert psychological testimony about child complainants in sexual abuse prosecutions: A foray into the admissibility of novel psychological evidence. *The Journal of Criminal Law & Criminology, 77,* 1-68.

McCormick, M. (1982). Scientific evidence: Defining a new approach to admissibility. *Iowa Law Review, 67,* 879-916.

McGaugh, J. (1989). Dissociating learning and performance: Drug and hormone enhancement of memory storage. *Brain Research Bulletin, 23,* 339-345.

McGough, L. (1989). Asking the right questions: Reviving the *voir dire* for child witnesses. *Georgia State University Law Review, 5,* 557.

McGough, L. (In press). Expert testimony: Assessing a child's credibility and interpreting behaviors. In L. McGough, (Ed.), *Fragile voices: Child witnesses in the American legal system.* New Haven, CT: Yale University Press.

McMartin case called a fiasco. (1990, January 21). *Omaha World Herald.*

Megaw-Nyce, J. S. (1979, March). *Perception of reversible and irreversible events by pre-schoolers.* Paper presented at the Meeting of the Society for Research in Child Development, San Francisco.

Melton, G. B. (1981a). Children's competency to testify. *Law and Human Behavior, 5,* 73-85.

Melton, G. B. (1981b). Procedural reforms to protect child victim/witnesses in sex offense proceedings. In J. Bulkley (Ed.), *Child sexual abuse and the law* (pp. 184-198). Washington, DC: American Bar Association.

Melton, G. B. (1984a, May 22). *Testimony before the United States Senate Subcommittee on Juvenile Justice Committee on the Judiciary,* Washington, DC.

Melton, G. B. (1984b). Developmental psychology and the law: The state of the art. *Journal of Family Law, 22,* 445-482.

Melton, G. B. (1984c). Child witnesses and the first amendment: A psycholegal dilemma. *Journal of Social Issues, 40,* 109-123.

Melton, G. B. (1990). Sexually abused children and the legal system: Some policy recommendations. *The American Journal of Family Therapy, 13,* 61-67.

Melton, G. B., & Wilcox, B. L. (1989). Changes in family law and family life: Challenges for psychology. *American Psychologist, 44,* 1213-1216.

Meriwether, M. H. (1986). Child abuse reporting laws: Time for a change. *Family Law Quarterly, 20,* 141-171.

Mischel, W., & Mischel, H. N. (1976). A cognitive social-learning approach to morality and self-regulation. In T. Lickona (Ed.), *Moral development and behavior* (pp. 84-107). New York: Holt, Rinehart & Winston.

Moely, B. E. (1977). Organization factors in the development of memory. In R. V. Kail, Jr. and J. W. Hagen (Eds.), *Perspectives on the development of memory and cognition* (pp. 203-236). Hillsdale, NJ: Lawrence Erlbaum.

Myers, J. E. B. (1985-1986). The legal response to child abuse: In the best interest of children? *Journal of Family Law, 24,* 149-269.

Myers, J. E. B. (1987). *Child witness law and practice.* New York: John Wiley.

Myers, J. E. B. (1988). Examining the young witness: Paint the child into your corner. *Family Advocate, 10,* 42-47.

Myers, N. A., & Perlmutter, M. (1978). Memory in the years from two to five. In P. A. Ornstein (Ed.), *Memory development in children* (pp. 191-218). Hillsdale, NJ: Lawrence Erlbaum .

Nelson, K., & Kosslyn, S. M. (1976). Recognition of previously labeled or unlabeled pictures by 5-year-olds and adults. *Journal of Experimental Child Psychology, 21,* 40-45.

Nichols, J. F. (1980, July). The marital/family therapist as an expert witness: Some thoughts and suggestions. *Journal of Marital and Family Therapy,* 293-299.

Nigro, G. N., Buckley, M. A., Hill, D. E., & Nelson, J. (1989). When juries "hear" children testify: The effects of eyewitness age and speech style on jurors' perceptions of testimony. In S. J. Ceci, D. F. Ross, & M. P. Toglia (Eds.), *Perspectives on children's testimony* (pp. 57-70). New York or Berlin: Springer Verlag.

Ochsner, J. C., & Zaragoza, M. (1988, March). *Children's eyewitness testimony: Accuracy and suggestibility of a memory for a real event.* Paper presented at the Biennial Meeting of the American Psychology-Law Society, Miami.

Office of Juvenile Justice and Delinquency Prevention. (1989, May/June). The child victim as a witness. *NIJ Reports*, pp. 11-14.

Ornstein, P. A., & Naus, M. J. (1978). Rehearsal processes in children's memory. In P. A. Ornstein (Ed.), *Memory development in children* (pp. 69-99). Hillsdale, NJ: Lawrence Erlbaum.

Packer, H. L. (1964). Two models of the criminal process. *University of Pennsylvania Law Review, 113,* 1-68.

Paris, S. G., & Lindauer, B. K. (1982). The development of cognitive skills during childhood. In B. B. Wolman (Ed.), *Handbook of developmental psychology* (pp. 333-349). Englewood Cliffs, NJ: Prentice-Hall.

Parisi v. Superior Court, 144 Cal.App.3d,. 211, 192 Cal.Rptr. 486 (1983).

Parker, J. (1982). The rights of child witnesses: Is the court a protector or perpetrator? *New England Law Review, 17,* 643-717.

Parker, J. F., Haverfield, E., & Baker-Thomas, S. (1986). Eyewitness testimony of children. *Journal of Applied Social Psychology, 16,* 287-302.

Penfield, W. (1969). *Speech and brain-mechanisms.* Princeton, NJ: Princeton University Press.

People v. Buckey (not reported) (Cal. [1990]).

People v. Kelly, 17 Cal.3d 24, 549 P.2d 1240, 130 Cal.Rptr. 144 (1976).

People v. Matthews, 17 Ill.2d 502, 162 N.E.2d 381 (1959).

People v. McDonald, 208 Cal.Rptr. 236, 37 Cal.3d 351, 690 P.2d 709, 46 A.L.R.4th. 1011 (1984).

People v. Murphy, 526 N.Y.S.2d 905 (Supp. 1988).

People v. Parks, 41 N.Y.2d 36, 359 N.E.2d 358, 390 N.Y.SS.2d 848 (1976).

Perlmutter, M. (1984). Continuities and discontinuities in early human memory paradigms, processes, and performances. In R. V. Kail & N. E. Spear (Eds.), *Comparative perspectives on the development of memory* (pp. 253-287). Hillsdale, NJ: Lawrence Erlbaum.

Perry, N. W., Docherty, C., & Kralik, R. (1988, April). *Expert testimony and child witness behavior: Effects on jurors' decisions.* Paper presented at the Annual Meeting of the Southwestern Psychological Association, Tulsa, OK.

Perry, N. W., Nielsen, D., Burns, D., Cunningham, E., & Jenkins, S. (1987, April). *Young children's ability to provide accurate testimony following a witnessed event.* Paper presented at the Spring Meeting of the Nebraska Psychological Association, Lincoln, NE.

Perry, N. W., Nielsen, D., Silvius, R., and Rosenthal, P. (1986). *Effects of visual stimuli cues on time-lapse recall.* Unpublished manuscript, Creighton University, Omaha, NE.

Perry, N. W., & Teply, L. L. (1984-1985). Interviewing, counseling, and in-court examination of children: Practical approaches for attorneys. *Creighton Law Review, 18,* 1369-1426.

Peters, D. P. (1990, March). *Confrontational stress and children's testimony: Some experimental findings.* In S. Ceci (Chair), *Do children lie? Narrowing the uncertainties.* Biennial Meeting of the American Psychology-Law Society, Williamsburg, VA.

Piaget, J. (1932/1965). *The moral judgment of the child.* New York: Free Press.

Piaget, J. (1952). *The origins of intelligence in children.* New York: International Universities Press.

Piaget, J. (1969). *The mechanics of perception.* New York: Basic Books.

Piaget, J., & Inhelder, B. (1973). *Memory and intelligence.* New York: Basic Books.

Pynoos, R. S., & Eth, S. (1984). The child as witness to homicide. *Journal of Social Issues, 40,* 87-108.

Raskin, D. C., Boychuk, T., McGough, L., & Stellar, M. (1990, March). *Psychological experts and evidence in cases of child sexual abuse: Scientific, professional, and legal issues.* Biennial Meeting of the American Psychology-Law Society, Williamsburg, VA.

Raskin, D. C., & Stellar, M. (in press). Assessing credibility of allegations of child sexual abuse: Polygraph examinations and statement analysis. In H. Wegener, F. Loesel, & J. Haisch (Eds.), *Criminal behavior and the justice system: Psychological perspectives.* New York or Berlin: Springer Verlag.

Raskin, D. C., & Yuille, J. C. (1989). Problems in evaluating interviews of children in sexual abuse cases. In S. J. Ceci, D. F. Ross, & M. P. Toglia (Eds.), *Perspectives on children's testimony* (pp. 184-207). New York or Berlin: Springer Verlag.

Reed v. State, 283 Md. 374, 391 A.2d 364 (1978).

Research upholds credibility of children's testimony in abuse cases. (1989, March 20). *Behavior Today,* pp. 4-5.

Rex v. Braddon and Speke, 9 How St. Tr. 1127 (1684).

Rex v. Braiser, 11 Leach 199, 168 Eng. Rep. 202 (1779).

Rich, J. (1968). *Interviewing children and adolescents.* London: Macmillan.

Richman, C. L., Nida, S., & Pittman, L. (1976). Effects of meaningfulness on child free-recall learning. *Developmental Psychology, 12,* 460-465.

Richmond Newspapers, Inc. v. Virginia, 448 U.S. 555, 100 S.Ct. 2814 (1980).

Rose, D. (1979). *Dentate granule cells and cognitive development.* New York: Columbia University Press.

Rosen v. United States, 245 U.S. 467 (1918).

Ross, D. F., Dunning, D., Toglia, M. P., & Ceci, S. J. (1989). Age stereotypes, communication modality, and mock jurors' perceptions of the child witness. In S. J. Ceci, D. F. Ross, & M. P. Toglia (Eds.), *Perspectives on children's testimony* (pp. 37-56). New York or Berlin: Springer Verlag.

Ross, D. F., Miller, B. S., & Moran, P. B. (1987). The child in the eyes of the jury: Assessing mock jurors' perceptions of the child witness. In S. J. Ceci, M. P. Toglia, & D. F. Ross (Eds.), *Children's eyewitness memory* (pp. 142-154). New York or Berlin: Springer Verlag.

Roth, V. (1985, March). *Thinking better by ourselves.* Unpublished presentation at the March colloquium of the Creighton University Department of Psychology, Omaha, NE.

Rothenberg, R. E. (Ed.). (1981). *The plain-language law dictionary.* New York: Penguin.

Rueger v. Hawks, 36 N.W.2d 236 (1949).

Salatas, H., & Flavell, J. H. (1976). Retrieval of recently learned information: Development of strategies and control skills. *Child Development, 47,* 941-948.

Santostefano, S. (1967). Children cope with the violent death of parents: The effect of severe trauma discussed from the viewpoint of adaptation. In D. Moriarty (Ed.), *The loss of loved ones: The effect of a death in the family on personality development* (pp. 151-166). Springfield, IL: Charles C Thomas.

Saywitz, K. J. (1988). The credibility of child witnesses. *Family Advocate, 10,* 38.

Saywitz, K. J. (1989). Children's conceptions of the legal system: "Court is a place to play basketball." In S. J. Ceci, D. F. Ross, & M. P. Toglia (Eds.), *Perspectives on children's testimony* (pp. 131-157). New York or Berlin: Springer Verlag.

Saywitz, K. J., Goodman, G. S., Nicholas, E., & Moan, S. (1989, April). *Children's memories of genital examinations: Implications for cases of child sexual assault.* Paper presented at the Biennial Meeting of the Society for Research on Child Development, Kansas City, MO.

Schaffer, H. R. (1971). *The growth of sociability.* Baltimore: Penguin.

Selman, R. L. (1981). The child as a friendship philosopher. In S. R. Asher & J. M. Gottman (Eds.), *The development of friendships* (pp. 242-272). New York: Cambridge University Press.

Simon, R. J. (1969). Judges' translations of burdens of proof into statements of probability. *Trial Lawyers Guide,* 103-114.

Smith, V. L., & Ellsworth, P. C. (1987). The social psychology of eyewitness accuracy: Misleading questions and communicator expertise. *Journal of Applied Psychology, 72,* 294-300.

Smith, V. L., Kassin, S., & Ellsworth, P. C. (1989). Eyewitness accuracy and confidence: Within- versus between-subjects correlations. *Journal of Applied Psychology, 74,* 356-359.

Spaulding, W. (1987). *Interviewing child victims of sexual exploitation.* Louisville, KY: National Center for Missing and Exploited Children.

Spitz, R. (1946). Anaclitic depression: An inquiry into the genesis of psychiatric conditions in early childhood. In A. Freud (Ed.), *The psychoanalytic study of the child* (Vol. 2, pp. 313-342). New York: International Universities Press.

Sprayberry v. State, 174 Ga.App. 55741, 330 S.E.2d 731 (1985).

State v. Chapple, 660 P.2d 7208 (Ariz.App.1983).

State v. Clark, 765 P.2d 916 (Wash.App. 1988).

State v. Cook, 485 So.2d 606 (La.Ct.App. 1986).

State v. Eggert, 358 N.W.2d 156 (Minn.Ct.App. 1984).

State v. Eiler, 762 P.2d 210 (Mont. 1988).

State v. Fairbanks, 171 P.2d 845 (1946).

State v. Guy, 419 N.W.2d 152 (Neb. 1988).

State v. Mannion, 19 Utah 505, 57 P.542 (1899).

State v. Moon, 726 P.2d 1263 (Wash. App. 1986).

State v. Orona, 92 N.M. 450, 589 P.2d 1041 (1979).

State v. Pomerleau, 363 A.2d 692 (Me. 1976).

State v. R.W., 104 N.J. 14, 514 A.2d 1287 (1986).

State v. Sheppard, 197 N.J.Super. 411, 484 A.2d 1330 (1984).

State in re S.H., 293 A.2d 181 (1972).

Stellar, M., Raskin, D. C., Yuille, J. C., & Esplin, P. W. (In press). *Child sexual abuse: Forensic interviews and assessments. New York or Berlin: Springer Verlag.*

Straus, M. A., Gelles, R. J., & Steinmetz, S. K. (1980). *Behind closed doors: Violence in the American family.* Garden City, NY: Doubleday.

Telling it to the judge: On being an expert witness. (1989, March). *Children & Teens Today,* pp. 1,3.

Texas Code of Criminal Procedure art. 38.071 (2).

Todd, C. M., & Perlmutter, M. (1980). Reality recalled by preschool children. *New Directions in Child Development, No. 10: Children's Memory,* 69-86.

Undeutsch, U. (1982). Statement validity analysis. In A. Trankell (Ed.), *Reconstructing the past: The role of psychologists in criminal trials* (pp. 27-56). Stockholm: Norstedt & Soners.

United States v. Addison, 498 F.2d 741 (D. C. Cir. 1974).

United States v. Baller, 519 F.2d 463 (4th Cir.), cert. denied, 423 U.S. 1019 (1975).

United States v. Fatico, 458 F.Supp. 388 (E.D.N.Y. 1978).

United States v. Ridling, 350 F. Supp. 90 (E.D. Mich. [1972]).

Use of child witness sparks concerns. (1983, November 7). *Omaha World Herald*, p. 3, col 1.

Utah Code Ann. § 76-5-410 (Supp. 1986).

Vera v. State, 709 S.W.2d 681 (Tex.Ct.App. 1986).

Vurpillot, E., & Ball, W. A. (1979). The concept of identity and children's selective attention. In G. A. Hale & M. Lewis (Eds.), *Attention and cognitive development* (pp. 23-42). New York: Plenum.

Wald, M., Ayres, R., Hess, D. W., Schantz, M., & Whitebread, C. H. (1967). Interrogations in New Haven: The impact of *Miranda*. *Yale Law Journal, 76,* 1519-1648.

Waller v. Georgia, 467 U.S. 48 (1983).

Walsh, F. (1982). Conceptualizations of normal family functioning. In F. Walsh (Ed.), *Normal family processes* (pp. 3-42). New York: Guilford.

Warren-Leubecker, A., Bradley, C., & Hinton, I. D. (1988, March). *Scripts and the development of flashbulb memories.* Paper presented at the Conference on Human Development, Charleston, SC.

Warren-Leubecker, A., Tate, C. S., Hinton, I. D., & Ozbek, I. N. (1989). What do children know about the legal system and when do they know it? First steps down a less traveled path in child witness research. In S. J. Ceci, D. F. Ross, & M. P. Toglia (Eds.), *Perspectives on children's testimony* (pp. 158-183). New York or Berlin: Springer Verlag.

Wehrspann, W. H., Steinhauer, P. D., & Klajner-Diamond, H. (1987). Criteria and methodology for assessing credibility of sexual abuse allegation. *Canadian Journal of Psychiatry, 32,* 615-623.

Weinstein, J., & Berger, M. (1987). *Weinstein's evidence.* New York: Matthew Bender.

Weiss, C. H. (1987). Diffusion of child development research to legal audiences. In G. B. Melton (Ed.), *Reforming the law: Impact of child development research* (pp. 63-85). New York: Guilford.

Weithorn, L. A. (1987). Professional responsibility in the dissemination of psychological research in legal contexts. In G. B. Melton (Ed.), *Reforming the law: Impact of child development research* (pp. 253-279). New York: Guilford.

Wells, G., L., & Leippe, M. (1981). How do triers of fact infer the accuracy of eyewitness identification? Using memory for peripheral detail can be misleading. *Journal of Applied Psychology, 66,* 682-687.

Wells, G. L., Lindsay, R. C. L., & Ferguson, T. J. (1979). Accuracy, confidence and juror perceptions in eyewitness identification. *Journal of Applied Psychology, 64,* 440-448.

Wells, G. L., Lindsay, R. C. L., & Tousignant, J. P. (1980). Effects of expert psychological advice on human performance in judging the validity of eyewitness testimony. *Law and Human Behavior, 4,* 275-285.

Wells, G. L., Turtle, J. W., & Luus, C. A. E. (1989). The perceived credibility of child eyewitnesses: What happens when they use their own words? In S. J. Ceci, D. F. Ross, & M. P. Toglia (Eds.), *Perspectives on children's testimony* (pp. 23-36). New York or Berlin: Springer Verlag.

Wenar, C. (1982). *Psychopathology from infancy through adolescence.* New York: Random House.

Werner, J. S., & Perlmutter, M. (1979). Development of visual memory in infants. In H. W. Reese & L. P. Lipsitt (Eds.), *Advances in child development and behavior* (Vol. 14, pp. 1-56). New York: Academic Press.

Wheeler v. United States, 159 U.S. 523 (1895).

Whitcomb, D., Shapiro, E. R., & Stellwagen, L. D. (1985). *When the victim is a child: Issues for judges and prosecutors* (Contract #J-LEAA-011-81). Washington, DC: National Institute of Justice.

White, B. L. (1971). *Human infants: Experience and psychological development. Englewood Cliffs, NJ: Prentice-Hall.*

Whitehurst, G. J. (1982). Language development. In B. B. Wolman (Ed.), *Handbook of developmental psychology* (pp. 367-386). Englewood Cliffs, NJ: Prentice-Hall.

Wiehl, L. (1990, January 12). National rules for child witnesses? *New York Times,* p. 24.

Wigmore, J. H. (1935/1940/1976). *Evidence in trials at common law* (revised by J. Chadborn), (Vol. 6). Boston: Little, Brown.

Wilson, J. C., & Pipe, M. E. (1990). *The effects of cues on young children's recall of real events.* Manuscript in preparation.

Wrightsman, L. S. (1991). *Psychology and the legal system.* Belmont, CA: Brooks/Cole.

Yakovlev, P. I., & Lecours, A. R. (1967). The mylogenetic cycles of regional maturation of the brain. In A. Minkowski (Ed.), *Regional development of the brain in early life.* Oxford, UK: Blackwell.

Yarmey, A. D., & Jones, H. P. T. (1983). Is the psychology of eyewitness identification a matter of common sense? In S. M. A. Lloyd-Bostock & B. R. Clifford (Eds.), *Evaluating eyewitness evidence.* (pp. 13-40). Chichester, UK: John Wiley.

Yates, A. (1987). Should young children testify in cases of sexual abuse? *American Journal of Psychiatry, 144,* 476-480.

Young, M. de (1986). A conceptual model for judging the truthfulness of a young child's allegation of sexual abuse. *American Journal of Orthopsychiatry, 56,* 550-559.

Yuille, J. C. (1988). The systematic assessment of children's testimony. *Canadian Psychology, 29,* 247-261.

Zaporzhets, A. V. (1965). The development of perception in the preschool child. In P. H. Mussen (Ed.), *European research in cognitive development. Monographs of the Society for Research in Child Development, 30,* 82-101.

Zaragoza, M. S. (1987). Memory, suggestibility, and eyewitness testimony in children and adults. In S. J. Ceci, M. P. Toglia, & D. F. Ross (Eds.), *Children's eyewitness memory* (pp. 53-78). New York or Berlin: Springer Verlag.

Zaragoza, M. S. (In press). Preschool children's susceptibility to memory impairment. *Proceedings of the Cornell Conference on the Suggestibility of Children's Recollections.*

Legal Cases Cited

Birmingham Ry., Light & Power v. Wise, 149 Ala. 492, 42 So. 821 (1906).

Bole v. Bole, 76 Cal. App. 2d 344, 172 P.2d 936 (1946).

California v. Green, 399 U.S. 149 (1970).

Callicott v. Callicott, 364 S.W.2d 455 (1963).

Chambers v. Mississippi, 410 U.S. 284 (1973).

Cleaveland v. State, 490 N.E.2d 1140 (Ind.Ct.App. 1986).

Commonwealth v. Anderson, 552 A.2d 1064 (Pa.Super. 1988).

Commonwealth v. Berry, 355 Pa.Super. 243, 513 A.2d 415 (1986).

Coy v. Iowa, 108 S.Ct. 1798, 487 U.S. 1012 (1988).

Frye v. United States, 293 F. 1013 (D.C. Cir. 1923).

Globe Newspaper Co. v. Superior Court, 457 U.S. 596 (1982).

Gonzales v. State, 748 S.W.2d 513 (Tex. App.—Beaumont 1988).

Harrold v. Schluep, 264 S.2d 431 (Fla. App. 1972).

Herbert v. Superior Court, 117 Cal.App.3d 661, 172 Ca.Rptr. 850 (1981).

Higgs v. District Court, 713 P.2d 840 (Colo—Douglas County 1985).

Idaho v. Wright, 110 S.Ct. 3139 (1990).

In re R.R. 79 N.J. 97, 398 A.2d 76 (1979).

Kentucky v. Stincer, 482 U.S. 730, 107 S.Ct. 2658 (1987).

Kirby v. United States, 174 U.S. 47, 19 S.Ct. 574 (1899).

Maryland v. Craig, 110 S. Ct. 5157, 111 L.Ed.2d 666 (1990).

Parisi v. Superior Court, 144 Cal.App.3d 211, 192 Cal.Rptr. 486 (1983).

People v. Buckey (not reported) (Cal. [1990]).

People v. Kelly, 17 Cal.3d 24, 549 P.2d 1240, 130 Cal.Rptr. 144 (1976).

People v. Matthews, 17 Ill.2d 502, 162 N.E.2d 381 (1959).

People v. McDonald, 208 Cal.Rptr. 236, 37 Cal.3d 351, 690 P.2d 709, 46 A.L.R.4th. 1011 (1984).

People v. Murphy, 526 N.Y.S.2d 905 (Supp. 1988).

People v. Parks, 41 N.Y.2d 36, 359 N.E.2d 358, 390 N.Y.SS.2d 848 (1976).

Reed v. State, 283 Md. 374, 391 A.2d 364 (1978).

Rex v. Braddon and Speke, 9 How St. Tr. 1127 (1684).

Rex v. Braiser, 11 Leach 199, 168 Eng. Rep. 202 (1779).

Richmond Newspapers, Inc. v. Virginia, 448 U.S. 555, 100 S.Ct. 2814 (1980).

Rosen v. United States, 245 U.S. 467 (1918).

Rueger v. Hawks, 36 N.W.2d 236 (1949).

Sprayberry v. State, 174 Ga.App. 55741, 330 S.E.2d 731 (1985).

State v. Chapple, 660 P.2d 7208 (Ariz.App.1983).

State v. Clark, 765 P.2d 916 (Wash.App. 1988).

State v. Cook, 485 So.2d 606 (La.Ct.App. 1986).

State v. Eggert, 358 N.W.2d 156 (Minn.Ct.App. 1984).

State v. Eiler, 762 P.2d 210 (Mont. 1988).

State v. Fairbanks, 171 P.2d 845 (1946).

State v. Guy, 419 N.W.2d 152 (Neb. 1988).

State v. Mannion, 19 Utah 505, 57 P. 542 (1899).

State v. Moon, 726 P.2d 1263 (Wash. App. 1986).

State v. Orona, 92 N.M. 450, 589 P.2d 1041 (1979).

State v. Pomerleau, 363 A.2d 692 (Me. 1976).

State v. R.W., 104 N.J. 14, 514 A.2d 1287 (1986).

State v. Sheppard, 197 N.J.Super. 411, 484 A.2d 1330 (1984).

State *in re* S.H., 293 A.2d 181 (1972).

United States v. Addison, 498 F.2d 741 (D.C. Cir. 1974).

United States v. Baller, 519 F.2d 463 (4th Cir.), cert. denied, 423 U.S. 1019 (1975).

United States v. Fatico, 458 F.Supp. 388 (E.D.N.Y. 1978).

United States v. Ridling, 350 F. Supp. 90 (E.D. Mich. [1972]).

Vera v. State, 709 S.W.2d 681 (Tex.Ct.App. 1986).

Waller v. Georgia, 467 U.S. 48 (1983).

Wheeler v. United States, 159 U.S. 523 (1895).

Name Index

Ainsworth, M.D.S., 81
Albert, M. L., 58
Alberts, F., 230
Alvarez, W., 86
Amador, M., 110
Aman, C., 150, 187, 193, 194
American Bar Association, 230, 232, 256
American Jurisprudence, 37, 50
American Jurisprudence Trials, 108
American Psychiatric Association, 86, 91
American Psychological Association, 213
Anglin, J. M., 126
Appelbaum, P. S., 230
Atkinson, R. D., 107
Avetissian, I. V., 110
Ayres, R., 166

Baker-Thomas, S., 57, 68
Ball, W. A., 67
Barbieri, M. K., 16-17, 18, 72, 135
Beach, L. H., 16, 31
Bekerian, D. A., 187
Belli, R., 130
Bendek, E. P., 247
Berger, M., 47
Berliner, L., 16-17, 18, 72, 135, 214, 224
Birmingham Ry, Light & Power v. Wise, 3
Blau, T. H., 230
Blehar, M. C., 81
Bloom, L., 125
Bole v. Bole, 3
Bond, E. C., 37
Bones, V., 159
Bottoms, B. L., 31, 33, 36, 120, 121-122
Bowers, J. M., 187
Boychuk, T., 200, 201
Boys Town Conference, 251
Bradley, C., 194

Bransford, J. D., 114
Brant, R.S.T., 4
Brigham, J. C., 3, 25, 27-29, 30
Brooks, C. M., 151, 183, 236, 256
Brown, A. L., 114
Bruner, J., 70
Buckley, M. A., 31, 32, 82
Bulkley, J., 4, 36, 46, 48
Burns, D., 110, 111, 123
Burton, R. V., 83, 106
Bussey, K,, 194

California v. Green, 144
Callicott v. Callicott, 3
Campione, J. C., 114
Carey, S., 63, 109
Ceci, S. J., 24, 25, 30, 32-33, 34, 38, 39, 82, 109, 185, 190, 196, 235, 247, 260
Chambers v. Mississippi, 189-190
Chance, J. E., 109
Chase, S., 73
Chi, M.T.H., 116
Christiaansen, R. E., 187
Clark, E. V., 126
Clarke-Stewart, A., 120, 121
Cleary, E. W., 43, 46, 50, 51, 148, 152, 162, 171
Cleaveland v. State, 149
Cohen, G., 110
Cohen, R. L., 110, 118, 190
Collins, G. B., 37
Collins, W. A., 65
Commonwealth v. Anderson, 46
Commonwealth v. Berry, 162
Cornell, C. P., 4
Cousins, C., 3, 25
Coy v. Iowa, 18, 143, 158-159, 174, 215, 218, 229, 251
Crewdson, J., 227
Cunningham, E., 110, 111, 123
Cutler, B. L., 212

Dale, P. S., 191
Damon, L., 185
Davies, G. M., 16, 73, 100, 104, 119
Day, M. C., 67, 68
Deffenbacher, K., 199, 203
DeFrancis, V., 137
Dent, H. R., 26, 64, 122, 248, 249-250
DeSimone, M., 190, 196
Dexter, H. R., 212
Diamond, R., 63
Docherty, C., 35
Doek, J. E., 4
Doherty, E., 4, 34
Doherty, S., 134, 174
Duggan, L. M., III, 4, 34
Duncan, E. M., 117
Dunning, D., 24, 25, 32-33, 34, 35, 82
Dziech, B. W., 226

Egan, D., 64
Egeth, H. E., 203
Elkind, D., 63
Ellsworth, P. C., 192-193, 199
England, P., 135, 136, 137, 138, 194
Erickson, M. T., 91, 92
Erikson, E., 81, 86
Esplin, P. W., 201
Estrada-Mullaney, T., 149, 150, 151
Eth, S., 19, 71, 80, 86, 87, 88, 89, 90, 106,
    136, 137, 138
Expert Witness: Psychology and Beyond,
    230
Faller, K. C., 26, 106
Fantz, R. L., 130
Faust, D., 203, 204
Federal Rules of Evidence 24, 41, 43, 45,
    46, 47, 53, 153, 157, 162, 163, 169,
    206, 229
Ferguson, T. J., 210
Ferrara, R. A., 114
Firstenberry, I., 110
Fisher, R. P., 110, 111
Flapan, D., 65
Flavell, J. H., 56, 114, 115, 116
Flin, R., 100, 104
Foley, M. A., 104
Folkman, S., 90
Fraser, B. G., 214

Freeman, H. A., 128, 241, 245
Freeman, K. R., 149, 150, 151
Frye v. United States, 206-207, 208-209,
    210, 211
Furth, H. G., 75, 115
Gaithe, A., 69, 77
Galin, D., 60, 61, 62
Gander, M., 78, 79
Gardiner, H., 78, 79
Geiselman, R. E., 110
Gelles, R. J., 4
Georgia Code Annotated, 43
Giannelli, P. C., 206, 207, 208, 209, 210-
    211
Gibbens, T.C.N., 137
Gibson, E. J., 64
Gilligan, C., 83
Girdner, E., 191
Globe Newspaper Co. v. Superior Court,
    135, 141, 142, 214
Gold, P. E., 194
Golding, G. M., 31, 32, 34, 91, 117
Goldsborough, C. L., 230
Goldstein, A. G., 64, 109
Gonzales v. State, 45
Goodman, G. S., 10, 24, 31, 32, 33, 34,
    36, 38, 39, 57, 61, 66, 67, 73, 75-76,
    80, 82, 91, 109, 110, 117, 119, 120,
    121-122, 135, 136, 137, 138, 145,
    150, 185, 186, 187, 193, 194, 196,
    212, 213
Gothard, S., 225
Graham, M. H., 46, 143, 165, 168
Greenberg, M. T., 120
Greenhouse, L., 146
Grisso, T., 101
Grossberg, S. J., 99
Guth, M., 71, 112, 118, 186

Hafemeister, T. L., 180
Hagen, J. W., 113
Hahn, A., 110
Haith, M. M., 31, 32, 34, 91, 117
Hale, G. A., 66
Hall, E., 62, 63, 64, 69, 70, 83, 107-108,
    113, 124, 126
Hall, M. D., 111, 177, 178, 189, 204, 205
Harnick, M. A., 118, 190

Harris, J., 77, 95, 114
Harrold v. Schluep, 3
Hartshorne, H., 83
Haugaard, U. J., 41, 49
Haverfield, E., 57, 68
Hecaen, H., 58
Hebbs, D., 185
Heckler, D., 5, 226
Heeney, T. L., 135, 152-153, 154, 155, 160
Helgeson, V. S., 31, 34, 57, 61, 66, 67, 73, 75-76, 80, 82, 117, 120, 186, 187, 193
Herbert v. Superor Court, 157
Herron, J., 60, 61, 62
Herscovici, B. B., 31, 33, 36
Hess, D. W., 166
Hetherington, E. M., 69
Higgs v. District Court, 150
Higgins-Trenk, A., 69, 77
Hill, D. E., 31, 32, 82
Hinton, I. D., 99, 100, 101, 102, 103, 104, 106, 156, 194
Hirschman, J., 195
Holland, H., 110
Hollingsworth, J., 227
Holmes, D. L., 71, 112, 118, 186
Hopkins, E., 139, 140
Horowitz, M. J., 86
Hosch, H. M., 212
Howson, R. M., 139, 246, 247
Hubel, D. H., 58
Hutton, L. A., 110

Idaho Code S 9-202, 41
Idaho v. Wright, 170, 220, 251
Imwinkelried, E. J., 148, 209-210, 222
In re R. R., 171
Inhelder, B., 69, 71, 74, 75, 77, 96, 107, 109, 110
Isquith, P., 4, 34

James, W., 56
Jenkins, s., 110, 111, 123
Jewish Encyclopedia, The, 37
Johnson. J., 227
Johnson, M. K., 104

Johnstone, J., 60, 61, 62
Jones, D.P.H., 10, 13, 15, 80, 135, 136, 137, 138, 163, 194, 237, 238, 239-240, 242, 243, 244, 247, 257
Jones, H.P.T., 24, 26, 31
Jurkevich, L. M., 110

Kagehiro, D. K., 211
Kail, R. V., Jr., 113
Kalish, R., 88
Kassin, S. M., 199
Kastenbaum, R., 87
Katz, S., 135
Kelly, R. J., 4
Keniston, A., 65
Kentucky Revised Statutes, 46
Kentucky v. Stincer, 164, 216, 229
King, P., 134, 174
Kirby v. United States, 144
Klajner-Diamond, H., 183, 186, 200, 202
Kobasigawa, A., 115, 116
Koeske, R. D., 116
Kohlberg, L., 83-84, 85, 106
Kosslyn, S. M., 78-79, 109, 123
Kovac, P., 71, 112, 118, 186
Kralik, R., 35
Krugman, R. D., 10, 13, 15, 80, 163, 238, 257
Kultreider, N., 86
Kübler-Ross, E., 88, 95
Kunen, S., 117

Lahey, M., 125
Lamb, M., 62, 63, 64, 69, 70, 83, 107-108, 113, 124, 126
Landwirth, J., 37, 164, 165, 166, 168, 256
Lazarus, R. S., 90
Lecours, A. R., 60
Lee, J. M., 190, 196
Lefrancois, G. R., 56
Leippe, M. R., 3, 24, 25, 27-29, 30, 32, 68
Lenneberg, E. H., 71
Lepore, S., 120, 121
Levine, M., 4, 34
Levy, R. J., 139-140, 149, 151, 188, 222, 244

Liebert, R., 77, 95, 114
Lickona, T., 84, 105
Linberg, M., 116
Lindauer, B. K., 66, 67
Lindsay, R.C.L., 210
Lipton, J. P., 122
Loftus, E. F., 16, 63, 72, 119, 187, 191,
    192, 212, 213, 245
Loftus, G. R., 187, 245
Luus, C.A.E., 25

Macaulay, S., 100-101, 104
Macfarlane, A., 109
MacFarlane, K., 4, 26, 121, 185
MacKinnon, D. P., 110
Maclean, P. D., 58
Mahady-Smith, C. M., 49
Mandler, J. M., 73
Marin, B. V., 71, 112, 118, 186
Marvin, R. S., 120
Maryland v. Craig, 36, 143, 146-147,
    157, 159, 164, 166-168, 174, 183-
    184, 185, 195-196, 214, 215, 216,
    217, 218, 229, 251
Mass. General Laws Ann., 46
May, M. A., 83
Mazur, M. A., 135
McCauliff, C.M.A., 211
McCloskey, M., 203
McCord, D., 201, 202
McCormick, M., 203, 204, 206, 209, 211,
    212
McDaniel, A., 134, 174
McGaugh, J., 194
McGough, L., 135, 145, 159, 174, 184,
    185, 189, 200, 215, 230, 235
McGraw, J. M., 247
McQuiston, M. D., 238, 239-240, 242,
    243, 244
Megaw-Nyce, J. S., 64
Melton, G. B., 17, 19, 49, 65, 134, 135-
    136, 138, 141, 144, 159, 163-164,
    180, 229
Michelli, J., 31, 34, 137-138
Milchman, M. S., 151, 183, 236, 256
Miller, B. S., 15, 34
Milgram, N. A., 115
Mischel, H. N., 83

Mischel, W., 83
Moan, S., 185, 196
Moely, B. E., 115
Moran, P. B., 15, 34
Mossler, D. G., 120
Myers, J.E.B., 37, 38, 40, 41, 42, 43, 45,
    46, 47, 48, 49, 50, 51, 52, 54, 95,
    99, 142, 145, 147, 148, 152, 153,
    154, 155, 157, 160, 161, 162, 168-
    169, 170, 172, 174, 190, 197, 235,
    237, 243, 254
Myers, N. A., 109, 110

Nakell, L., 60, 61, 62
National Center on Child Abuse and
    Neglect, 4
Naus, M. J., 114
Nelson, J., 31, 32
Nelson, K., 109
Nicholas, E., 185, 196
Nochols, J. R., 230, 232, 233, 234
Nida, S., 116
Nielsen, D., 63, 110, 111, 123
Nigro, G. N., 31, 32, 83

Ochalek, K., 187
Ochsner, J. C., 187, 194
Office of Juvenile Justice and Delin-
    quency Prevention, 256
Omaha World Herald, 5, 9, 10
Ornstein, P. A., 114
Ozbek, I. N., 99, 100, 101, 102, 103, 104,
    106, 156

Packer, H. L., 2
Palmer, J. C., 72
Paris, S. G., 66, 67
Parisi v. Superior Court,d 161
Parke, R. D., 69
Parker, J., 135, 145, 256
Parker, J. F., 57, 68
Penfield, W., 187
Penrod, S. D., 212
People v. Buckey, 4-10
People v. Kelly, 207
People v. Matthews, 50

People v. McDonald, 29
People v. Murphy, 42, 51
People v. Parks, 43
People Weekly, 30
Perlmutter, M., 62, 63, 64, 69, 70, 83, 107-108, 109, 110, 113, 124, 126
Perry, N. W., 35, 63, 65, 110, 111, 112, 123, 237
Peters, D. P., 194
Piaget, J., 65, 69, 71, 74, 75, 77, 83-84, 96, 107, 109, 110
Pipe, M. E., 121
Pittman, L., 116
Pittner, J., 64
Port, L. K., 135, 136, 137, 138, 194
Prado, L., 135, 136, 137, 138, 194
Prince, J., 137
Prosk, A. L., 110
Putnick, M., 190, 196
Pynoos, R. S., 19, 71, 80, 86, 87, 88, 89, 90, 106, 136, 137, 138

Quigley, K. L., 111

Raskin, D. C., 26, 200, 201, 202, 244, 246, 247
Rathburn, L., 191
Raymond, D. S., 110
Reed, R. S., 109, 119, 120, 186, 187, 193
Reed v. State, 207
Rex v. Braddon and Speke, 38
Rex v. Braiser, 39
Rich, J., 73, 237
Richman, C. L., 116
Richmond Newspapers, Inc. v. Virginia, 141
Ritchie, V., 225
Romanczyk, A., 3, 24, 25, 27-29, 30, 32
Rose, D., 58
Rosen v. United States, 40
Rosenthal, P., 63
Ross, B. M., 75
Ross, D. F., 15, 24, 25, 30, 32-33, 34, 38, 39, 82, 109, 185, 190, 235, 247
Roth, V., 79
Rothenberg, R. E., 168, 203
Rudy, L., 135, 136, 137, 138, 185, 194

Rueger v. Hawks, 3
Rumpel, C., 210

Sachsenmaier, T., 120, 121-122
Salatas, H., 115, 116
Sandza, R., 134, 174
Santostefano, S., 87
Saywitz, K. J., 99, 100, 101, 102, 103, 155, 185, 196, 199
Schaffer, H. R., 124
Schantz, M. 166
Scheiner, J., 4, 34
Schetky, D. H., 247
Schudson, C. B., 226
Schwartz-Kenney, B., 120, 121-122
Selman, R. L., 77
Shapiro, E. R., 3, 4, 100, 139, 224, 225, 237, 239
Shaver, P., 31, 33, 36
Shiffrin, R. M., 107
Silvius, R., 63
Simon, R. J., 211
Smith, V. L., 192-193, 199
Spaulding, W., 237, 239, 248
Spitz, R., 80
Sprayberry v. State, 51
State v. Chapple, 29
State v. Clark, 43
State v. Cook, 50
State v. Eggert, '148
State v. Eiler, 44
State v. Fairbanks, 3
State v. Guy, 47
State v. Mannion, 157
State v. Moon, 29
State v. Orona, 147
State v. Pomerleau, 42
State v. R. W., 50
State v. Sheppard, 164-165
State *in re* S. H., 3
Steinhauer, P. D., 183, 186, 200, 202
Steinmetz, S. K., 4
Stellar, M., 200, 201
Stellwagen, L. D., 3, 4, 100, 139, 224, 225, 237, 239
Stephenson, G. M., 64
Stevenson, Y., 100, 104
Straus, M. A., 4

Sullivan, S. J., 110
Surtes, L., 110

Tate, C. S., 99, 100, 101, 102, 103, 104, 106, 156
Taub, E. P., 135, 136, 137, 138, 194
Teply, L. L., 65, 112, 237
Thompson, W., 120, 121
Tisza, V. B., 4
Thomas, S., 120, 121-122
Todd, C. M., 113
Todd, J., 185
Toglia, M. P., 24, 25, 30, 32-33, 34, 38, 39, 82, 109, 185, 190, 196, 235, 247
Tousignant, J. P., 210
Turtle, J. W., 25

Undeutsch, U., 186, 201, 202
United States v. Addison, 207
United States v. Baller, 209
United States v. Fatico, 211
United States v. Ridling, 210
Utah Code Annotated, 49

Vera v. State, 149
Vurpillot, E., 67

Wald, M., 166
Wall, S., 81
Waller v. Georgia, 142
Walsh, F., 74
Warhaftig, M. L., 110
Warren-Leubecker, A., 99, 100, 101, 102, 103, 104, 106, 156, 194
Waters, E., 81

Wehrspann, W. H., 183, 186, 200, 202
Weihofen, H., 128, 241, 245
Weinstein, J., 47
Weiss, C. H., 179
Weithorn, L. A., 180
Wellman, H., 65
Wells, G. L., 25, 68, 210
Wenar, C. 89
Werner, J. S., 107
Westby, S., 65
Wheeler v. United States, 3, 40, 41
Whitcomb, D., 3, 4, 100, 139, 224, 225, 237, 239
White, B. L., 81
Whitebread, C. H., 166
Whitehurst, G. J., 126
Whitney, P., 117
Wilcox, B. L., 229
Wiehl, L., 134
Wigmore, J. H., 36, 38
Wilner, M., 86
Wilson, J. C., 121
Wolfskeil, M. P., 27
Wrightsman, L. S., 3, 20

Yakovlev, P. I., 60
Yarmey, A. D., 24, 26, 31
Yates, A., 250-251
Young, M. de, 26
Youniss, J., 75
Yuille, J. C., 26, 200, 201, 202, 244, 246, 247

Zaporzhets, A. V., 62
Zaragoza, M. S., 185, 186, 187, 194, 197
Ziskin, J., 203, 204

Subject Index

Accuracy of child witnesses, 57, 63, 99, 100, 228; and age of children, 28, 107, 120; assumptions about, 24, 26, 117; criteria for determining truthfulness, 202; fabrication and, 26, 33, 45, 66, 186; how to determine, 199-200, 202; of knowledge about the court system, 100, 101; reactions of attorneys, investigators, police, judges, and jurors, 24-29; and suggestibility, 117-120; and Susie, case of, 13

American Psychology-Law Society, 213, 235

Amicus curiae brief, 213

Animism, 79

Association of Trial Lawyers in America, 197

Attorneys: children's understanding of, 102-103; comparison of prosecutors and defense attorneys, 27, 28; reactions to children as witnesses, 26-28; recommendations to, 127-128, 252-256; use of manipulative techniques with jurors, 28-29

Betrayal of secrets, 120-121

Brain, development of, 58-62, 69, 79

Buckey, Peggy McMartin, 4-10

Buckey, Raymond, 4-10, 191

Centrality of information to be remembered, 187

Cerebral transfer, 60-61

Child development, 55-96; attention, 66-68; brain, 58-62; cognition, 68-77; emotional and social development, 80-85; exceptional children, 90-93; grieving, 87-90; language, 71-72, 124-126; morality, 83-85, 104-106; perception, 62-65; reasoning, 79; scanning and selectivity, 67-68

Children with behavioral or emotional disorders, 92-93

Children's Institute International, 5, 6, 185, 191

Children's rights, 17-19, 212-214

"Clinician-as-researcher" model, 236-237

Cognitive limitations of young children, 77-80

Communication, by children, 16, 32-33, 126-128, 195

Competence of children, 14, 15-17, 39, 57, 177, 181-198, 229, 235; age and, 61-62, 63, 64, 65, 66, 67-68, 70, 71, 73-74, 75, 76, 77-78, 101-104, 105, 181-182; age limit and, 38, 39, 40, 41-43, 48; ancient and common-law traditions about, 37-41; assumed age of competence to testify, 25; cognitive limitations and, 77-80; compared to adults, 63, 64, 65, 6, 68, 70, 107, 182; determinants of, 17; individual differences in, 16; jurors' reactions, 15-16, 28, 29-36; legal views of, 37-49; recent trends regarding, 41; states differ in rules on, 41-49; statutes about, 41

Competency examination, 43, 49-52, 228, 254; abuses in, 50; attorney's role in, 51, 52, 254; and Federal Rules of Evidence, 46-47; psychologist's role in, 51; trial judge's role, 49-51

Comprehension by children, 64; and age, 68-100; of attorneys, 102-103; of concepts of the court and courtroom, 101-102; of court proceedings, 99-106, 183; of the judge, 102; of the jury, 103; of witnesses, 103;

Confidence and accuracy, 199, 200
Context reinstatement, 110-111
Country Walk case, 226, 227
Court Appointed Special Advocates
    (CASA), 160, 174
Credibility of children, 57, 99, 177, 198-
    213, 235-236, 246; and age, 32, 34;
    beliefs about, 24; compared to
    adults, 24, 31, 34, 57; and confi-
    dence, 82; demeanor and speaking
    style, 198; at different points of the
    trial, 35; factors influencing, 17;
    ways of detecting, 200; witness
    credibility vs. statement credibil-
    ity, 200-201
Crime control model, of criminal justice,
    2, 3
Cross-examination of child witnesses,
    152-155, 189-195, 197, 255; form
    of questions, 191; interviewer's
    knowledge of alleged crime, 192-
    193; intimidation, effects on, 193;
    limits on, 215-216; in McMartin
    Preschool trial, 5, 7; status of ques-
    tioner, 190-191; stress, effects of,
    193-195; techniques for, 190

Defendants' rights, 2, 19-21, 177, 217-
    219; confrontation clause, 10, 143-
    144, 158, 164, 165, 170, 195, 196,
    216, 218; constitutional rights, 10,
    14, 134, 135, 138, 140-145, 153,
    229; dilemmas in, 19-20, 134; First
    Amendment and, 134, 140-141,
    142; protection from false charges,
    135, 139-140, 150, 151; right to a
    public trial, 134, 141-143; right to
    confront accusatory witness, 10,
    14, 19, 134, 143-146, 147, 152-155,
    148, 164, 165, 170, 195, 196; Sixth
    Amendment, 10, 19, 134, 140-141,
    143-145, 160, 164, 189
Demonstrative evidence, 148-149;
    children's drawings as, 151
Differing roles in the justice system,
    178-181
Dilemmas, psycho-legal, 4, 10, 13, 19,
    20-21, 57, 177, 224

Direct examination, of child witnesses,
    145, 147-151, 185-188
Disabled children, 92
Distortion, deliberate, 66
Dolls, anatomical, 29, 111, 123, 148,
    183, 222; authors' views on, 189;
    court decisions re. admissibility,
    148-149, 188; empirical work
    with, 150, 189; history of use, 149;
    protocol for use of, 151; training in
    use of, 188; use before trial, 188;
    validity of, 188-189
Due process model, of criminal justice,
    2, 3

Eriksonian stages of psychosocial devel-
    opment, 81-82, 86
Errors, in children's communication,
    126-128
Exceptional children, 90-93
Expert witnesses, 29, 230-231, 232-234;
    admissibility of evidence by, 205,
    206, 207; authors' views on, 212-
    213; benefits of, 212-213; contro-
    versy about use of, 203; "do's and
    don'ts," 234; eligibility, 203-204;
    failure to admit, 29; Frye stan-
    dard, 206-209, 210-211; functions
    in child-witness cases, 202-203;
    mandated use in Germany, 202;
    purpose of, 205; and relevance and
    helpfulness, 204; resources for,
    230; role of psychologist as, 205,
    212, 213; and two-pronged test,
    204;

Fabrications, by children, 26, 33, 45, 66,
    186
Fears about the court system, by chil-
    dren, 100
Frye standard, 206-209, 210-211

Grieving, process of, 87-90

Hearsay evidence, 30, 168, 169, 229-230

Imagery, as memory strategy, 114-115
Importance displacement hypothesis, 31
In camera testimony, 144, 163-164
Inducements to keep secrets, 120-122
Information-processing model, of cognitive development, 69-70, 107
Innovative procedures, for children's testifying, 14, 18, 19, 30, 133-134, 155-172, 184, 229, 251, 254; acceptability of, attorneys, 29, 30 134; alteration of the courtroom and its procedures, 156-172; and appeals, 134; authors' views on, 185; and constitutional issues, 134; examples of, 19, 133-134; excluding witnesses from the courtroom, 152-163; interpreter, use of, 171, 172; legal opinion on, 185; neutral questioner, use of, 163; preparation of child witness, 155-156, 254; and prosecutors vs. defense attorneys, 29; providing support persons, 160-161; recesses and postponements, 159-160; screens, use of, 156; videotaped testimony, 164-172, 216-217
Internal cues, as e memory strategy, 115-116
Interviewing the child witness, 191-193, 231-232, 236-247

"Jeanette," case of, 136-137, 138
Jordan (Minnesota) case, 226, 227
Judges: children's comprehension of 102; factors in determining child's competency, 51; reactions to children as witnesses, 36-37; re-education of, 250-252; topics for cross-examination to be evaluated, 153
Jurors: effects of child's age on, 34; effects of deliberation, 35; issues of credibility, 15; reactions to children as witnesses, 15, 28, 29-36, 57; re-education of, 255; summary of reactions, 35

Kohlberg's theory of moral development, 83-85, 106

Language and communication, by children: age norms for understanding questions, 125; child's powerful speech style, 32-33; and confidence, 35; development of language, 71-72, 124-126; enhancing through alternative procedures, 195; errors in children's communications, 126-128; linguistic representation, 71; of questions and suggestibility, 191-192; and transforming memory, 72; use of simple, 198
Leading questions, 145, 147-148, 185-188, 191-193, 196, 252; authors' view on, 196-197; "enabling," 243, 244; mis-, 192-193; "stacking and counterstacking," 245

McMartin preschool trial, 4-10, 16, 31, 34, 49, 185, 191, 222, 223, 225, 226, 227, 228, 257
Memory, in children, 15, 106-124; age differences, 108, 109, 112, 113, 114, 116, 193; deficiencies in, 114-117; interviewer bias, 16, 122; maximizing, 122-124; models of, 106-108; photographic, 71; recognition memory, 108-110; reconstruction memory, 110-111; search, 115-116; stereotype of poor rememberers, 36; strategies for remembering, 114-117; stress, effects of, 120, 193-195; Susie, case of, 15; types of remembering, 108-114
Mental health professionals, and children as witnesses, 57; beliefs about children's ability to testify, 26; decision to encourage testifying, 19; functions, 228-247; preparation for court, 229; researchers, 235; responsibility to report abuse, 4

Mental representations of the world, 70-72

Oath, understanding of, 43-45
Obligation to tell the truth, 43-45, 104-106, 254
Overextension and underextension, 126-127

Pedophilic acts, 4
Photographic memory, 71
Physical abuse of children, incidence of, 4
Piagetian approach to cognitive development, 69, 74-75, 76, 107, 110
Plea bargains, in sexual abuse cases, 139
Police officers, and children as witnesses, 25-26, 248-249
Policy recommendations, 255-257
Post-traumatic stress disorder, 86
Putnam, Ann, 39

Raleigh, Sir Walter, 143
Rehearsal, as memory strategy, 114
Retarded children, 90-91
Reversibility, and age, 64

Salem witch trials, 38-39
Sexual abuse of children, 2, 4, 16, 41, 66, 72, 121, 135, 165, 201; books on, 226-227; and competency to testify, 48, 191-198; definition of, 4; and grieving stages, 87-90; incidence of, 4, 224-225; reporting rate, 224; Susie, case of, 10-13
Sixth Amendment right to confront accuser, 10, 19, 134, 140-141, 143-145, 160, 189
Social science findings and legal decisions: on children's rights, 213-214; in conflict, 20-21, 178-179; on credibility, 198-199; use of, 180
Stages: of cognitive development, 69-74; of grieving, 87-90; of mental representation, 70-71; of morality, 83-

85; of psychosocial development, 81-83
"Statement validity assessment," 200-201
Steinberg, Lisa, 227
Stress, 120, 187, 193; "confrontational," 194; effects on memory, 193-195; effects on testimony when cross-examined, 193-195
Subpoena and subpoena duces tecum, 233
Suggestibility, 14, 28, 75-76, 117-120, 186, 191, 197; assumptions about children's, 117; comparison of children and adults, 117-118, 119-120
Suggestion, 25, 244, 245; and distortion of memory, 72, 118-119
Susie, case of, 10-13, 14, 15, 16, 257; issues of credibility in, 15; traumatization, 17-18

Therapeutic effects of testifying, 18
Time estimation, 65-66
Traumatization of child witnesses, 80, 85-87, 135, 213, 214, 218-219, 236; compared to adults, 135-136; and compromising reliability of testimony, 182-185; considerations in deciding to testify, 18-19; effects of sexual abuse, 225; empirical research on, 137-138; extent of, 136; and grieving, 87-90; post-traumatic stress disorder, 86; procedures to reduce, at trial, 155-172; programs to deal with, 214-215; protecting children from, 135-138; at trial, 17, 134, 137

Understanding of the legal system, by children, 99-106, 252

Victims of Child Abuse Laws (VOCAL), 139
Videotaped testimony, of sexual abuse victim, 11, 12, 13, 133, 144, 164-172; court decisions, 36, 146-147, 183-185

About the Authors

Nancy Walker Perry (Ph.D., University of Nebraska, 1982) is Associate Professor of Psychology at Creighton University, Omaha, where she teaches classes in child development, psychopathology, and psychology and the law. She has received the Nebraska Psychological Association's Distinguished Teaching of Psychology Award and the Robert F. Kennedy Memorial Student Award for Teaching Achievement. She has been conducting research on children as legal witnesses for six years and has served as an expert witness regarding children's developmental abilities. She is sole contributing author to J. E. B. Myers's *Child Witness Law and Practice*. In addition to nine years of academic experience, she has served as staff psychologist for two community mental health centers and as Director of Children's Services for one.

Lawrence S. Wrightsman (Ph.D., University of Minnesota, 1959) is Professor of Psychology at the University of Kansas, Lawrence. He has been doing research on legal processes for fifteen years and is director of the Kansas Jury Project. He is author or editor of five books relevant to the legal system, including *Psychology and the Legal System* (1991), *The American Jury on Trial* (1988), *In the Jury Box* (1987), *On the Witness Stand (1987), and The Psychology of Evidence and Trial Procedure* (1985). He has testified as an expert witness on the issue of the accuracy of eyewitness identification, and he has assisted defense attorneys in jury selection in various types of trials ranging from criminal murder cases to civil malpractice suits. He is a former President of the Society for the Psychological Study of Social Issues and of the Society of Personality and Social Psychology.